The Taoist Inner View of the Universe and the Immortal Realm

The Taoist Inner View of the Universe and the Immortal Realm

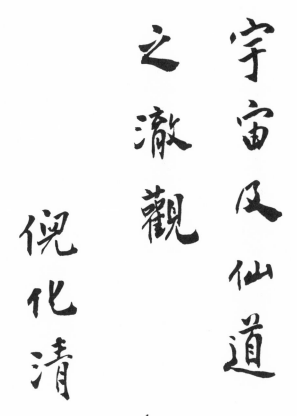

by

Hua-Ching Ni

SEVEN STAR
COMMUNICATIONS
SANTA MONICA

The College of Tao offers teachings about health, spirituality and the Integral Way based on the teachings of Hua-Ching Ni. To obtain information about Mentors teaching in your area or country, or if you are intereted in teaching, please write the Universal Society of the Integral Way, PO Box 28993, Atlanta, GA 30358-0993 USA. To obtain information about the Integral Way of Life Correspondence Course, please write the College of Tao, PO Box 1222, El Prado, NM 87529 USA.

We wish to thank the Bildarchiv Foto Marburg in Marburg, West Germany, for the use of the photograph on the cover.

Published by:
Seven Star Communications Group Inc.
1314 Second Street
Santa Monica, CA 90401 USA

The paper used in this publication meets the minimum requirements of the American National Standard for Information Sciences Permanence of Paper for Printed Library Materials, ANSI 239.48-1984.

First Printing August 1979
Second Printing: September 1982
Third Printing: July 1986
Fourth Printing: April 1991
Fifth Printing: May 1996

*This book is dedicated to those who search
for the inner truth of the universe
and possibly find that the truth of the outside world
is the same truth of the inner self.
Thus, they may also find the immortal essence of Life.*

To female readers,

According to Taoist teaching, male and female are equally important in the natural sphere. This is seen in the diagram of Tai Chi. Thus, discrimination is not practiced in our tradition. All my work is dedicated to both genders of human people.

Wherever possible, constructions using masculine pronouns to represent both sexes are avoided; where they occur, we ask your tolerance and spiritual understanding. We hope that you will take the essence of my teaching and overlook the superficiality of language. Gender discrimination is inherent in English; ancient Chinese pronouns do not have differences of gender. I wish for all of your achievement above the level of language or gender.

Thank you, H. C. Ni

Warning - Disclaimer

This book is intended to present information and techniques that have been in use throughout the orient for many years. The information offered is to the author's best knowledge and experience and is to be used by the reader(s) at their own discretion. The information and practices utilize a natural system within the body and natural spiritual response, however, there are no claims for absolute effectiveness.

Because of the sophisticated nature of life and the limited information contained within this book, it is recommended that the reader of this book also study the author's other books for further knowledge about having a healthy lifestyle and practicing energy conducting exercises.

People's lives have different conditions. People's growth has different stages. Because the background of people's development cannot be unified, no rigid or stiff practice is given that can be applied universally. Thus, it must be through the discernment of the reader that the practices are selected. The adoption and application of the material offered in this book must be your own responsibility.

The author and publisher of this book are not responsible in any manner whatsoever for any injury which may occur through following the instructions in this book.

CONTENTS

Prelude

"Tao is the destination of all religions and spiritual effort, yet it leaves behind all religions just like the clothing of different seasons and different places. Tao is the goal of serious science, yet it leaves behind all sciences as partial and temporal descriptions of the Integral Truth.

"The teaching of Tao includes all religious subjects, yet it is not on the same level as religions. Its breadth and depth go far beyond the limits of religion. The teaching of Tao serves people's lives as religions do, yet it transcends all religions and contains the essence of all religions.

"The teaching of Tao is not like any of the sciences. It transcends the level of any single subject of science.

"The teaching of Tao is the master teaching of all. However, it does not mean that the teaching relies on a master. It means the teaching of Tao is like a master key which can unlock all doors leading to the Integral Truth. It teaches or shows the truth directly. It does not stay on the emotional surface of life or remain at the level of thought or of belief. Neither does it stay on the intellectual level of life, maintaining skepticism and endlessly searching. The teaching of Tao presents the core of the subtle truth and helps you to reach it yourself."

Preface

In the total human cultural achievement, three outstanding cultures have guided the human life and mind. Each of these cultures, in its time, became the most influential way of human life. According to historical order, the first and the least popular today is the Integral Way of Taoism, which was the main culture of ancient China. The Taoists developed an integral view of the universe, and formalized their life in the Integral Way. The influence of this culture diminished as the other two ways of development advanced.

The second culture, still popular today, is the godly religious way. With its establishment, the human mind of the West learned the distinction between good and evil, and began to nurse strong emotions towards loving good and hating evil. Each religious group believed that they had received the true word of God, and that their codes set forth the only way to live. They therefore judged human behavior with certainty, tending to pursue rewards from God and to extend punishment to others in the name of God. That way has been the force behind some of history's most violent intolerance.

The social foundation of the West is rooted in the supposed godly way. When the existence of God could not be confirmed by the rational scientific mind, the ethics and social order of the West began to collapse.

The third culture, the most prevalent today, is the modern physical scientific way. The first western scientists were considered witches, and suffered persecution from the conventional religious society. When the time was right and scientific achievement was sufficiently impressive, the western mind became convinced that the world was most accurately seen from a scientific viewpoint.

In the scientific way, observation and experiment became the means of determining reality. Technology replaced the bare organic capability of human sense; the world revealed itself in an entirely different way. But new narrowness was built on the denial of other human capabilities, such as the intuitive faculty and the spiritual responsive reality operating in daily life. In my work, I take advantage of being a born "integralist." "Integralism" was the only subject I learned and the way I have lived. In this book, I speak about human intuitive development and the universe's spiritual capability to respond in all situations.

As I see it, the godly religious way needs to extend more understanding instead of imposing judgement, condemnation, and punishment. Any strong emotion, whether religious or non-religious, is a separation from the true, godly way. Divinity must embrace what is eternal and universal, and not just suit one particular society at one time in history.

As for the scientific way, we do not need to cut our friends open to learn more about them, as scientists cut the frog open in order to know the frog, or test the monkey in order to know the human being. The source of real understanding is much greater than dissection and examination.

The universe moves beyond logic, analysis, and the evidence of the five senses. If the scientific way hopes to find the total truth, first they must discover that the established methods of observation and experimentation are incomplete perceptions, and that their way is their limitation, at least in regard to the expectation of containing all aspects of knowledge.

If the world's eminent physicists are willing to learn the Tao, despite their conventional training, it would not be hard for them to know the existence of the universal subtle responsive system of spiritual oneness.

If the world's most eminent physicians are willing to learn pulse reading from the subtle change of the arterial pulse waves, it would not be hard for them to know the blood changes within the human body and other information, without needing to use insufficient methods like counting the blood cells. They would also learn to cure many diseases without having to cut the body open. They would learn the healing of human diseases by treating the body as a living entity rather than collecting information from dead bodies. A Taoist does not depend on cutting, hypnosis or brainwashing, but on the plain truth revealed to the delicate human mind.

In general, I offer the Way of no partiality, the Way of keeping the essence of life. Be simple, act simply with godly nature and the integral nature of the mind. But in this book the width and depth of my exploration reaches farther to share the inner view of the universe and the truth of immorality from the attainment of my ancestors and teachers.

The inner view of integral beings (shiens) that is known by the name of Taoism dates back to the pre-history of China. At that time, over 6,000 years ago, there existed no written language, no nations and no royal courts. All human beings were equal as manifestations of nature. One tradition, now entitled Taoism, was also a manifestation of nature and did not belong to any nation or culture in particular. It belonged only to great nature itself.

The human race emerged as the manifestation of a combination of the energies of the sun, moon, earth and all the stars. Through the great cooperation of these energies, humankind took form in this universe. According to the way of traditional thinking, the first human beings came into existence as the result of the union of the universal, creative yang energy with the universal, receptive yin energy, thus giving birth to all humanity.

The first ancestors of the human race in the Chinese region originated from the yellow earth highlands in Asia, near the beginning of the Yellow River in ancient China. According to Taoist classics, Fu Hsi, the great Taoist sage, succeeded many great pre-historical sages. He lived approximately 8,000 years ago and it was he who began the use of the eight kua (trigrams) of the *I Ching*. At that time, the method of tying knots in rope was employed to record significant events in human society. This time and before was the golden of no social interference. It was the day of Taoists. All of the significant books written in later Chinese history are reminiscent of the anecdotes and sayings of the past Taoist sages of that era. There are also many precious discoveries preserved by this tradition, because all the esoteric knowledge has been orally transmitted from generation to generation.

From the Taoist perspective, humankind was born into this world as a natural and supernatural being, with an independent spirit and natural integrity. The original human beings were endowed with great spiritual and physical abilities, and the mind shared its part in the orderliness of their being. As the human mind developed a dualistic mode of functioning later on, it destroyed the original balance of body, mind and spirit. As its mental faculty became more and more developed, humanity's spiritual and mental faculties withered until people finally diminished themselves in body, shortened their years, and segmented and disintegrated themselves in spirit. In the process of perception, the human mind came to habitually separate the perceiver from the perceived, and thus destroyed its connection with universal oneness. Humankind lost its natural completeness, independence and well-being.

As history progressed, in an attempt to remedy the problem, humanity came to seek the truth through secondary, twisted, so-called spiritual teachings and religions, not realizing that the path to integrity is within oneself, and that the subtle essence as Tao is inherent in one's own nature. Then came Taoism, which works to enable individual beings to eliminate the false sense of duality from their poisoned minds and to reunite themselves with their true nature. Thereby it allows people to actualize their pristine, complete harmony with the eternal truth, Tao. This means to enhance the re-integration of individual beings with their total environment of time and space and energy.

In ancient Taoism, which is the source of all ancient Chinese cultural achievement, the title shien means a being who possesses and enjoys spiritual independence and completeness. Once you revivify this spiritual independence in yourself, you restore your natural and supernatural qualities. This is not just a myth. One can prove this for oneself rather than simply accept these words from reading. Taoism is a natural way of developing the mind. At the same time, its mental discipline keeps the mind in the right channel, which makes it more serviceable to one's life. Taoism is also an integral way to protect the mind.

The spirit of a human being has the ability to know the whole, but the mind, in its learning, can only know the parts. As humankind multiplied, its spiritual qualities decreased through the worldly, segmented way of life, which developed and distorted the mind. Human beings then became selfish, foolish, ambitious and insane because they began to focus on external profits and undertake unnecessary contests which were mostly motivated by tension and vanity rather than the reality of survival.

This kind of behavior is not the true nature of human beings. It results from incomplete knowledge and is the product of an ill mind. The human mind, through the activity of comparing, tends to imitate the reactions of others instead of acting for itself. This causes people to forsake their spiritual ability of intuitive and complete knowledge. Becoming addicted to the incompleteness of fragmentary mental knowledge, they do not realize their own blindness. Much of the misery of today's human beings is due to this separation from the original integrity.

In this world, most people are still interested in religions rather than in the growth or development of one's spirit. When one has rectified one's mind and has a true base of sanity, then spiritual development can take place. Few people truly pay attention to their own character and improve their personality and psychological sanity. To follow Tao is to first rebalance oneself and restore one's original, independent spirituality as an integral being in the universe.

At the beginning of human society, people gathered into groups for natural reasons. The original family unit expanded into groups of families or tribes, which naturally united for either cultural or geographical reasons to form the early communities. At the beginning, the natural leader was the head of the group. Later, the wise people of the tribes and small communities came to be the natural leaders, not by using force to make themselves leaders, but by rendering their selfless service and setting an eminent example of the Integral Way of life.

The tradition of the Union of Tao and Man dates back to the original integral example and naturally formed a subtle educational system in the ancient Taoist community of prehistoric times. During these ancient times in China, society was composed of people with a pristine nature. Nobody had ambition to conquer another tribe, hoping to become a leader or teacher. To hold leadership was not a cause for fighting. This was because life was natural, noncompetitive, nondualistic and nonfragmentary. Each individual had his or her own true nature of self-sufficiency. In this way, there was no spur of ambition.

Leadership and teaching work were the natural responsibility of the wise. All persons with naturally good and high energy contributed to their community in any appropriate manner, with absolutely no rivalry. At that time, no titles were created or were of interest to the leaders. This was the master key of the high energy harmony in ancient Taoist society. Beings of high energy and supernatural beings (shiens) were titled as Emperors because they could manifest independence and the integrity of their own spirits. They were high beings who had sovereignty over themselves and people as well. They used their virtues and good example to influence people and did not have to resort to force.

It was not until the end of the Chou dynasty, when the so-called "Time of the Warlords of Spring and Autumn" (1052 B.) began, that the abuse of force appeared. In order to achieve their goal of independence and integrity, Taoists retreated at that time from the overgrown society to the high mountains or remote wilderness, or lived quietly and plainly in society. Some of them took high positions and responsibility at that time, but spiritually they still enjoyed their own integral being as hermits, remaining untouched by the rule of force.

Thus, my tradition guided itself to a place which was beyond the influence of the worldly power fever and the destruction of natural balance. It has kept a pure way of life and teaching system. As a result of the drastic changes which have taken place in China, I came forth as the nourishing milk from the breast of old mother China by the pressure and stirring of the world. I now have this chance to come and share my training with the people of the world.

Taoism is a subject which is evasive to the mind. It reaches far beyond the ordinary function of mind. Merely looking at words forms a separation from the direct participation in the truth, beauty, goodness and sacredness of the entire whole. However, to establish communication, to transmit the Tao, and to show the Way, I am risking the use of words and writing this book. The basic knowledge of my tradition is treated in this book as well as in my other books. Each book has a different function in transmitting Tao. In most areas they can help explain each other, as long as the reader does not confuse the practical, plain truths of Taoism with the mental discipline of self-cultivation.

The nation with the five thousand year old history, China, is a metaphor and a myth. Yesterday's myth cannot help today's reality, and yesterday's endeavor cannot replace today's effort. But most of the old prescriptions have been proven still effective and useful in Taoists medicine, in my own practice and for many other Chinese medical practitioners. I truly know all those ancient "metaphors" and "myths" may serve you well when you are ready. All the books I write are my dedication to my beloved readers who have real comprehension and accurate insight.

Taoism belongs to no nationality, no race, no locality. Taoism belongs to universal mind. Though it originated in the ancient Chinese region and was developed by Chinese ancestors, these good Masters never established nationalism, racialism or localism in their minds. They always treated themselves as the plain life of the universe. That was their background. That was the standpoint from which they started their development and reached their destination. China is a place in which to remember all the shiens, but the real land of the shiens is not limited to that particular place and people. It belongs to my beloved readers.

Ni, Hua-Ching
Los Angeles
December 1979

Introduction to Taoism

A Dialogue With My Western Friends and Students in 1976

Q: Master Ni, would you tell us something about your background and training?

Master Ni: Traditionally, a Taoist follows the example of impersonal nature in guiding oneself. Thus it is not the Taoist's style to talk about oneself as a special, individual existence. However, this is a special occasion. First, let us understand that traditionally the esoteric knowledge of the ancient Chinese was transmitted from Master to disciple through an apprentice system and through family heritage. I was born into one of those families with a Taoist heritage and with the responsibility to preserve this culture.

Besides my father, who was my first traditional teacher, I had the special opportunity to learn from three other great Masters and many others who lived as hermits at that time in some beautiful, high mountains in mainland China. They passed their esoteric knowledge and traditional techniques down to me. Having foreknowledge about the coming of drastic changes in the world, they trained me as a spiritual descendant of the Union of Tao and Man to continue this prehistoric tradition in the present time. This tradition is the mainstream of ancient, integral Taoism.

Taoism holds as true that human beings are born with the Tao as their inherent, true nature. However, people lose and separate themselves from the Tao through worldly life by developing a dualistic mind. Thus, the Taoist's goal in worldly life is to reunite oneself with one's true nature-the reunion of Tao and Man. Or we may put it this way: when humankind originally appeared on earth, the spiritual and physical energies of human beings were harmoniously balanced. But after living in the world, desire eventually outgrew intelligence and spirituality. This imbalance took us far away from our true nature and created disaster and misery in life. This is why we need Taoist self-cultivation: so that we can rediscover ourselves and reconstruct within ourselves the original essence of an immortal divine being, a shien, who is simply an integral being united in body, mind and spirit with nature. This is my simple background as well as my tradition.

Q: Why have you come to America?

Master Ni: I came to the United States at the invitation of some American students who first came to study with me in Taiwan, where I taught at that time.

After studying with me for some time, they invited me to come to this country. Before coming here, I practiced traditional Chinese medicine, taught Tai Chi movement and passed on Taoism. Also, while I was in Taiwan, I wrote many books on Taoism with a wide readership interested in learning Taoism through me. The reason for my accepting the invitation to come here was based on my own understanding of today's world crisis.

The decisive power of human destiny is humankind itself. There is an old Chinese proverb which says: "When nature makes difficulties, humanity still has the opportunity to avoid the problem and survive. But when man himself creates disaster, it is hard for him to avoid the consequences." Today's social conflicts are based mainly on the fact that people are ignorant of their own true nature and the cosmic principles of life. With the realization of their true identity and adherence to the cosmic laws which govern all manifestations in the universe, it is within humanity's potential to transform the quality of life on this planet.

We all know that our view of the universe influences our view of life. This view of life in turn influences a person's personality. What view of the universe does the modern person hold? One can look in a college astronomy text book and find that there are two main theories of the beginning of the universe. One is that the universe had no beginning at all. What exists now is the same thing that has always existed. This is one theory. The second main theory is what is called the "Big Bang" theory, which states that there originally existed a "cosmic egg" of primordial energy and then there was a big explosion. As a result of this explosion, the universe, with its innumerable galaxies, was created. This is modern society's heritage and culture. From a Taoist perspective, the Big Bang theory presumes the existence of time and space prior to the creation of the universe, whereas the Taoist sees time and space as one of the developed attributes of the universe.

I mention this because the view one holds of the universe is so important in influencing one's activities and the whole of human society. Through the study and application of the principles of Taoist cosmology, one may know and experience cosmic law. You may call it Tao. Tao is the substance of the universe. As Tao extends, develops and evolves, duality manifests as the tai chi principle, which is the principle of the dynamic equilibrium of opposites. The tai chi then splits and becomes three levels of existence, manifesting as the spiritual, mental and physical planes. You might say that from the point of view of physics, mind is the most sensitive energy, spirit is the most subtle, and physical energy is the grossest.

Taoist cosmology holds a peaceful and orderly view of the universe. Such a view can bring a peaceful mind and a creative attitude. You may also know that to connect yourself with the deep root of the universe, the highest subtlety, you must utilize your calm mind, your high level energy; not the lower emotional force, which is the energy of the biological sphere. Emotion, the lower sphere of the mind, is mostly connected with physical, relative activity. It is not an attribute of the deep inner view of the absolute world.

I came to America with the hope that through my teaching, people would be able to see a reasonable and integrated view of the universe. Through such an understanding, the development of humanity's future will be bright. An individual, with the foundation of understanding the origin and nature of the universe, can know that life does not finish at the end of physical life. Life is connected with the whole universe. This understanding can help eliminate the conflict in the world's thinking. This conflict arises out of different, erroneous views of God, of humanity and of the nature of life. Generally, all religions are a way of thinking. If you follow an incorrect way of mind, you will arrive at an incorrect result.

The religion and culture of a people are the manifestation of the mental energy of the people. If the correct way of mind is applied, the resulting manifestations will be harmonious.

Q: Master Ni, what is Taoism? How does it differ from other spiritual traditions?

Master Ni: Religions and most spiritual traditions are involved with the worship of a personalized concept of God. The Tao is not another mental concept of a personalized God. Tao is the primary, essential energy of the universe, not merely the products fashioned from it. Tao is beyond personalization. It may take form, yet it may also remain formless. It is beyond definition. To attach an "ism" to Tao is an attempt to limit or title Tao, which is not really appropriate. However, in order to verbally communicate, we must rely on such limited words and concepts to point our mind in the direction of the truth, knowing all the while that the truth which can be spoken is not the absolute, ultimate truth.

The Taoist tradition has become an old school of universal knowledge and wisdom which has accumulated over thousands of years dating back to prehistoric times. The title of Taoism was used only to differentiate it from other traditions. You may say that Tao is the essence of the universe which exists before the formation of heaven, earth, or anything else. It is the unmanifest potentiality from which all manifestations proceed. It is being, it is non-being, and yet it is neither of these. After things manifest mentally or physically, they are then given name or titles. The names and titles are not the Tao, but its descriptions.

This process can also be applied to describe our mind. When our mind is perfectly still and we have not yet formed our mental energy into ideas, concepts, images or attitudes, it is the pure, cosmic mind itself. This is so even if one is not aware of its existence. Actually, it is only when one is involved in something, excited or disturbed, that one is aware of one's mind. Pure mind in Taoist terms is called po. This may be translated as the primary essence. It is the fundamental power of mind. When pure mental energy connects with the universal, unmanifest, creative energy, it is referred to as the Original Simplicity. In its unmanifest aspect, the Original Simplicity is infinite and boundless. When it becomes manifest, it then becomes finite and limited.

Taoism is not a religion in the ordinary sense. It is a Way of Life. One may also say that it is a highly developed integral science. Ordinary religions were originally created for psychological or social reasons, but Taoism is for the purpose of continual development. <u>Religions offer you their awareness, whereas Taoism offers you the way to find your own awareness.</u> Religions generally emphasize worship, while Taoism is self-cultivation. In order words, in Taoism, you work on yourself. You do not worship or admire other divine beings, but you cultivate your own divine nature. It is similar to becoming rich and productive through your own efforts, instead of remaining poor and needy while admiring the rich.

When people stimulate your mind by creating the sentiment of worship, you fashion something outside of yourself as the object of your worship. By so doing you trap your mind in the illusion of duality, which is only furthering the disintegration of the wholeness of one's being. In reality, the worshiper and the worshiped are one. When Taoists engage in worship, they are revering the objectification of their own true nature, but this is still not the main practice of Taoism. Relatively speaking, the goal of Taoism is the reunification of oneself with the primal, creative energy which is the essence of the universe. The highest, most refined energy within us is of the same frequency as the primal energy referred to as Tao.

Your life is one hand of the primal energy of the universe extending itself outward as your Self. It is not like a fish which jumped out off the ocean. We are an extension of the universal power which has stretched itself outward, not only into human-kind, but into all manifestations. Since we have lost our Original Simplicity or original essence in our habitual mental perception of duality and multiplicity, we need to restore it within ourselves once again. In Chinese, Original Simplicity is called yuen chi, the primal, creative energy. With yuen chi we can do anything. If we disperse or scatter the yuen chi, we can do nothing. So the Original Simplicity is not a doctrine, it is the subtle essence of all beings.

Taoists cultivate their energy in order to realize their true nature. The Taoist Way is not merely a weekly worship and donation to keep up one's membership in a church. Rather it is a daily self-cultivation. Self-cultivation is essentially practicing various techniques for the purpose of refining one's energy to progressively higher and purer states to ultimately unite oneself with the highest realms of the universe. It is mostly related to one's way of life such as diet, exercise, sex and so forth. As an aspect of self-cultivation, the Taoist tradition also includes the practice of certain rituals or formulas in order to bring about a response from the divine, cosmic energy of the universe. These are some of the activities and non-activities which comprise today's Taoism.

At the end of the Han dynasty (between 140 and 185 A.D.), a Taoist religious cult involving social and political issues came into being which vulgarized the ancient tradition of spiritual Taoism through their involvement with superficial issues. Since that time, the pure tradition of Taoism has been affected by the confusion between it and popular Taoism. Popular Taoism, nevertheless, also preserves the spiritual root underneath its many religious ceremonies. I belong to the pure tradition, and maintain the original simplicity of Taoism. My tradition is recognized as being the tradition of the shiens or immortal divine beings, whereas the local religious customs of various Chinese villages are the so-called Taoist folk religion.

Q: What is the basic philosophy underlying the teachings of Tao?

Master Ni: Taoist philosophy is not merely an idea; it is a Way of Life. Most philosophies are just concepts. Generally, when philosophers intentionally invent a philosophical system, they are usually motivated by bitterness. Then they try to spread their ideas by finding followers of their system. Then their followers try to find followers. But Taoist cosmology starts with a basic understanding of the universe. Taoism came into being in a way similar to the invention of the Chinese written language, which imitates nature's evolving images of universal mental energy tracings.

First we have life, then we have a Way of Life. In language, first we have the language, then we have grammar. We do not create grammar and therefore have language. What I mean here is that truth always exists before description. Absolute Tao existed before Taoism, which is not like religions or philosophies which were created through the spreading of ideas or the publication of books. The daily life of the ancient Taoists is the model of the embodiment of Taoist cosmology and truth itself.

Q: What is the I Ching?

Master Ni: The *I Ching* is the foundation of all Chinese knowledge systems. All eminent achievements of China, i.e., acupuncture, herbology, geomancy (the discovery of subtle energy rays and their use in personal development), political and military philosophy and strategy, architecture and so forth, are all derived from the *I Ching*. The study of the *I Ching* has reaped an abundant harvest of knowledge throughout its long history, which dates back over 6,000 years. Even a native-born Chinese scholar still has difficulty comprehending its profound immanence. As heir to the heritage of the mainstream of Taoism, I was given the opportunity to thoroughly study the *I Ching*, which is the foundation upon which Taoism developed.

Originally, the *I Ching*, which is also called *The Book of Changes*, contained no written words at all. It only had signs made up of three or six lines, either broken, representing yin energy, or unbroken, representing yang energy. At first, the signs were composed of three lines. All of the possible combinations of three yin and/or yang lines resulted in eight main signs known as the Pa Kua or Ba Gua. As time passed, some other sages doubled the signs, making six lines, which had sixty-four possible combinations. These signs are a concrete indication of all the energy manifestations of the universe, how they are formed and how they function.

The foundation of *I Ching* is the principle of yin and yang. The ancient Taoist "cosmic scientists" discovered through their highly developed insight that there is essentially one primal cosmic energy. In the stillness of the unmanifest aspect of the universe, the primal cosmic energy expresses a state of oneness. As it extends itself in the process of creation, its movement causes the polarization of the one primal energy, giving birth to duality. The polar aspects of the effects thus created were designated as yin and yang. Yin and yang have many translations, such as the two sides of positive and negative, expansion and contraction, construction and destruction, masculine and feminine. Yin and yang are not two separate energies or activities. The activity of one is inherently contained within and created by the other. For example, a symphony is composed not only of musical sounds, but the silent pauses between the sounds are also intrinsic aspects of the composition. In the English language, the contradictory sense of positive and negative is strong. But in the Chinese way of thinking yin and yang unite themselves, and through this union the existence of all things is made possible. If one side is excessive, its state of balance is lost, thereby creating the possibility of destruction.

In modern thinking, positive and negative must fight each other on opposite sides. But the Chinese concept of yin and yang shows us that the great harmony of universal development is based on the cooperation and union of apparent opposites. The *I Ching* shows that the universe is one whole, but with two wings, like man with two legs. In order to function effectively, the two legs do not fight each other, but they work together to help each other. For example, in movement, when you produce one kind of force to push yourself up and forward, at the same time you also produce a kind of rejecting force.

This principle can be applied to everything with yin and yang united as a tai chi. The tai chi then evolves into three levels of existence: physical existence, spiritual existence, and the combination of the two, which is mental existence. Human beings are one manifestation of mental existence, and are a good example of the unification of the physical and the spiritual. Through the study of the *I Ching*, one may come to know and experience the subtle universal energy and the mysterious generating origin of the universe. One may also learn how to achieve integral development and keep pace with the universal evolution.

Q: Why do you teach the I Ching, or Book of Changes and the Unchanging Truth, as the main textbook of Taoism?

Master Ni: Some of my students have brought various translations of the *I Ching* to me. It is difficult to make a translation because the Chinese mental structure is so different from that of Westerners-especially the intuitive language of the ancient Taoists. Even the most excellent translators and elucidators have difficulty. Therefore, none of the translations are perfect. Many misunderstandings and shallow truths about the original material are presented to the reader. Only a person who is educated in the Taoist tradition has the same intuitive mental quality. With the added advantage of Taoist enlightenment training comes the development of high comprehension of cosmic law and familiarity with all the historical aspects involved. This shall greatly deepen the understanding of exactly what is meant in the *Book of Changes*. Its quality changes by transferring the intuitive enlightenment into words. In China, there have been over 1,000 books discussing it. The books in themselves do not have too much meaning; it is the training through their use which can bring about the development of high intuitive capability. My own translation and elucidation serves as a useful tool for English-speaking students.

The reason I use the *Book of Changes* as the first material in my teaching is that when one practices and learns the *I Ching*, one can find external evidence showing the connection between oneself and the subtle energy of the universe. With this evidence, one may experience the melting of apparent subjectivity and objectivity. When one perceives oneself as subject and all that is external to oneself as object, one is bound and limited within that context of perception. Practice of the *I Ching* can guide you and encourage you to move forward into the mysterious realms of the "unknown" and to the ultimate realization that what each person truly is cannot be bound or limited. In this way, one may unite so-called subject and object into one whole and restore one's intrinsic integrity.

Q: What is "internal alchemy," so often mentioned in Taoist cultivation? This is something not generally discussed in other spiritual traditions.

Master Ni: According to the Taoist understanding, the whole universe is a big nuclear reaction furnace in which energy transformations are constantly taking place. Non-being becomes being. Being becomes non-being. This results from the constant transformation, sublimation, evolution, or devolution of energy. Through objective understanding, one can see that it is necessary to make subjective effort to consciously adjust oneself in order to achieve and maintain harmony, balance and progressive evolution. The whole human body, like the universe, is also like an alchemical furnace in which energy changes and transformations are continually taking place.

The Taoist tradition teaches that we can make our body into a small workshop of the universal process of energy transformation by subtly adjusting our own internal energies. In this way, we may gain the self-mastery necessary to dissolve our apparent physical bondage. When certain terms and environmental conditions are present, specific results must appear. This is the basis of all experimental science. This principle can also be applied to Taoist cultivation. As far as the human external form is concerned, since it is already completely formed, we are limited in our ability to change and improve it. However, everyday, even every minute, the inside of the body is constantly working and changing.

The energy produced within us has three manifestations: physical essence, as gross energy; mind, as refined energy; and spirit, as subtle energy. These correspond with the three general manifestations of universal energy. These three manifestations of energy are not three separate entities. They are essentially one energy, existing in grosser or finer states. The normal order of energy development is from the lower to the higher. The energy arrangement of a highly evolved being is for the spirit to control the mind, and the mind to control the physical energy. However, the opposite order predominates in the majority of the world's creatures, with physical desire controlling the mind and the mind overpowering the spirit. Consequently, much confusion abounds and man-made disasters are prevalent.

To a Taoist, spirit is the manifestation of high energy as heaven within us. Our physical essence, which produces our vital power, is the physical energy in our body, which represents the earth. Our mind can develop in the time/space context to make social relationships and things of that nature. This is the human level of existence, the human energy structure. The human body is a combination of heaven or "spirit," human being or "mind," and earth or "body" in one great unity, an exact microcosm of the harmonious universe. It can be a small workshop of the subtle power which operates as the subtle performer of the universe.

The purpose of Taoist cultivation is to refine our energy. It is to refine desire to become wisdom, refine physical essence to become mental power, and ultimately, to refine one's high level mental power to become spirit. This spirit can unite with the immortal divine nature of the universe. One can achieve immortality by using one's own spirit to thrust through the illusion of duality of the physical realm and thereby unite with the eternally unfolding universe.

The Taoist concept of immortality is not to be confused with the Egyptian attempt to achieve immortality through the preservation of the body after death through mummification. True immortality involves more that the continuation of individual existence after the final stage of the life cycle referred to as death. It is a state of being which may be experienced here and now.

As the universe exercises itself through the universal law of tai chi, the principle of dynamic equilibrium of opposites is expressed. Thus, with the manifestation of the phenomenon of evolution, devolution is also manifested. The physical body has evolved to its highest potentiality. Nature has already done its job.

To continue the process of personal evolution and thereby transcend our biological destiny, we must cultivate our spirit. Through the cultivation of our divine energy, we may achieve immortality here and now. This experience, in Taoist terminology, is referred to as a state of "ever-spring," which means that every moment of life is a process of rebirth in which one may have the continual experience of springtime. This is not merely an idea. There are specific methods through which past Taoist Masters have, since ancient times, fulfilled this goal in their lifetimes. They have maintained a life responsive to the three Realms of Purity and have entered the realm of true immortality.

These realms have been referred to as "Heaven." The Taoist notion of Heaven must be differentiated from the concept of Heaven which is promulgated by shallow, dualistic religions. The Taoist does not think of heaven as a place where one may go after death as reward for having lived a virtuous life. Taoism does not try to present an enticement or temptation to the worldly mind by stating that there is a reward or punishment after death. Some religions teach that people are born into this life as sinners and must spend their lifetimes in repentance and retribution. They claim that if a person manages to atone for one's sins, after death one will go to heaven. If one does not, one will spend eternity in hell. This may be true to them, but Taoism does not create illusory stories to spoil, confuse and control people's minds. Taoists believe that the kind of energy arrangement a person manifests here and now is one's reward or punishment. The Taoists define Heaven as an arrangement or formation of clear, creative energy which is sublimely harmonious. It is not necessary to wait until after death to be in Heaven. It is possible to experience every moment of time as Heaven, right here and now throughout all one's life, if only one can perceive and experience one's own true nature without corruption by mental ornamentation.

Everything that exists in the universe exists as an arrangement or formation of energy. All energy formations, however, are impermanent and changeable. It is only the productive, essential energy of the universe that is above the universal law of transformation. Consequently, Taoists do not waste their time trying to manipulate energy formations in order to achieve a desired result. Instead, they cultivate the essential energy of the universe within in order to both achieve true enlightenment and effect positive transformation in their lives and environment.

To achieve true enlightenment means to fulfill the true nature of your being. When we fulfill our true nature, we fulfill the responsibility of our lives. Our nature of beingness is an extension of the nature of the universe. Thus, when you fulfill your life, you already accomplish the completeness of the nature of the whole universe. Your individual being ends in a certain year, but your nature of beingness is endless through its continuation with the nature of beingness of the universe. Your physical form dies, but your true nature can never die.

Q: In Taoism, immortality is frequently mentioned. Exactly what is meant by this term?

Master Ni: The deep nature of the universe is invariable and constant, as the subtle reality of universal law and as the subtle performer of all transformation. As this energy exercises itself, its movement causes the energy to become polarized. This polarization creates myriad manifestations which are in a state of incessant change. If one can once connect with the energy of the divine nature of the universe, one may achieve immortality.

In other words, from the relative standpoint, life is unstable. One minute you have life, the next minute you lose it, just like the one-celled bacteria. It is not worthy for one to live at this low level of existence as a prisoner of time and space. But from the absolute standpoint - through unification with the Tao - time, space, and the unceasing transformation of the universe are transcended and the unchanging peace and harmony of one's true nature of beingness are achieved. If you respect and revere your life, there is only one way to go - that is, to consciously harmonize with the progressive evolution and unify yourself with Tao.

Q: How is T'ai Chi Ch'uan or T'ai Chi movement related to Taoist self-cultivation?

Master Ni: Although T'ai Chi Ch'uan is considered to be a martial art, it is not really involved with fighting. It is actually the practice of Taoist cosmology. Through the practice of T'ai Chi, the universal law may exhibit itself, both within and outside of the body, so that one may reunite with it. It is a necessary cultivation, because what a person learns and the kind of activities one engages in, influences one's personality. For example, a person who studies and practices martial arts with only the fighting aspect in mind tends to be easily inclined to fighting, has less self-control and is hot tempered. T'ai Chi movements are a method of balancing oneself physically, emotionally and spiritually. T'ai Chi is a self-healing process which may be practiced every day by anyone in any physical condition. The correct way to practice T'ai Chi is as an implement to the universal law which is expounded in Lao Tzu's *Tao Teh Ching*, or Way of Life, and in the *I Ching*.

In my teaching I sometimes mention the martial arts application of T'ai Chi because its principles are so high and subtle that it is necessary to use some tangible illustration for a better understanding. The practice of T'ai Chi movement is a part of Taoist self-cultivation. It is a way of gaining real natural health and is an effective method of self-defense, but mainly it is a practice for the integration of one's physical, mental, and spiritual energies.

Q: Is Taoism related to acupuncture and other Chinese healing methods?

Master Ni: Yes, you may say that the entire ancient Chinese culture is essentially Taoist culture. All traditional Chinese knowledge originates in Taoism. Acupuncture and Chinese herbology are practices which are integral parts of Taoism.

The principles underlying all Chinese healing systems are derived from Taoist cosmology and deal with the human body as a small model of the universe. This is clearly illustrated in the *Nei Ching*, the most ancient book on Chinese healing.

Q: How do Taoist choose their diet?

Master Ni: Diet is an important topic to a Taoist. In addition to the health consideration, what you eat and the way you eat can determine your energy situation, thereby influencing your disposition and temperament. Disposition and temperament form your character. The most basic principle of a Taoist diet is to eat simply. This indicates that not many items should be consumed during one meal in order not to stir up your desire, either psychologically or physically. We eat clean food and avoid bloody meats. This is a general idea of the Taoist approach to diet.

Q: How does your system of meditation differ from the many other meditation techniques which are taught?

Master Ni: Primarily, Taoist meditation focuses on forming the positive habits of self-control, self-balance and self-development in quietude through the practice of quiet sitting. This is the traditional preventative method of "self-help." It is used to avoid the occurrence of difficulties, but is not meant as a brooding over already-existing problems and nurturing of the negative mind. Taoist meditation is the continuation of the evolution of one's self-awareness and the transcendence of one's biological destiny. In meditation, we are aware that the vital or physical energy, the mental energy and the spiritual energy within us are the main generators of all our activities. Our work is to harmonize these energies and to refine them to higher levels of development. We do not develop our energies fragmentarily, but work to integrate them into one harmonious entity.

Generally, when one's spirit is strong, nothing can disturb one's mind, but one's vital energy also needs to be directed in support of one's spiritual goal. Only through the refinement of one's whole being is high attainment possible. In addition to this meditation practice, one may also learn the high technique of Taoist internal alchemy.

Q: In Taoism, there is am emphasis on nature and on following what is natural. What is meant by this?

Master Ni: It is true that Taoism emphasizes following what is natural in order to achieve the restoration of one's true nature. However, some people mistake this for an excuse to protect their own self-indulgence. For example, there are people who, despite a certain degree of understanding or enlightenment attained through reading books or spiritual training, still keep bad habits. Smoking, taking drugs, alcohol, laziness, or whatever their particular defect, are done with the rationalization that they are "following what is natural." In effect, what they are following is their own blind impulse which is controlled by their hormonal secretions.

They fail to understand that the Taoist doctrine of "being natural" means to be simple, pure, innocent, and perfectly clear. It is obvious, however, that if one does not follow the internal completeness of one's true nature, one will never be able to lift oneself out of the pit of all kinds of traps of the mind and unite oneself with the original, eternal Tao. A Taoist is basically the same as everyone else. We are all born with the same strong desires. The way in which Taoists differ from others is in the fact that they choose not to follow their physical nature or allow their hormonal secretions to control them. Instead, the goal of Taoist cultivation is the transcendence of one's physical nature in order to restore oneness with eternal nature.

Q: Generally speaking, Westerners have been raised differently from the people of the East and therefore have a much different mental structure. With this consideration, is it possible for Westerners to truly absorb and digest the teachings of the East?

Master Ni: I understand that all human beings have the same true nature. The only differences are those of cultural background. All culture has the danger of stiffening people's minds. However, if you thoroughly understand the quality of a culture, you will know that it is just like a suit of clothes. For instance, I come from China. I can wear Chinese clothes. I look like a Chinaman. But I can also wear Western clothes. That looks nice, too. I do not emphasize cultural differences too much. They are simply historical accumulations of much confusion.

Humans thus have lost their true nature in their many cultural creations. Yet if one's mind is open and unprejudiced, then one's spirit is high.

If in your house you have Western antiques with Oriental decorations-you feel it all fits, it is all good. Nothing fights anything else, because your high spirit is in the position to enjoy it. If any culture or religion makes you feel confused or troubled, I tell you, those cultural decorations are unnecessary and unhealthy and can often become hindrances and obstacles to your growth. You should recognize and respect your true nature. Then you may enjoy all the creations of all cultures. If you cannot enjoy the culture but instead let all the world cultures confuse you, they cease to be a tonic and instead become a poison. Therefore, they can be eliminated from your mind. Today many people cannot make good use of all cultures; instead they try to blindly emphasize the differences or specialness of one particular culture, making the world even more confused. This is humanity's own defect and is not consistent with ancient Taoism.

Q: Would you give us some general outlines which describe the fundamental teachings and viewpoints of Taoism?

Master Ni: Yes, there are twelve fundamental principles which may be considered as principles or guidelines for Taoist understanding.

❯ ✳ The Twelve Fundamental Principles of Taoism
(From the Tradition of the Union of Tao & Man)

1. Tao is the Subtle Origin and primal energy of the universe. We recognize the Subtle Origin of the universe as the mysterious mother of existence and non-existence. The universe is naturally so. It was neither created nor designed. Even though there is no personified creator, Tao, the primal energy which exercises and develops itself, brings forth all the manifestations of the universe. The universe can be comprehended by the human mind without creating a personified God. The original energy becomes the law of its manifestations. Everything manifested and

unmanifested is a spontaneous expression of the nature of the Subtle Origin; no intentional design is needed.

The universe forms an energy net for its own connection. All individual beings and things are under the influence of the energy net in the vast arena of the universe. The energy net is the natural administrative system. The freedom of all things and beings is prescribed exactly. As human beings, if we indulge in our strong passions, emotions, desires and ambitions, the influence of the energy net will be strong. If your energy is light, the influence of the energy net would also be light. If you lead your life normally and in harmony with the universe, you would have no sign of the existence of an energy net at all.

In this universe, each life is responsible for itself. Nobody can assign an external God to be the savior. However, occasionally some kind and highly evolved or natural beings will sometimes subtly stretch out helping hands. Or the person's energy may move to a favorable section of the cycle. Or the problems created through one's tenseness will turn into a comical emotional outburst.

2. The existence of Tao is absolute. Whether one is aware of Tao or not, all receive their life energy from Tao. Some follow Tao consciously, some follow it unconsciously; yet whether or not we are aware of it, Tao is the essence of all life. To be ignorant of Tao is to live in blindness; to know Tao is to see clearly. Therefore, we follow only the absolute, nameless, original Oneness of the universe, which is the essence of our lives. If we violate the Tao, we annihilate our own lives. We cannot exist without Tao. We reject all man-made names and religious concepts which were created for the second-rate mind. They cause confusion and obstruction to our direct experience of truth. The external Way is gentle. Brutal, emotional force is the low-level teaching of some religions. It is never the spiritual truth of high nature.

3. Our inner intention is to clarify and purify our own spirit. Our outer intention is to extend care and kindness to all beings and things. We refine our emotions and desires to be as light as possible in order to maintain ourselves as a high level being. We do not indulge in passionate love or hate. Temper and passion are by no means our ruler. In this way we avoid any downfall.

We also avoid religious emotionalism. As a spiritual child, religious emotionalism may function to initiate one's journey back to the source. But as a spiritual adult, religious emotionalism will prevent direct union with Tao. To follow Tao is to follow the integration of the universe with harmonious, life-giving energy, while to follow religious emotion is to form prejudice and nurture hostility. As a consequence of this, people invite death.

4. We practice conservation in our lives, particularly with regard to our energy. Thus, we do not scatter our energy or distract our minds with frivolous, unnecessary activities. We avoid wasting energy through arguments, restless boondoggle (busy work), fidgety behavior and meddling into others' affairs. In this way, we preserve the integrity of our spirit and enjoy harmony with the universe. We keep the spirit of a Taoist hermit in a busy worldly life.

5. We bravely and earnestly face the bare truth of our lives. We do not mistake Taoist cultivation as an escape from the reality of life, as may be the case in some religions. A simple plain and natural life is essential to spiritual completeness. Wu Wei, non-deviation and non-duality, is the highest discipline.

6. We take the constant virtue and normal steadiness of the universe as the model of our lives. The guideline of a Taoist life is to keep a clear mind and have few desires.

7. We in no way practice either ignorant asceticism or wantonness. We enjoy the beauty, richness and nobility of life and we practice the principles of right purpose, right method and right timing according to the universal subtle law of energy response. This sacred spiritual tradition can be maintained only by disciples who lead disciplined, simple and righteous lives. Initially, this discipline is rendered to the awakening disciples by the Master. An aspect of self-discipline is the abstinence from drugs, coffee, excessive consumption of alcohol, and other similar things, which are an obstacle to spiritual refinement. The developed individual is guided directly by the Tao. If one does not heed this guidance, one loses the Tao.

8. Sincerity, purity of heart and good deeds can lift an ordinary life to the divine realm. However, we do not disrupt the simplicity of life to create artificial opportunities to do good. This kind of effort is unnecessary, for a simple life in itself is divine. To learn Tao, fundamentally, is to live a simple, natural and essential life. It means we would deny trivialities and avoid unnecessary activities. In this way, we maintain the integration of spirit.

9. The Masters of this ancient Taoist tradition and of Ch'an (a branch of Taoism in Buddhism) are our spiritual pioneers and examples.

10. The clarity, purity and harmony of our own energy are the reality of union with Tao. Heavy energy (including emotional force and psychological cloudiness) is an obstruction to one's true spiritual growth. Taoism is not an ordinary religion. Most religions of different forms and levels depend on the psychological weakness of human beings. Some use hypnosis in their attempt to help and to control people's cloudy minds. Hypnosis uses only part of the mind, whereas Taoist cultivation is to integrate one's wholeness of being with the wholeness of the universe. Some practices mistake emotionalism for spirit. Such religious practices foster self-assertiveness, prejudice, and hostility. But in truth this is a pitfall for spirit. Sons and daughters of Tao must be above this and all things.

11. Sanity is the essential foundation for learning Tao. It is the basis for the development and subjective evolution of one's own being. Without a sound body and mind there is no hope of attaining Tao. Temporal phenomenon of madness are not encouraged in the path of Taoist cultivation. Criminal stories, ghost stories or religious stories in any form are not the food of a good mind.

12. Those who positively respond to the spiritual principles expounded above can be recognized by this tradition as its spiritual friends and heirs through their natural spiritual affinity.

Chapter 1

Taoist Inner View of the Universe

The Spheres, Manifestations and Realms of the Universe

According to the ancient Chinese Taoist inner view, the reality of the entire universe is comprised of three simple spheres of existence:

1. the subtle or pure law, which is narrowly termed Tao
2. the chi, the subtle energy
3. the phenomena, the transformations of the basic types of energy

In the furthermost depth of reality, there is no separation between these three spheres. One vast integrity, their substance is contained in their function, and function in substance.

"Heaven" is the ancient term designating the realm in which energy remains in a pure and subtle state. "Earth" is the realm in which it becomes gross and rigid. The Subtle Origin of the universe is the source of all "Heavens" and "earths," of all beings and things. The chi generates from the Subtle Origin at all times. The first beings who directly receive the original pure energy of the universe are called shiens, the beings of truth, purity and subtlety. Thus the realm of pure chi is the sphere in which the shiens are active. The center of this pure realm is the pivotal energy of the universe.

With respect to the whole universe, everything is a transformation of energy, including the field in which the energy transformations occur. Movement of energy brings forth all phenomena. Taoist Masters say that "the subtle law appears within the event and the event appears within the subtle law." They recognize that the law is not beyond events and that events are not beyond the law, because these two cannot possibly be separated. The Masters also say that when the law becomes "the multiple variations," all things are formed. Conversely, when united, all things and beings become one with the law. Looking at the diagram of the tai chi, ☯ we see the black and white embracing each other. This means that the law and the variations of things and beings are interwoven in oneness.

Ancient Taoists developed the capability of unobstructed insight into the universe as clear as the exposition of their own lives. By instinct and intuition, they discovered that there are four manifestations which represent the Tao in its original sense. These have always been the subject of the novice's research and, at the same time, have typified the Taoist's intuitive, natural approach toward all aspects of life. Exploration of the four manifestations is not pursued as a decorative philosophy. Rather, from the beginning, these categories have developed naturally into the available and applicable Taoist integral science. Penetration into those subjects becomes the Taoist integral life. These manifestations are:

1. the subtle law
2. number
3. the chi, either as subtle or as gross material energy
4. phenomena, all the different energy formations and transformations

The Taoist Masters understood that all events and phenomena in the universe must be subject to law, which is not only the origin of all things, but which also permeates everything. Thus to study the law is a way of knowing the universe. The numerology of the *I Ching*, or *Book of Changes*, is the ancient cosmological mathematics. It provides the calculative science of all phenomena, not only on the abstract level, but also on the practical level of daily application. The *I Ching* is the best instrument for exploring the subtlety of the universal process.

Without chi or energy, however, the law cannot manifest itself. The subtle law of the universe is not lifeless and limited as are human laws. Its subtle influence is always present, weaving through every moment and constantly expanding in all directions and dimensions.

All things in all realms of existence consist of law, number, energy and form. As for law, everything can be categorized as being or non-being, partial or whole. As for number, it must be odd or even, singular or plural. As for energy, it must be yin or yang, apparent or hidden. As for form, it must be concrete or subtle, flexible or rigid. Law, number, energy and form are the four manifestations of movement which can be observed because of the principle of polarization. Any movement has innate polarization; that is to say, any movement manifests the describable attributes of the mover. The ancients discovered that all things in stillness contain duality, or liang yi, which means "two sides." Thus all phenomena within the sphere of existence are exposed to the state of relativity.

The "One" is called in Taoism "the unborn universe," or "the stage prior to Heaven." At this stage there is only unnameable unity. The manifestation of "two" is called "the born universe," or "the stage of birth after Heaven." This stage is the world of all the transformations. Thus when the oneness becomes two, it has become the second stage of self-manifestation of the origin, the second stage of the universe.

All transformations can be traced back to liang yi and yin/yang. Liang yi returns to oneness, the original chi. This original one chi, the subtle energy, is the root of Heaven and earth, the origin of all things and beings. The original chi is the absolute and the infinite. When the Subtle Origin transforms into beings and things, it immediately transfers itself from the sphere of absolute and infinite into the sphere of relativity and finitude, i.e., from the unborn universe to the born universe. Once the universe transforms itself from the unmanifested sphere to the manifested sphere, then the indescribable Subtle Origin becomes describable things and beings.

The processes of the whole manifested universe can be calculated by means of an accurate science of description and prediction. Such a science is available to the student of Taoism in the system of the *I Ching* and the symbology of tai chi which are composed mainly of yin and yang with variations.

The Three Pure Realms of the Universe

The realm of pure law has no specific location and no direction. However, for the sake of convenience in understanding, we may refer to it as the "center of Heaven," or "the axis of the universe," where the pure, subtle, yang energy resides. In its pure state it manifests as law. When it forms itself it becomes events. In time and in space, energy may be classified according to its purity into early, middle and later phases. The early energy phase is the Subtle Origin; the middle energy phase, the subtle pure beings; the later, the tangible world. Above the world exists the Heavenly Realm of Great Purity, the Heavenly

THE REALMS, SPHERES & BEINGS OF THE TAOIST INNER VIEW

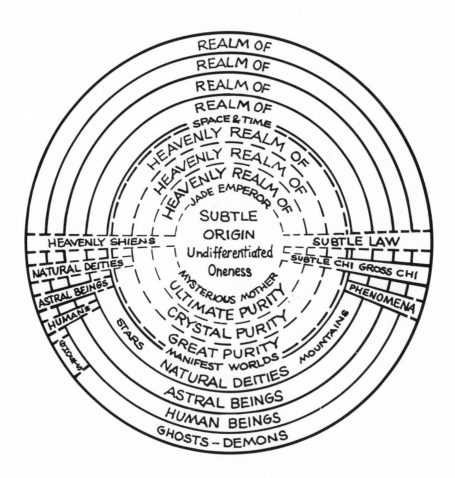

Realm of Crystal Purity, and the Heavenly Realm of Ultimate Purity. These are the three pure Heavenly realms, the attainment of which is the goal of a Taoist's self-cultivation through consistent purification and refinement.

The Heavenly Realm of Ultimate Purity is the original energy of the universe. Its unmanifested stage is entitled "the mysterious primal mother of the universe" and its manifested stage as the Jade Emperor or "Undecayed One." This realm is the energy in its most pure state, the indivisible oneness of the universe. An individual human being's spirit or the higher functions of one's mind, as the functional center of the physical body, corresponds to this realm of pure law which is the harmonizing, functional center of the universe.

The realm of pure law is narrowly represented by the harmonizing, functional center of the universe. It contains the original purity which manifests as truth, goodness, beauty and sacredness in their uncontaminated and unformed state. It is the source of the most mystical energy revealed as the fullness and perfection of the universe. Following the Heavenly Realm of Ultimate Purity is the sphere of the Heavenly Realm of Crystal Purity, the realm of the middle level of energy. It has its own Jade Emperor. Then comes the Heavenly Realm of Great Purity, also with its own Jade Emperor. These Heavenly realms are above the realm of humankind.

The energy from all different universal realms congeals to form the soul, mind and body of the human. If it is not blocked, the extended energy of the Jade Emperor dwells in the individual beings as integrating energy which can be further strengthened to increase one's power and uplift oneself. Not only is this energy the nourishment for one's own integral life, but it also serves to maintain the light which will help one to higher achievement, to become healthy and virtuous. An individual can then realize Heaven in one's own nature and life. On the other hand, if one uses one's good energy to indulge in only material desires, one will block the light of the Jade Emperor. Then a dark hell is created as the light becomes gradually extinguished.

So one may find everything within. The potential either to nourish and develop one's true self so as to realize the Heaven in one's being or to twist oneself and consequently experience hell - both are decided only by the development of self-awareness and proper living.

The Beings in the Three Realms of Purity

The Heavenly shiens are able to directly absorb pure energy and communicate with the Subtle Origin of the universe; therefore, the energy they embody is of the highest purity and is the most powerful.

Following the Heavenly shiens, the beings of absolute freedom are the most superior among the astral beings. The beings in this phase of evolutionary development receive energy in its primal simplicity. Their chi is also highly developed and powerful.

The next level of evolutionary development is that of humankind which receives its chi from all the neighboring stars, the sun, moon, earth and ocean. With all these factors as the source of life, human energy is a combination of the different influences. Each individual is thus composed differently with varying degrees of purity, essence and energy which is often disordered and confused. Since beings are not the first shape of energy of the universe, but only the third phase of the great transformations, they do not receive direct energy radiation from the Subtle Origin. Nevertheless they still contain the "extended" energy, or energy to spare, from the Jade Emperor.

The Recognition of Other High Beings

In the universe, human beings rank fourth from the pivotal energy of the universe, which Taoists respect as the Jade Emperor. Those above humankind are the focus and also serve as the locus of subtle interconnecting energy. They are the immortal divine beings known as shiens, and the starry or astral shiens, which are superior beings on this and other planets. Through Taoist cultivation, one is able to retrace oneself back step by step by refining one's energy from the gross level to the essential and spiritual level; from the mortal human to the undecayed Jade Emperor, the most exquisite energy of the universe. This is achieved through refining and purifying one's organic energy within and without to become the superior subtle energy, which then becomes one with the universal subtle center.

Is Self Real?

The Yellow Emperor posed a question over five thousand years ago: "My spirit returns through the gates from which it came, and my bones go back to the source from which they sprang. Where does the ego continue to exist?" If self is not real, how can one commune with the Jade Emperor? If self is solidly real, how does the Jade Emperor join in our being?

The establishment of self is never right. It is the result of the double vision of the dualistic mind. The external building up of the Jade Emperor is also never right; because the high truth of spirit can never be external only. The origin of the multi-universe is the unanalyzable mystery. It is beyond the mind.

To Know the Jade Emperor through the Taoist Teaching:
The Daily Communion with the Jade Emperor

In the vastness of the universe
there are many Heavenly realms.
In the center of each
resides its own Jade Emperor,
the universal central energy of harmony and integration.
While appearing as many,
in substance, all Jade Emperors are one.
"The Undecayed One" is his divine title,
but his true name is "Self So."
The universe is his body,
cosmic law his connection.
He is the mind of the known,
the eye to the unknown.
The giving and taking of life
is his self-expression and the exercise of his eternality.
People are his offspring,
the Heavenly born nobility.
Because they are self-corrupting,
they lose the healthy, virtuous qualities
held by pristine, high beings.
He reestablishes himself in humankind
in a still and flexible mind.
The self-commanded and easy mind
is the government of the Jade Emperor in man.
The only command he gives to his moral descendants
is to live in harmony with the natural cosmic order.
He educates them with self-knowledge;
Self-effacement is the venerable rank he confers.

He bestows his blessings
upon those of self-cultivation.
Self-contentment is the reward
he gives to his divine lineage.
To those of high self-awareness
his Heavenly assignment is self-realization
of their divine nature.
He fulfills the one who has self-dignity
and establishes the one who renounces himself.
He subdues no one as he regulates the universe.
He favors those who help themselves
and hinders those who are slothful and inert.
He gives energy to those who have positive virtue
and takes it away from those who have self-doubt.
Self-contradiction is the punishment
he gives to the vulgar-minded.
He brings calamity to the overly self-concerned
and delivers tragedy to the self-indulgent.
Shock and misfortune are his warnings
to those who are self-deceived.
He shackles those who have self-pity
and binds the self-opinionated.
He chains the self-centered
and penalizes excessive self-love and self-hate.
Simplicity is his great teaching,
harmony his abiding principle.
Egolessness is his key
for the attainment of greatness.
Selflessness is his secret
for the achievement of immortality.
The process is his immortal path.
He is the most supreme
because he is self-forgetting.
The clarity and purity of his being
are the source of all fulfillment.
He is the unruling ruler of my life and all lives.

Chapter 2

Introduction to the Subtle Beings

As we start our journey on the shien's pathway, it is essential that we have an understanding of its destination. As the old Chinese saying advises us, "know where you are going lest you become lost before you start."

The subtle realm is vast. It comprises subtle beings which range from the purest energy of the highest frequency of vibration existent in the universe to the energy which is so dense, heavy and muddled that it is almost on a par with the energy of the material plane. There are also subtle beings which can form themselves at will on any level.

There are five general categories or subtle states of being which exist in the universe comprising what is referred to as the "subtle realm."

As Taoist cosmology shows us, there is a Subtle Origin which is the beginning of the universe. All beings and things were born and nursed by the womb of the Universal Mother as the Subtle Origin of the universe. The Subtle Origin is beyond conceptual understanding. Through the practice of self-cultivation one cannot only re-experience its existence, but also its all-encompassing profundity. It is not an invented dogma which can be imposed on the minds of worldly people.

Between the Subtle Origin and the dense and gross material or semi-material beings and things, there is an intermediary world. We can say that the Subtle Origin is the pure energy of absolute infinity which contains the potentiality of all existence. It is the essential substance of everything in the universe. The other sphere is the visible, limited, definite, individualized physical world. Between these two there is a realm referred to as "Heaven" which is easily confused with the fictitious or religious concept of Heaven. But it is actually far beyond human imaginative abilities. It is also not the philosophical world of pure thought. It is pure reality. It is the realm of pure "yang" or subtle, active, creative energy. The energy of the physical realm is "yin" or inert, receptive, and gross.

In the realm between the Subtle Origin and the physical world reside the subtle beings, things and places which function as the higher creations of the Subtle Origin. This might be a debatable issue to the worldly mind; however, shallow perceptual abilities may detect only shallow truth. The Subtle Origin contains the subtle and all other realms, yet the Subtle Origin is still far beyond the subtle realms. Words cannot reach or define them. We are not capable of mentally describing the subtle realms.

When we face the "new" reality, there are two pitfalls of which we need to beware. One is the tendency to personalize, individualize or distinguish the energy of the subtle realms. Although it is true that they can be classified into many groups and levels, this is of no benefit for the integration of one's personal energy. The other tendency to avoid is perceiving the subtle realms within the limited concept of time and space and other frames of mind. The subtle energy may personalize and individualize itself and many manifest in time and space, and yet it may also exist transcendent to all human concepts. A beginner is easily confused about the difference between the teaching of mental discipline, the reality of subtle realms and the fictitious effects of children's and religious stories. Therefore, it is important to achieve clarity of one's mind.

The first category of subtle beings in the universe is that of Heaven and the Heavenly shiens. Heaven and the Heavenly beings are the first energy to emanate from the Subtle Origin. The Subtle Origin is the direct insubstantial substance of the Heavenly shiens, as well as being the subtle essence of the entire universe. The body of this energy is sometimes referred to in Taoist terms as the "Jade Emperor." The Jade Emperor is impersonal, creative energy which exists within the essence of all high beings and things everywhere, visible and invisible to human eyes. The subtle origin is the reality of the Heavenly shiens, and the Heavenly shiens are the function of the Subtle Origin. The reality and function are one, not two things.

The second category is that of natural "deities," as the energy transformations of some special locations. Natural energy is able to gather and form itself, and to be responsive to human beings. This energy comprises the natural "deities" of the universe, as the ancient innocent mind titled them. They can communicate in different ways with human beings according to their mutually sensitive capability.

Look at the stars. The stars are not merely the physical manifestations they appear to be. All stars have different personal characters because of their different energy formations, and they radiate different energy rays. Thus, they are natural deities with undeniable influence upon each other and the human world. Even on the earth, some beautiful lakes or high mountains or certain spots on the earth are energetic and may also form a special kind of energy which can be classified as a natural "deity." Natural deities exist within the realm of time and space. They are not equal to the omnipresent Heavenly shiens.

The third category is that of the spirit and astral beings as spiritual shiens, who reside in special places of the universe. In ancient times, those special places had communication with the earth, but now they no longer do. The original species of human beings had a strong relationship with those places. Some highly developed human beings can find those places. The astral beings came to this planet, finished their work and went away. Examples of this would be the Yellow Emperor and Master She Sen, who restored themselves after making a great social contribution and then ascended on high. The Yellow Emperor ascended on a yellow dragon, which is a transformation of the subtle energy. Master She Sen brought his whole family and some students with him when he ascended. Some of these super-beings came to earth to show the people how to plant rice and other crops.

Some people, through cultivation and spiritual evolution, can change their energy and respond well with the subtle realm. Also, when their spiritual evolution is consummated, they can bodily fly away to those places of higher energy. There are many historical stories of shiens coming to this world to help people, practicing miracles and then returning to their own place.

There are certain spots on the earth where the energy is strongly connected with those special places, so that once you enter into the circle of that energy ray, you may be attracted somewhere unknowingly. For example, in the Tien Tai Mountains where my tradition started, Liu and Yuan were picking herbs and gathering firewood, and as they wandered off the road, they found themselves deep in the woods. They met two beautiful female shiens whom they married. When they returned to their town, several generations had already passed. Nobody could recognize them and the descendants of their families barely remembered what had happened to their ancestors. In this universe, there are many spaces like this where the energy can respond to the special subtle realm and where people will immediately disappear if they wander there.

The fourth category we call the Immortals. Through cultivation, a person can change his or her energy. At last, this person sheds the old body like worn-out clothes and ascends to places which we call cave-Heavens. These places are openings of the universal high energy. Once you consummate your spiritual evolution during your lifetime and come into one of these energy "eyes" as the wonderland, you suddenly lose the sense of time and space, and thus become immortal. These "eyes" are sometimes called shien islands. Shiens dwell there and sometimes travel to the world and then return to that space again. They can also visit another one of the "eyes" or caves of energy. They can communicate with other "eyes" and know all the "eyes" of the universe according to their level of power. This is the reality of immortality.

The fifth realm is that of the ghosts. A ghost is the remaining energy of a human being who has died. It is like when you burn a piece of wood and it is transformed into smoke, but the human soul remains much longer than the smoke. When people die, they have energy remaining which may transform into another life or into anything else. It is uncertain. In this realm, because the ghosts are attached to their past lives, they try to gather a kind of impure, heavy energy in order to personalize themselves. Their minds form illusory lives with all the elements of their past lives - their families, professions, friends, etc. When they lived, they lived in an illusion like one of numberless bubbles on the ocean as it surfs to the shore. Some of the bubbles have "admirable" colors. The bubble is the life and the color is the glory of life. They play in bubbles and illusions. When they lived in this world, their lives were as bubbles. When they go to the shadow world, they are still playing bubbles without certainty of being.

They stay on the earth, but because their energy is different and intangible, they generally go unnoticed by humans. There are some places like old communities, which are so heavily populated with ghosts, that you may say the place is suffering with ghost pollution.

Usually students of this tradition cultivate themselves in high mountains because this kind of environment is not overly populated by people and ghosts. Because of ghost pollution, the ordinary world is not suitable for cultivation, as there is spiritual interference. The high level ghosts are called ghost shiens. These are ghosts who understand that life was just a bubble, and are spiritually detached. They can cultivate themselves and become pure yin energy. If ghosts have some prior spiritual training during their lifetime, it is possible for them to cultivate themselves, but with less opportunity than a human being. However, if they had much religious conceptual dominance, they may still depend on their faith, having no better opportunity than an ordinary ghost. This is because faith is only an emotion, and emotions are primarily a manifestation of gross, physical energy. They may have no effect after death. But the ghosts may still be attached to some religious ideas as their limitation.

The Heavenly shiens are the source of the spiritual tradition of the Union of Tao and Integral Man. Thus, this tradition is derived from the source of the Subtle Origin. These shiens brought the species of human beings to this planet and also enlighten their descendants. The Subtle Origin is connected with everything directly and indirectly. It is the most unspecial thing, but the most precious thing. The formula of being a divine immortal is passed down to the human descendants, and with it we can return to the Subtle Origin or any of the other high realms. We can integrate with the creative Heavenly energy and connect with the Heavenly beings of that realm and achieve that state of being. Because we are natural beings, we can also achieve the level of natural "deity." If we do not waste all of our fortune, our wealth of natural energy as manifested in physical, mental and spiritual essence, then the positive direction of our life is forward and upward toward the realm of the shiens.

Chapter 3

The Fivefold "Bodies"

Three Steps for Cultivating Qualities of a Divine Immortal
The ancient masters have deep sympathy for the people of the world. They guide people with the truth of life. If one has a disharmonious or partially harmonious body, one must first achieve a balanced body. After achieving this balanced body, one should not linger and remain attached to worldly pleasures, but rather make the effort to further refine oneself.

Through refining one's essences, one develops superior energy. When one combines this superior energy with wisdom and virtue, one may attain the great harmonious body and enjoy the fruits of being an earthly shien. After reaching the level of an earthly shien, one must refine and cultivate one's mental energy into subtle spiritual energy and thereby transform the harmonious body into the crystal body (i.e., the starry astral body). This body is more subtle than the physical body; it has more freedom and exists for a longer time. With the astral body, one achieves the illumination of one's mind. From the level of the astral shien, one must continue to cultivate in order to unite oneself with the eternal, egoless Tao. After the subtle body is achieved, one may then reach the level of the high Heavenly shien.

The "Basic Principles of Three Steps" necessary for cultivating the qualities of a shien are: (1) first, to refine one's essence to develop pure energy, then (2) to refine one's pure energy to become subtle essence and (3) to refine one's subtle essence in order to embody the Tao. This procedure is absolutely essential. We must follow this sacred method of the Integral Way and diligently cultivate ourselves.

All highly achieved shiens from the human world had to first work through these procedures of cultivating the body, mind and spirit to personally experience the three bodies internally and externally, to gain control of the one chi, and at last to ascend to Heaven. All the proof must be gathered during one's lifetime. After knowing the truth, one may live an ordinary life in one's community, or one may serve and teach people so that they can also realize and fulfill the purpose of the reunion of Tao and the integral person.

In this way, one can show one's gratefulness for the grace received from living in the world. One can then entrust oneself to the great nature of the universe. After one has already achieved the truth of immortality, one must keep in harmony with the great transformation to avoid damaging one's own nature. But one must also follow the evolutionary procedure for a shien to transform one's body through the spiritual selection of a nature.

This allows one to develop the essential energetic form, to return to one's Heavenly center or even to the subtle origin, and to achieve the final fulfillment of Tao. It is not necessary to display one's unusual abilities and startle the vulgar world in order to show that one is an achieved Heavenly shien. The Taoist method of cultivation is precise and systematic. One must fully understand all the steps in order to experience the fruits of achievement.

The Heavenly Emperor's Body of Oneness

The Heavenly Emperor's "body" is the "absolute one" and is composed of pure subtle law. It is not like the Heavenly shien's "twofold body," the astral shien's "threefold body," or the ordinary person's "fivefold body." When it exercises the function of law, it is always just and omnipresent. This body embraces the oneness to govern the myriad beings and things in a subtle way. It is the absolute one and has no comparative or relative parallel.

When it expands, it can permeate all directions and dimensions. When it contracts, it can conceal itself within the realm of mystery. Yet its virtue is constant, and is distinguishable by people with developed minds who know how to harmonize themselves with it. In the ultimate truth, it expresses itself in expansion and contraction, and at the same time as non-expansion and non-contraction. This subtle body exists both inside and outside of space and time, because it is the true realm of non-action.

Creative and productive and without end, it uses nine chi to adjust and govern the infinite and develop into the fullness. Its color is lucid and its light is simple and mild. If one embodies oneself with it, one will understand and experience its abundance and treasure of goodness, beauty and truthfulness. Nothing can compare with the wonders of its way. But it is always in a state of being not completely full, for there is always something left unfinished and untouched.

To see its dignity is to know its greatness. When the Heavenly sovereign shows itself, many beautiful colored energies embrace and worship it, and many respectful purple clouds reflect and clothe it. The magnificence and majesty of its subtle model is the highest form of nature. It is the unnameable and the indescribable. No thing and no being can compare with it. From ancient times until now, achieved Taoists have been paying homage to this supernatural sovereign and titled him the "Jade Emperor" ("Jade" meaning non-decaying). This has been a long tradition and is the terminal station of a Taoist's spiritual journey.

The Twofold Body of the First Ranked Supernatural Beings, the Heavenly Shiens

The Heavenly shiens have a "twofold body." Their bodies are composed of the interweaving of the subtle law with flexible high energy. Yet, their bodies respond more to the subtle law and are less formative, so nothing can obstruct them. They are free to do whatever their nature tends to do. Their light is blue when they rest and yellow when they produce goodness. These "two wonders" in one body never create friction with each other, for they exist together in perfect harmony.

The Threefold Body of the Astral Shiens

The astral shiens have a "threefold body" consisting mostly of subtle law and superior energy, but also having form. They transform themselves endlessly without changing their high natural spiritual qualities in their transformations, while they enjoy full freedom and happiness according to their own heaven-given nature and virtue. The main rays of the five bushels of high astral Heavenly shiens are mostly pure colors of light. The next are mixed with three colors. These are purple, blue and green. The source of their violet color is from the Heavenly sovereign and it ranks them high above other beings. The blue color shows they possess the sharpness of true wisdom combined with a quick mind and right reactions. The green color confirms their individualization.

The Fivefold Body of Human Beings

Human beings have a "fivefold body." They combine their bodies with the body of pure law, the subtle body, and the crystal body from above, in addition to their own human ordinary organic body and the potentiality of the development of the great harmonious body. Therefore they are composed of a "fivefold body." Their bodies consist less of subtle law and superior energy, and instead have more formative energy. Human beings hold on to their form tightly, so they are puzzled by the meaning of life and death. Through their worldly life, human beings have strong concepts about the body. Thus, they reincarnate over and over, but the stories of their next lives are not necessarily better. Sometimes they are even much worse, because of greater contamination. Reincarnation is dependent on the individual being's contamination.

There are different levels among those who have the shien's cultivation. Some have more formative energy and some adhere more closely to the subtle law and their spiritual ability. Average human beings hold onto the gloomy body of an ordinary soul. Therefore, their spare energy remains in the realm of the gloomy body long after the death of their bodily form. Even before their death, this gloomy body of an ordinary soul may appear in an individual's dreams or as visions. Through the process of cultivation, human beings must one by one remove each layer of their "fivefold body" until they return to the realm of the eternal Tao.

The high astral shiens with "threefold bodies" need to remove only two folds in order to return to the eternal Tao. The Heavenly shiens with "twofold bodies" need to remove only one more fold to become the eternal Tao, and the universal sovereign, the Heavenly emperor, has no need to remove anything. His being is the Subtle Origin. The process of removing the folds in some way resembles someone taking off their clothes to go to bed. In the realm above the astral shiens, the highest supernatural beings have absolute freedom, and put on and take off their clothes easily. Their bodily existence is beyond humankind's inferential ability.

Chapter 4

The Realm of Pure Law

The Subtle Origin

The Subtle Origin is the subtle root of the multi-universe. Through its advances and retreats it appears in all universes and all things and beings. It is the source of the creation of pure yang energy. All things and all phenomena are brought about by the universal yang energy. This energy vibrates subtly and continuously in all directions and dimensions, exercising itself like waves in the ocean with one wave pushing another, productively creating all phenomena. Unceasingly, this center of pure yang energy is the axis of the movement and circulation of all Heavenly bodies, the spinal bone of the entirety of the multi-universe.

The Subtle Origin as the Primal Mysterious Mother of the Universe

The Mysterious Mother cannot be talked about.
If she could be talked about
  She would not be the Mysterious Mother.
The name we give her is not the eternal name.
As the origin of all Heavens and earths
  She is nameless.
As the Mother of the multi-universe
  She is so named.
As ever-hidden behind all things
  We apprehend her wonders through the development
  Of our spiritual eyes.
As always manifest
  We can see the outer form of her offspring
  Through the development of our ability to observe.

Although seeming to express duality
  Spirit and matter flow the same source
  And each performs a different function.
That opposites are really one
  May appear mysterious.
But the mystery of the mysterious is the gate
  Through which the universe is born.

When the world recognizes beauty as beauty
The mind gives birth to ugliness also.
When the world recognizes goodness as goodness
Evilness is also brought forth.
Truly, the hidden and the manifest
Give birth to each other
And nurture each other's nature.

Difficult and easy complement each other.
Long and short exhibit each other.
High and low set measure to each other.
Voice and sound harmonize each other.
Back and front follow each other.
Therefore, the Mysterious Mother
Manages the world without ado
And imparts her teaching without words.

She disciplines without servitude.
She denies nothing and embraces all.
She rears her offspring
But lays no claim on them.
She accomplishes her task
But takes no credit.
And yet it is because she takes no credit
That nothing can be taken away from her.

By not exalting the talented
She discourages rivalry and contention.
By not prizing goods difficult to acquire
She deters coveting and stealing.
By not displaying what is particularly desirable
She encourages our hearts to remain undisturbed.
Therefore, she governs by emptying the heart,
Filling the body,
Weakening the ambitions,
Strengthening the bones.
In this way she causes the universe
To live without false knowledge and evil desire
And spares the knowing ones from any bother.
Practice non-concern and everything will be in order.

The Mysterious Mother is like a boundless valley
  which is neither empty nor full.
Fathomless, she seems to be
  the origin of all things.
She blunts all sharp edges.
She unravels all tangles.
She harmonizes all aspects of life.
She unites the world into one whole.

Hiding in the deep
  She seems to exist forever.
I do not know whose offspring she is.
She seems to be the common ancestor of all,
  Existing even before any divinity.

The Golden Carriage of the Jade Emperor

The center of the subtle energy is called the "Palace of the Golden Carriage." Its majesty and solemnity is beyond description. It is neither tangible nor idealistic in nature, but is original. It transcends the sense of time and space. The Palace of the Golden Carriage is the throne of the Jade Emperor, who is the subtle center of the entire multi-universe. The external energy flow evolves all phenomena, bringing its appearance into different forms. From the Palace of the Golden Carriage toward all directions and multi-dimensions, the subtle light of the Jade Emperor radiates into many circling light layers forming energy whirlpools surrounded by many golden rings, many light curves and many light zones. Each layer in succession pushes against the next, permanently surrounding the Palace of the Golden Carriage. There are thirty-six great universes, and the center of each is called a "Heaven." This center is the most profound! These Heavens can create many additional Heavens, each with a Golden Carriage and a Jade Emperor. The Jade Emperor with his Golden Carriage reaches each universe and sub-universe at the same time.

Exaltation to the Jade Emperor Within and Without

Your Heaven has no Heavens above it.
It is a wonderful and mysterious realm.
Your Golden Carriage is the vehicle of protection;
  It brings all essence to the infinite.

You are the primal oneness.
You are the source of subtle light, purity,
Quietude and impartiality.
With your wonderful harmonizing gentleness
You integrate all things and beings in all ten directions.
Through the profound everlasting Way,
You connect all the shiens.
Compared to you, the blue sky is young.
Your boundless wisdom is so quiet and pure.
Because you are so wise you do not contend.
Your Way and power are the most helpful and untraceable.
You are the true model of the three realms of purity.
You are the remote ancestor of all life.
All life comes from your constant virtue.
You encompass all virtues.
Your kindness reaches out in all dimensions.
Your profundity is immeasurable.
You revive all lives integrated with you.
You are the most kind teacher of all the wise and honest.
You are the wordless book for all the untaught generations.
You are the generator of Heavens and earths.
You are the strict reviewer
Of a thousand beautiful cultures.
Through the practice of non-action
You tame the untamed world.
Your pathway is opened by the truth.
You are the most exalted of all in all ages.

The Heavenly White Jade Capital

The energy range nearest to the Palace of the Golden Carriage is full of auspicious light which forms the center of the upper subtle realm called the White Jade Capital. This is the place where the Heavenly beings convene. The Subtle Origin and the White Jade Capital together compose the true realm of pure law, which is the most influential of all Heavens.

Request to All Divine Beings

My vibration of jade and gold
Accumulates nature's subtle energy.
This invites the effective divine chi
Which envelops this shrine.

With my positive breath
   I extend protection to all beings
   In all directions and dimensions
   In order to realize my true nature of divinity.

I use all my power
   So that this humble intention will come true.
Tai Chi begins with the undivided oneness.
It protects my essence and keeps my spirit.
The supernatural power of all the true shiens
   Is the boundless grace of the Jade Emperor.
The Tao is unifying and impartial
   To everything it reaches.
Divine energy is more than smoke or fire.

The Jade Girls spread flowers.
The Golden Boys spread good wishes.
I request all the positive spirits to present themselves.
Heavenly majesty envelops my shrine.
The subtle power exists everywhere.
It is effective and responsive.
With my subtle invocation I can touch the true Tao.
No spirit is insensitive to this invocation.
With my head up in sincere dedication
   I respectfully request all the spiritual beings
   To use my shrine as a shelter for all beings.
My heart is open like the enormous valley.
Only Tao is to fill the vacant center.
I employ this invocation
   So that my selfless intentions will be realized.
The subtle energy responds.
And so it is commanded.

Chapter 5

The Realm of Coloration

The Source of Coloration

> In the interpretation of the high truth of the universe, color precedes language. All subtle light energy rays originally emanate from the Palace of the Golden Carriage, signifying the universal primal yang energy. The nine kinds of color rays which correspond with the nine spiritual realms function as specialized vehicles through which subtle beings may communicate, impart blessings and transmit life-giving energy.

In this tiny portion of the energy playground, the nine color rays radiate outward from one of the many Palaces of the Golden Carriage in a spiral movement. They move around the "Jade Maiden" as one source of the young feminine energy, and become the manifestation of the active yang and the inactive yin. This spiral energy stream flowing from the Subtle Origin creates and contains all manifestations. The rays of light energy are in their purest and most powerful state when they are closest to the origin. In other words, when they originate in the purest energy states referred to as "The Nine Heavenly Realms," they carry the vitality of the young paternal energy to this planet.

As they radiate outward via the spiral energy stream, the colors intersect and intermarry, creating new energy formations, some of which are harmonious and some, inharmonious. The farther away from the Subtle Origin the spiral energy stream flows, the less pure the colors become and the more the energy is dispersed. As the subtle energy is weakened, it loses its subtlety, becomes more inert and rigid, and descends to the level of the gross, physical yin sphere.

As a result of reaching a less stable state, the energy undergoes a process of unceasing transformation, thereby evolving all the physical phenomena of the universe. The Palace of the Subtle Golden Carriage radiates its subtle influence outward to all beings and phenomena, conveying to them the energy necessary to sustain life, to attain light and to reveal wisdom. It is transmitted by the sun, moon, and other influential stars and planets to this small human world.

The Subtle Rays of Light Energy

The "Heavenly Capital" is the subtle center, the pivot of all Heavens, the realm containing supreme beings and harmonious energy. It is from this realm that Heavenly shiens respond with remedies for the universal mechanical maladjustments and disasters created by inferior beings. To the shiens, the Jade Emperor is the source of pure energy from which they continually refresh their subtle bodies and refill their productive spirit. They radiate auspicious light rays, pure energy, and are the true source of Heavenly blessings. By using the subtle light of different frequencies, the Heavenly shiens radiate various luminous colors of blue, orange, yellow, frozen green, violet and snow white as an expression or performance of their being and doing. The Jade Emperor uses ten main colors, while the Heavenly shiens use five. The main principle to be applied to color classification is that all colors correspond to the five phases of energy transformation. Each color classification has a specific meaning and interrelationship with other colors and with the energy transformations. This chapter will illustrate how useful a foundation this principle is for subtle practice.

Each color ray is interpreted as having a specific meaning which conveys Heavenly blessings and different kinds of messages from the Heavenly energy realm to the beholder. The subtle color rays are not like the grosser manifestations of ordinary colors which we perceive with our physical eyes. Nor are they the high frequency color rays such as the ultra-violet and infrared rays which have been discovered scientifically. Many color rays may be perceived by the sensory organs, and others through scientific devices which are extensions of the sensory organs, but these are far from the subtle colors of the high spiritual realms.

The subtle radiations from the Subtle Origin are only perceived spiritually. The appearance of a spiritual color ray during formal or informal meditation is the result of the harmonious interaction between the subtle energy developed through an individual's self-cultivation and the specific spiritual realm represented by the color manifestation. The process involved during this phenomenon is one in which an individual, through achieving a state of egolessness, initiates a response from a specific spiritual realm, and actually becomes united with the energy of that realm. The color of the subtle ray experienced during such a meditation indicates to which one of the purest energy realms the individual is attuned. The color is also an indication of specific mental qualities of an individual because it is through one's mental qualities that a color manifests.

The manifestation of colors, however, does not necessarily indicate that individuals are highly developed, but merely that their mental qualities are responsive to particular color rays. It is not important to experience colors, it is important not to immerse oneself in color rays with negative vibrations. Individuals who have attained the highest degree of purity, development and balance in the personal center of the Subtle Origin manifest no colors because of their even and undifferentiated state of being. This is especially true when they keep calm and quiet. The color rays begin to manifest only at the edge of the subtle realm when movement or response is indicated. Coloration has little value in the process of subjective enlightenment because it is still remote from the realm of the profound colorless subtle truth. Coloration is useful, though, as a tool of interpretation or a sign of power performance.

The Violet Ray of Subtlety

Of all the subtle rays, the violet ray is the most highly respected and beneficial. It is never harmful. Because it is of the highest frequency, this color ray passes through all other rays, inspiring virtue and dissuading viciousness. Traditionally the illuminated violet energy is called the "Violet Subtlety" and is exemplified by the color of the Big Dipper. The surroundings of the Jade Emperor's residence are abundant with violet subtle light. The subtle violet ray is a noble color, for it surrounds not only the Jade Emperor, but also the highly achieved Taoist sages on earth, who display rings of the same subtle violet in their bodies, especially around their heads. This phenomena occurs during spiritual practice and during most of their ordinary states of being.

The Blue Ray of Wisdom

Through the subtle blue ray of wisdom, one may know all the subtleties and secrets of the universe, because the frequency of its energy vibrations is the same as that of the secret knowledge of the universe. The subtle blue light energy is traditionally called the "Heavenly Secret" or the "Heavenly Pivot."

The Yellow Ray of Righteousness

The subtle yellow ray expresses good luck and kindness. Traditionally, the subtle yellow ray is called the "Heavenly Minister" or the "Heavenly Supporting Beam," because it sustains righteousness and brightness.

The Orange Ray as Light Energy and Warmth

The subtle orange ray, like daylight, is related to the sun. It is also the energy foundation of all life and the source of all vitality. Traditionally, this ray is referred to as the "Great Yang Energy."

The Orange Ray of Abundance and Productivity

A variation of the subtle orange ray is called the "Heavenly Treasure." This ray influences the abundance of the universe.

The Green Ray of Prosperity

The subtle green ray becomes the productive and beneficial power of the universe. In our tradition, it is called "Heavenly Prosperity."

The White Ray of Equanimity

The subtle white color signifies amiable, congenial and flexible energy. Therefore it is called the "Heavenly Identity."

The Jade White Ray of Perception

The subtle energy of the Jade white color is connected with perception. Traditionally, it is named the "Great Stillness" and is illustrated by the moon. It is the source of elegance and grace and also relates to intelligence and accomplishment in literature and art.

The Gloomy White Ray of Hesitation

Gloomy white is concerned with critical problems or overcautiousness. In our tradition, it is called the "Great Opening," and it is the energy of finding fault and of argument over right or wrong.

The Red Ray of Greed and Conflict

When manifest, this subtle red ray usually indicates someone or something that can easily become radical. It means greed or conflict and was given the name of "Great Wolf." On some levels it signifies excitement and gives warmth.

The Strong Red Ray of Impatience and Anger
The strong red ray signifies impatience and anger, and causes destruction. Traditionally it is called the "Army of Destruction."

The Black Ray of Uncertainty
The color black signifies mystery, panic and death. Traditionally the color black is called the "Seven Killers." The black and gloomy white energy rays are twisted and distorted variations of the other rays. However, any ray may be twisted and distorted by coming into contact with various negative influences, which thus creates its negative or unhealthy aspect. Therefore, in its pure state, each ray has its positive, healthy aspect conveying blessings and supportive energy. In its improper emission or distorted, confused state, it has its negative, unhealthy aspect which conveys death and destruction.

The nine rays of subtle energy vibrate at different frequencies, creating different qualities. As light rays intersect, new varieties of energy are produced by their combination.

The Basic Application of Colors
This ancient system of color knowledge is a spiritual and symbolic one which is extremely effective in daily life as well as in all applications of spiritual power, such as healing, making rain or encouraging the growth of vegetation.

The elemental practice of spiritual coloration is the application of the colors red and black. Red symbolizes fire, whereas black signifies water. Because these two kinds of energy harmonize with each other, life springs from any form or stage of life. Taoist self-cultivation is generally thus the practice of harmonizing the energies of fire and water whether in individual or multiple cultivation. The use of red and black also comes into play in the application of mental color formation. Of course, one must be careful in this practice of color application, as in all other things, where following a rigid rule can be not only foolish but dangerous as well. In working with color rays, it is important to apply the color vibration with extreme accuracy, because

THE NINE SUBTLE LIGHT RAYS

(Applied to influencing personal destiny, military and social prosperity, weather, and even epidemics)

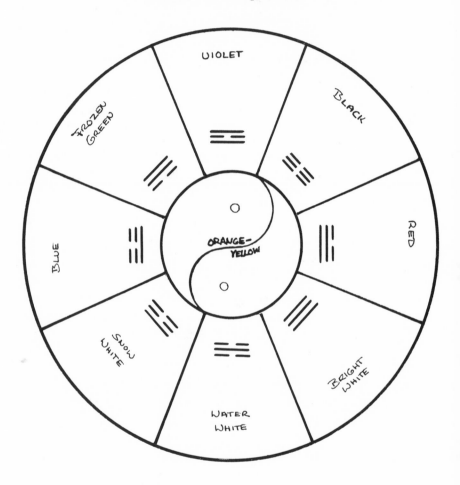

even with strong colors like red and black, there is a wide range of subtle differences among the length of the color waves.

Besides intensive meditation and cultivation, there are some basic applications of the colors signifying water and fire. One may use them to help adjust one to the climate, which affects the body through sensations such as hot or cold. Or one may purify oneself after sexual activity, for example, by visualizing the fire's color and sensation burning the body, and in this way disperse any odor or impurities. In the mental application of color, mind and body cooperate in adjusting the temporary congestion of energy in the abdomen which is caused by sexual activity. This practice is beneficial not only for spiritual purposes, but also for health reasons. It is important to maintain a balance in the body's energy flow without accumulating too much energy (or not generating enough energy) in any one part of the body. Both may provide the occasion for viral infections or other diseases.

It is quite common for Taoist Masters to apply their mental powers to assist people or to teach them. For example, they can summon orange and yellow color vibrations to accelerate the growth and ripening of crops. Sometimes the achieved Master will give a practical warning or punishment on a subtle level to a vicious person by the use of the black rays. But the transmission of black energy can be dangerous to the performer. The performer, because of his or her mental formation, is the first to receive the harmful energy before, during and after the projection of the subtle black colored ray. Also, the law of energy response dictates that what is projected by individuals will most certainly return to them. Thus a novice would do well not to experiment with the black color vibrations without thorough training by an advanced Master. This is a warning also to the practitioners of black magic. If the rebounding effect of one's actions is appreciated and if the truth of spirituality is understood, practices such as black magic would not be engaged in at all.

The Formation of Beings from Light Energy Rays

There are three great energy phases. The first is the phase of great purity. The second is the phase of diffusion, in which variation appears because of the different frequencies of the energy rays and their intersections. The third is characterized by stagnancy, rigidity and inertia, as on the physical level.

Subtle beings in the highest energy realm are composed of the original pure chi of the Subtle Origin, the first energy phase. The lucid bodies of spiritual beings are composed of the second phase of energy in the upper sphere. They have individualized characteristics and are strong and sensitive. The harmonious body of the original human being existing in the third phase, is composed of the energy diffused from the second phase, with the possibility of being refined into the highest first phase.

Diffused energy from the upper sphere becomes the so-called semi-gods, which are half-god and half-human, or half-spirit and half-animal. These beings are composed of a combination of various natural energies and unusual energy transformations. The diffused energy from human beings becomes the ordinary ghost or soul which manifests a gloomy, dark body.

The Rays of the Heavenly Shiens
The subtle bodies of the Heavenly shiens are a composite of the five rays of light energy, all of which are productive, creative, and graceful and without any negative aspects. The Heavenly shiens are the fountain of universal blessings and their colored rays of light energy harmonize with all things.

The lucid bodies of the superior beings in the astral Heavens, which reside in the central "Five Bushels of Subtle Energy Spots" of the multi-universe, receive the energy of the upper middle phase from the Subtle Origin. Their energy has many variations, is powerful, and influences the level beneath it which is the physical plane and human world. These superior beings of the "Five Bushels of Subtle Energy Spots" are the five main groups of the universal subtle Heavenly bodies. Existing more in a spiritual than physical sense, they have many different energy rays. The energy they receive from the Subtle Origin is the early developmental stage of yin and yang exposition with productive and destructive attributes in an equal balance.

 The Energy Rays of Man
The normal body of a human being, on the energy level, differs from that of beings with higher development. Human beings contain grosser energy than the beings of pure untouched light energy. The inferiority of human energy comes from its transformation through many indirect and winding channels and from its inferior energy source. Although the quality of human

energy is combinational and gross - that is, not in the original and subtle state - through self-cultivation it is possible to refine one's energy, thereby restoring its original, undistorted magnificence.

Heavenly shiens form themselves with the original, pure energy from the Subtle Origin. High astral beings are composed of the chi of the middle realm. The energy of the starry worlds below the central five bushels is more diffuse, less strong and more interrelated. However, if the energy of a being is balanced, peace and order are maintained. This is true whether we are concerned with the individual as such or as a member of a group or as an organism within a particular environment. If the energy is complexly interrelated, imbalances will occur as a result. It is disharmony occurring as a consequence of energy imbalances which creates what humankind defines as "misfortune." Throughout time, each individual is governed by the laws of energy balance.

The energy types of human beings are outlined in five categories which correspond with the five symbolic subtle forces - fire, earth, metal, water and wood. Some energies may manifest as the colors of green, blue, orange, red and yellow. The colors exhibited by humanity correspond exactly to the colors associated with the five types of subtle forces. This concerns the aura of individual human beings, not the color of their skin.

If an individual's energy formations exhibit predominantly red luminous chi, they will to be aggressive, quarrelsome and lustful. Generally speaking, their nature is troublesome and lacking virtue.

An individual whose energy formation exhibits predominantly orange luminous chi as his or her aura has a kind, favorable and spiritual nature, and is a good-natured person.

An individual whose energy formation exhibits predominantly yellow luminous chi is noble, kind, open-minded and gentle.

An individual whose energy formation exhibits predominantly green luminous energy is responsive, individualistic and conservative. They have high qualities similar to orchids, bamboo, pine trees, plum trees and evergreen trees, and are the finest of persons.

An individual whose energy formation exhibits blue luminous energy tends to have wisdom, a quick mind and to be quick acting. This person has the potential of being an excellent intellectual.

An individual whose energy formation exhibits luminous purple energy predominantly tends to be a superior person, a sage or a naturally good leader.

An individual whose energy formation exhibits predominantly luminous black energy is sick or dying.

There are seven possible colors of luminous chi which may be exhibited by a human being. However, the energy composition of most individuals is characterized by either red, orange, yellow, green or blue. The colors purple and black are unusual. If the five symbolic forces are balanced in individuals, they will be successful in their worldly careers. If the five subtle chi in individuals only develops partially, there will be a deficiency in some part of their life and they will not be able to enjoy life's fullness.

According to ancient Taoist tradition, we can make generalizations about a person's state of being by watching their energy aura. More importantly, though, is to know how to reform one's own chi in order to become harmonious with the natural order of life and to eliminate disorder and disaster.

The Significance of Balance in Individual Cultivation

When an individual becomes perfectly balanced, the inherent energies become harmonious and exhibit auspicious colors or no specific color. However, when the mind embraces particular attitudes or tendencies, colors manifest and the balance of the aura is disturbed. These colors alone can reveal an individual's good fortune or misfortune, and even an accidental death.

When a color is insistently produced by habitual mental tendencies, a person's nature becomes "stained" and overly defined. When an individualized personality is formed in this way, the flexibility of the universal personality is lost. By employing the cultivation and discipline of the integral Way, one may learn to transform oneself and rearrange one's energies so as to avoid any calamity created by an incomplete, imbalanced personality. For students of Tao, this becomes the first goal of their self-cultivation.

Certain individuals have an affinity to each other because their energies are harmoniously responsive to each other. However, although some individuals have strong subtle connection for each other, their energies may still be disharmonious and they may even dislike each other when they meet for the first time. To understand this, it is important to have the basic knowledge about the interrelationship of the five subtle forces.

Traditional Taoist disciplines apply the principles of energy relationship to self-cultivation. It is the rearrangement and reformation of the interrelationships from the prenatal and postnatal energy stages which affects an individual's development. Through diligent purification and self-refinement, one may transform one's imbalanced condition which stems from irregularity in the five subtle forces composing one's personality.

Correctness and honesty held in one's mind and lived through one's actions show the broad purpose of one's life, foretelling an auspicious destiny. Not by reforming the world, but through reforming oneself, can a person make practical improvement.

The Protection of the Golden Light

Spirituality denotes virtuousness. In the profound spiritual realm, helping others equals helping oneself, and helping oneself equals helping others.

The generation of the golden light creates a good and effective protection, mentally as well as spiritually and physically. As an illustration, you may begin to cultivate yourself with the "Golden Light Invocation" to nurture the golden light as your own protective power or energy transformation. When it becomes strong enough, it will be the best protection for you and for those who have not lost or destroyed their capability to be spiritually receptive.

The Golden Light Invocation

The mysterious origin of Heaven and earth is the source of many kinds of energy.

With this energy we can rectify the critical imbalances and make testimony of our communication with the spiritual realms.

Within and without the three spheres of the multi-universe, only the Tao is most revered.

From the Tao I receive the subtle golden light
to envelop and protect my body and soul.
It is so subtle that it cannot be seen or heard.
The subtle golden light permeates Heaven, earth and me.
It nourishes and educates all life.
I touch this invocation with my voice,
and with my subtle vibration of energy,
I attract and receive the golden light.
All spiritual beings gladly guard me.
The five emperors of the subtle five forces all come to meet me.
All the divine beings kindly accept me
for the golden light I have received,
which enables me to transcend all worldly troubles.
I am given power over all destructive forces.
Demons lose their courage and all evils are eliminated.
The shiens dam up their wisdom
and release it like thunder and lightning,
illuminating the dark clouds.
They inspire my clear wisdom to penetrate all things.
My five chi are shining and active.
The golden light quickly appears to envelop and protect me.
This edict is from the Jade Emperor.
May his golden light descend and guide me.

After reading this invocation, one can inhale golden light into the lower tan tien, which is located just below the navel; then visualize the light covering one's whole body. The water from the "beautiful pond," the saliva, should be swallowed and applied to the five directions.

Chapter 6

The Nature of Supreme Beings

The Divine Energy

Once an outstanding student of Tao said to his teacher: "Since there is leisure time today, I wish to ask about the Way of becoming immortal."

"Fast and obey the commandment of harmony! Cleanse your heart and mind, and make them become snow white! Brush away your know-hows!

"The immortal divine energy is too subtle for words to be able to describe it, but I will give you a rough outline of the immortal realm for you: the brightest of the bright is begotten from the darkest of the dark. The qualified is begotten of the shapeless. The spirits and divinities are begotten of the universal Mysterious Mother and the fundamentals of form are begotten of the sperm. Then from that point on, everything in creation begets itself a body.

"Divine energy comes without showing any traces, and its going recognizes no obstacles. To the divine energy, there is no door and no abode. Divine energy penetrates everywhere majestically. For those who obey the divine energy, the four limbs become strong, thought penetrating, ears and eyes keen, thinking effortless, and response to things universal. Without divine energy, the sky would not be lofty nor the earth broad. Without divine energy, the sun and moon would not move nor would creation prosper.

"And yet, expatiation upon the divine energy does not necessarily mean that one knows the divine energy. Discussion of divine energy does not mean that one understands. That is why the sage of Tao dispenses with such talk. If one adds to divine energy, the divine is not increased; if one subtracts, the divine energy is not diminished.

"The divine energy is the immortal essence of sages. Individual wisdom is like the streams that empty into the ocean. The divine energy is like the ocean. Individual wisdom of the sages is also like ascending a mountain peak, yet going to further to meet the divine energy, which is the highest. If the divine energy evolves all creations without fail, can divine energy be extraneous to the procedures of 'great' man? All creation turns to the Mysterious Mother, who does not fail them."

Can One Possess the Immortal Energy?

The ancient sagacious Emperor Shun (2255-2207 B.C.) asked his teacher, Ch'eng: "Is it possible to possess the divine, immortal energy?"

He answered: "For most people, even their body is not theirs, so how could they possess the divine energy? Your body is a shape that nature has given you. Your birth is not yours either, it is a harmony conferred by nature. This is why people travel, but do not know where they are going; they abide, but do not know what is holding them up; they eat without knowing that they are tasting. All this is the yin and yang breath of nature in action. How could you possess that? Divine energy is natural; it cannot be possessed."

The Heavenly Shiens

Through penetrating insight and spiritual communication, the ancient Taoists learned that the Heavenly shiens are the most supreme beings. They are the extension of the Jade Emperor's divine nature and virtue, and relate to the creative and productive functions of the universe. The bodies of the Heavenly shiens are subtle; that is, they exist without concrete form or solid qualities. Their form and qualities become manifest only through the performance of specific functions and are sometimes of an ethereal and luminous nature. They exist in response to the true nature of the universe and conduct themselves selflessly to integrate all Heavens.

A shien's body and activities are one. The behavior of a shien is not determined by conscious effort. Even so, it is always correct because the Heavenly shiens unerringly follow their positive, intuitive, true nature.

Generally speaking, all existence in the universe, both with and without form, is only transformation of the virtue and nature of the Heavenly shiens. Subtle energy sometimes manifests as the unification of reason and virtue; then its form becomes firmer and more understandable. When reason and virtue become more concrete and unified, the physical plane becomes manifest. Thus, the physical plane is the result of the materialization of subtle energy.

When related to the vastness of the rest of the universe, the physical plane is small. Indeed, the proportion of the physical plane to the spiritual realm may be thought of as being in a ratio of less than one to ten quadrillion. Thus, the physical world is merely an infinitesimal portion of the boundless and eternal subtle spiritual realm.

High beings descend to earth in order to teach and guide those who succeed in practicing the Taoist spiritual method. One attains this precious guidance, not through dualistic and idealistic faith, but through real experience of the truth. The profound Taoist spiritual method was accumulated and preserved through the practical minds of the Taoist descendants. Ancient Taoists usually cultivated themselves in high mountains or somewhere in the solitude of the wilderness for visitations and communication with divine beings. In later generations, lifestyles of Taoist practitioners differ widely. Some only cultivate themselves to reach enlightenment. Some cultivate only practical spiritual powers like healing and rainmaking. Some make it their cultivation to fly away with their astral friends. In my tradition, all these aspects of cultivation are necessary stages of one's spiritual achievement. For most people, all of these stages require a lifetime of devoted practice.

In the present materialistic age, ones who attain real achievement are few. They are as difficult to find as the feathers of the phoenix and the horn of the unicorn.

The subtle essence originates in the astral world. It is beyond normal human comprehension how the astral beings are created and are supplied with clothing, food, residence, communication, family and social life in a natural and effortless way. Their lives consist of self-adjustment and self-enjoyment, and although their beings are somewhat solidified, they maintain complete flexibility. Through their spiritual power, they can create industry, transportation, architecture and agriculture, all through the single-purposed actualization of pure being.

They create and accomplish things not with their hands and feet, but use the method of projection through invocations and incantations which cause the response of different frequencies of energy vibration. The astral beings or astral shiens depend completely on their own high energy to govern the inferior energies of the universe, and to properly arrange their modeless mode of life. They use their own energy to produce new types of energy or to transform energy from one kind to another. The myriad activities of the astral shiens produce innumerable influences on the natural creations and evolution of the universe.

The high astral shiens with their perfect self-awareness can take control of their own life span. They gather and renew their energy through certain practices. Through their high self-awareness, they adjust themselves so that they may live with ease and virtue within the subtle law.

The highest ones do not go against the Tao, thus, they receive no damage and are never imbalanced. They do not have any discrimination of time. When they become active, they appear as individual life. When they repose they return back to the indivisible oneness of the Subtle Origin. When the Masters of life inhale, they manifest life; when they exhale, they dissolve their being. Astral shiens can also transform the shape and features of their bodies as they wish.

The Heavenly shiens like to wander throughout all dimensions. They can make things and beings come to them when they wish. The astral shiens fly as fast as they wish and can reach any destination without the usual obstacles of time, space or gravity. They can manifest themselves in many different ways. They can do favorable and unfavorable things without any particular preference and, in turn, influence the inferior world. Because of this, Taoists are taught to cleanse themselves from any negative influences of the astral shiens. This kind of cleansing is much easier to accomplish than cleansing the influences of one's own impure mind.

The "Taoist Classic of Heavenly Revelations" and the "Taoist Classic of Spiritual Respondence," if applied correctly in practice, give one the power to cause the response of the astral shiens and deities, and to govern the inferior world.

Chapter 7

The Astral Realms

The Multi-Universe

The place we think of as the all-encompassing universe is actually only one universe in the entire, numberless multi-universe. The Subtle Origin of the multi-universe is formless, timeless, spaceless, ever-new and simple. The eternal flow of energy becomes apparent through the interaction of Yang and Yin and their exposition into categories of time and space. The expanding and extending movement of the subtle center reaches multiple dimensions. The interplay of different energies forms the shapes of things, beings and universes, all of which exist according to one pure law. Each universe has many astral groups, each with a different arrangement of energy which results from various compositions of interacting energy rays. The manifest sphere is actually very small compared to the unmanifest sphere.

Life in the Astral Realms

In the vastness of this universe, there are many stars and planets with beings much like humans. On the positive, subtle levels, there are such beings as "deities" and "nature spirits." On the harmonized subtle levels are astral beings. On the negative subtle levels dwell human beings and ghosts. All the beings on various levels are ranked by the quality and strength of their energy. The more impure or intermixed their energy is, the more physically and spiritually inferior they become. Only a highly developed human being with insight or higher, more subtle beings can attain knowledge of the entirely of the universe.

The Highest Subtle Astral Realms

The highest astral realms reach throughout all the space of almost all universes. These highest realms are hidden energy spots distributed throughout all territories of the visible universes. They may be described as branches of the Subtle Origin.

The Five Bushels[1]

The "five bushels" are groups of hidden subtle energy spots or subtle stars. They have a strong influence on the entire universe and are the highest energy resources and subtle connection centers for all the astral realms or stars.

The "central bushel" consists of three hidden energy spots which are significantly polarized in the shape of a triangle. The group of four hidden energy spots is called the "west bushel" and is significantly polarized like a rectangle. The five hidden energy spots titled as the "east bushel" are significantly polarized as , like the plum flower. The six energy resource spots of the "south bushel" are significantly polarized as , like a snowflake, and the seven energy resource spots called the "north bushel" are significantly polarized as . These are the basic hidden energy resource spots of the multi-universe, the origin of the energy which supports all positive action. They carry out their work as energy resources and balancing points for the entire universe, but can be perceived only through insight or intuition. Spiritually developed human beings can invite a response from these high energy realms for their personal rescue and spiritual power practices.

The Twenty-eight Constellations

Our ordinary physical senses enable us to perceive the twenty-eight constellations, which are our closest neighbors in this part of the universe. As the earth follows its "yellow path" around the sun, moving in a clockwise direction through the yearly cycle (i.e., from right to left), all of the twenty-eight groups of stars present themselves for our observation. If we imagine the constellations arranged on the face of a clock with the handle of the Big Dipper as its hand, we will see it pointing toward the different constellations as we experience seasonal changes here on earth. In reality, the handle of the Big Dipper can never point at different stars. Everything turns together. Four groups of seven constellations each mark the seasons of the solar energy cycle.

The ancient Masters used the constellations and the Big Dipper as examples in order to teach about the strong influence of the subtle rays emanating from all the important stars.

---

[1] also translated as "starry oceans."

The Astral or Starry Beings

The subtle energy center becomes the axis of the entire multi-universe up to the higher sphere. Surrounding the subtle energy center is the main zone from which high energy beings originate. These high energy beings are the astral or starry beings. They have individualized patterns of positive virtues and are furnished with some degree of form. They are the first typification of individual beings with form and function in the universe. The high energy of the five bushels begins to take form and be active as their lucid bodies. They can transform themselves and act at will, functioning naturally without even slightly going against the pure law. Besides their physical eyes, they have a Heavenly spiritual eye opened widely in the front of the head. They use the supernatural power of the universe to administrate, adjust and harmonize the multi-universe.

Astral shiens are responsive. They use positive energy to influence the beings of inferior worlds. They react to the subtle frequency of vibrations from spiritual practice. Through their profound and vast influence, they have a deep and long lasting effect on human beings. Astral beings were the ones who came to this planet as the ancestors of humanity.

The Three Levels of Pure Heaven

The "Heaven of Ultimate Purity" is the home of the most highly achieved beings who integrate themselves with the Subtle Origin and nurture the realization of their virtue and the subtle transformation of energy refinement.

The "Heaven of Crystal Purity" is the reward for achieved shiens who attain clarity of mind and supernatural qualities.

The "Heaven of Great Purity" is the Heavenly home for highly achieved beings, including the living achieved humans, who succeed in harmonizing themselves with the universe and maintaining the proper balance of their body, mind and soul.

These three Heavenly realms of purity as well as the rest of the universe is interlaced with negative elements. Ordinarily, people's lives range as wide as their mind and senses reach. All realms of purity are within reach of beings of high awareness.

The Ancestors of Humanity Before Fu Hsi

If one receives strong subtle energy rays from one of the superior astral worlds, one can become an excellent leader, manifesting special talents in one's vocation. A person with high and pure energy and spirit needs only some practice for refinement and cultivation. Originally, human beings are born as natural, complete and true beings; however, partiality appears later in the competitive way of life. The newly formed partiality and incompleteness cause one's energy and spirit to become degraded, impure and inferior.

Only the ancestors of mankind before Fu Hsi were beings with pure chi. They became perfect models for all their descendants. They directed their organic energy without any interference of the competitive mind. They balanced their minds through frequent adjustments without having any special attachment to the solidity or certainty of anything. Their spirit spontaneously balanced and harmonized all the elements of their lives without ever reaching exhaustion. They followed the principle of spontaneity in directing their energy from the gross levels of life towards the highest realms of spirit. They were rooted deeply in the origin of the entire universe and enjoyed complete freedom without having any concept of freedom. They followed the flow of the great transformation lightly, consistently and effortlessly, and were never trapped by death.

The Human Response to the Three Heavenly Realms

Humanity follows the positive nature of the universe through self-movement, self-adjustment and self-circulation on the physical and mental levels. The high astral beings and Heavenly shiens follow the nature of Tao, and in this way, reach their level of achievement. All three positive energy manifestations are based on the original one chi. This one true chi is the reality of the subtle Heaven and of the visible stars and planets, including the earth and the human sphere. With this basic understanding, a Taoist engages in his or her cultivation with the intention of rectifying his her energy projection in a positive direction. In the highest spheres, this one chi is less personified and sentimental. The spiritually inferior and ordinary spheres seek to be strongly personified and are sentimental about gains and losses, giving much attention to transient matters.

The great chi is pre-existent to the individual and the world. It is everlasting and can transform itself into anything, even back into its original state.

Therefore, to achieve any of the high and perfect states of being, one needs to purify and refine the present state of the chi of which one is composed. The pure energy of an enlightened being responds to the Subtle Origin. One's pure mind responds to the subtle center, and the senses respond to the high astral worlds and all the hidden supportive energy spots of the five bushels. One's eyes correspond to the sun, moon and stars, and the pores of one's body to the entire astral universe. One's spirit corresponds to the Jade Emperor, one's mind to the universal mind, and one's body to the body of the entire universe.

Thus a Taoist proves to be a real miniature of the universe. The pure spirit of a human being is the subtle universal energy as it is embodied by the divine immortals. It can be traced back to the Subtle Origin. With one's original purity, one proves the Heaven of Ultimate Purity. With one's restored simple mind, one proves the Heaven of Crystal Purity. With the harmonization and integration of one's life, one proves the Heaven of Great Purity.

The true Taoist pathway to divine immortality is first to refine the organic energy at the biological level to higher mental energy, then the higher mental energy to subtle spiritual energy, and then to rejoin with the essential center of the multi-universe with all its various high beings. This also means to regulate one's sensory activities in order to return to the simple mind, and to clear the mind to return to the pure spirit.

This is the healthy Way of life and the correct Way of spiritualization. This is the true evolution of the essential energy of a human being as a soul. Any fragmentary way equals the devolution of the soul. If you follow your physical nature, which corresponds only to the biological level, you unavoidably upset the natural order of your being by lowering the spirit to serve the mind and enslaving the mind to serve the sensory organs. When one has scattered and exhausted one's energy in this way, one can no longer enjoy physical, mental or spiritual well-being.

Having an excess of gross, physical energy which cannot dissolve or balance itself means to become an imprisoned ghost, as in the common concept of "hell," during and after one's bodily life. There are two distinct ways one may choose to live. One is to set one's spirit and mind free from enslavement to the physical sphere and to enjoy reaffirmed simplicity and purity. The other is to waste one's positive energy through ignorant materialistic struggling, thereby causing rigidity of mind, creating a prison of hell for one's solidified soul.

The Ancient Recognition of the Universal Energy Order

The energy rays from the Eastern seven stars,
   formed as a green dragon,
   are the source of
   Spring, life, vegetation and productiveness.
This energy is demonstrated by the activity of moving forward.

The energy rays from the Southern seven stars,
   formed as a red bird,
   are the source of
   Summer, fire, warmth and growth.
This energy is demonstrated by the activity of moving upward.

The energy rays from the Western seven stars,
   formed as a white tiger,
   are the source of
   Autumn, metal, ripeness and harvest.
This energy is demonstrated by the activity of contracting.

The energy rays from the Northern seven stars,
   formed as a black turtle,
   are the source of
   Winter, water, revival and storage.
This energy is demonstrated by the activity of reverting to the
   root.

The energy rays from the Central stars
   are the source of
   Earth, balance, harmony and sustenance.
This energy is demonstrated by the activity of keeping still.

The Ancient Invocation Causing the Response of Starry Energy in Spiritual Practice

May the energy rays from the Eastern stars,
   the Green Dragon,
   become the source of my revitalization.
May the energy rays from the Southern stars,
   the Red Bird,

become the source of my mellowness of spirit.
May the energy rays from the Western stars,
the White Tiger,
become the source of my abundant harvest of life.
May the energy rays from the Northern stars,
the Black Turtle,
become the source of my incessant revival.
May the energy rays from the Central stars,
become the source of my stability, harmony
and imperishable life.

Chapter 8

Shiens in the World

Humankind's First Ancestors

According to the tradition of the ancient Taoists, the ancestors of humanity were the Heavenly shiens. Pang Gu was the first integral, enlightened person to make distinctions about his environment. His name implies the undividedness of the ancient universe. Tien Wang, Jen Wang and Ti Wang are the source divided into three: Heaven, humanity, and earth. Chi Ti, Pai Ti, Ching Ti, Hui Ti and Hwang Ti are the five forces of natural structure. This was the period of natural sovereigns who guided the first people to live harmoniously with the cyclic energy rotation of the universe. This became the deep root of the nondualistic Way of life which is titled Taoism today. Tao literally means "the way."

Next came Fu Hsi who discovered the eight natural signs that are widely used as the basic principle of ancient cultivation to control humankind's subtle energy and predict events. Shen Nung, who invented agriculture and cultivated herbs for medical purposes, the Yellow Emperor, who invented the compass, clothing, political constitutions and the principles and theory of Chinese medicine, Emperors Niao and Shun, who were virtuous sages that led the people, and Emperor Yu, who tamed the great pre-historical deluge, were all outstanding shiens.

That was the period of the divine beings or shiens who worked with human wisdom for teaching humanity. They also used the techniques of the astral shiens to govern and regulate the public affairs of humankind. Those leaders and cultural heroes of ancient times came from a higher energy. They liberated the infant humanity from the difficulties of a primitive existence and put them safely under the warm mantle of their care.

The Astral Shiens

The astral world is profound and vast. The astral shiens are beings who keep their own energy order from going beyond their life orbit. Sometimes middle or low shiens would descend to earth as a human and after some time forget their astral nature because they lost themselves in worldly life. Nevertheless, they will still be dimly guided by the distant astral world. When they become desperate enough, they could regain their former level by awakening their former energy. Similarly, danger can also be changed to good fortune by one's returning to the original level in the astral Heaven.

Although the astral shiens have crystal bodies and complete freedom, they still respect the Heavenly order. Astral shiens might stray from their orbit, but they still have the tendency to restore themselves. Among the people of the world who learn Tao and become shiens, some were originally astral shiens who came to this world and through cultivation hope to restore themselves to their former level.

The starry shiens of the astral Heavens follow the Heavenly order and thus make it the order of their own lives. They gather together in a family-like group or community, and live according to the harmony of nature. Sometimes a new young shien comes to their sphere to live.

Shiens like to give help to the inferior human world. When a person's energy becomes harmonious, then this person too will have the possibility of ascending to the astral world of the shiens.

How Human Beings Corrupted Themselves

Human beings are a combination of three "bodies" which were originally pure and complete. Because we only make partial use of one body, we harm the wholeness of the other two. By overly amusing ourselves with physical pleasure, we hurt our spirit, so we cannot restore the integrity of our being without self-cultivation. Generally, people fall first from their "subtle body" to their "crystal body," and from their "crystal body" they fall further to their "harmonious body." They then become the body of an ordinary human being. Even in this stage, they can still enjoy a relatively long and happy life as a matter of course. Even when the "great harmonious body" declines into the "ordinary balanced body," they can still become heroes and leaders at some level. But next they decline to the level of the "partly harmonious body" or "disharmonious body," and finally become the "semi-harmonious" or "contra-harmonious body."

At this point they give birth to children that are weaker than they themselves and they in turn will have a tendency to become even more sick in general. Thus, humanity becomes sick and pained through its own self-created difficulties. This is because the pre-natal energy of the entire human species becomes impure. The perfect body containing the three precious energies and spirits begins to receive external pressure as its inner quality of strength is weakened due to unvirtuous or incorrect reactions to the sequence of events.

The pure energy is internally consumed by going against nature with excessive sex, excessive eating and excessive emotions and thinking. These excessive activities injure the three precious energies and throw the harmonious body into disharmony. People then look outside of themselves and run away with the wishful hope of passing through the gate of religion as a self-consolation and false salvation. Instead of asking for partial rescue, one needs to fulfill one's whole and complete nature in order to regulate one's life. Leading a life of dualism and self-deception goes against the true chi.

Taoist cultivation pursues the untying of mental and physical blocks in order to remove inaccuracy and restore the truth. This means to forsake the partial and follow the path of harmony. This is different from being socially and politically motivated by religious teachings which forsake this world out of pessimism.

The Problems of an Ancient Person Remaining in the Impure World

The human mind is sometimes pure and sometimes impure. It is sometimes clear and sometimes unclear. Thus it cannot maintain itself in a constant state. The histories of races and nations progress from one side or extreme to the other; they are like tottering drunks who can never walk in a straight line. Nevertheless, all people hold the possibility of cultivating themselves to the level of a shien. The only condition necessary to accomplish this is that they remove their impurities. If they can accomplish this goal, then they need not fear their ability to reach true and eternal life. The development of human society depends upon similar cultivation of pure energy in order to keep itself moving forward.

After living amidst the impure energies of the earth, a pure soul will become strained and will encounter some difficulty in instantly and thoroughly purifying itself. Then it becomes stagnant in the worldly domain and attached to a worldly existence. In general, human beings receive harmonious energy from Heaven and earth. If they can cultivate this energy and reach the level of the foundation of the harmonious body, then they can become earthly shiens with excellent knowledge and ability in life. They may live happily in this world as hermits. They are called earthly shiens because they have achieved the great harmonious body.

Those who have achieved the great harmonious body must use the two higher-level bodies in order to support the lower one; this is the price they pay for living in this impure world. If one lets the harmonious body strain the crystal body and the subtle body, one will experience disintegration again. The only exception to this are the ones who carry the truth to their fellow human beings. Their life is truth and truth is their life; thus there is no disintegration.

The Human Sphere

Those who receive the harmonious energy of the middle level from both Heaven and earth rank second in the human sphere to the earthly shien, the integral beings on earth. They may achieve the average harmonious body and thus they become the sages and heroes of human society. They are healthy, active, and positive, although they may sometimes suffer minor diseases.

Next in rank are those who are weaker in body and mind and have a half-harmonious body because they have injured their bodies and cannot receive the right energy.

It is difficult for people to perfect the composition of their energy. Therefore many misfortune befall them in the human sphere. In order to avoid these misfortunes, they need only to cultivate Tao, which means that they must regulate their lives. You can only refine the body you presently have. If you have a half harmonious body, you must first cultivate and attain the average harmonious body. With the foundation of the average harmonious body, you can go on to cultivate the great harmonious body. Once you have achieved the great harmonious body, you will have the energy to deal with worldly affairs. At this level you will have peace and happiness within and without, and you can always follow your own good will. Good will results from the health and wholeness of life and the balance of inside and outside. It is part of the manifestation of the great normality of the universal nature within you. With this energy, you achieve a connection with the great harmony that is the Tao.

Spirits of Mountains, Lakes and Lands
Mountains, lakes and countries are formed by their respective energies. They are shaped by the transformations of geographical energy and they take on their specific character due to their energy formation. Those with Heavenly eyes can see the beautiful and multi-colored light energy patterns as auras in nature. On occasion, the spirits of mountains, lakes and lands respond to particular human beings and transform themselves into a human image to establish communication with them.

> For the purpose of cultivating Tao, it is profitable to live in a place where there is a good accumulation of positive energy. In the high mountains and near the lakes of old China there are many human beings of self-cultivation who live and receive the benefits of their achievement of divine immortality. If they continue to bind themselves with the energy of the surrounding mountains and lakes, they will become spirits of the mountains and lakes.

Many lakes and mountain ridges of China have their origin in Kun Lun. At the top of Kun Lun is the famous and respected energy formation called the "West Pond of Jade Clouds." It is considered the main spiritual center of China and has become the Divine Territory of the Mysterious Mother.

The next rank to mountains and lakes are energy centers of nearby areas. This is also true of seas and oceans. From the Taoist point of view, geographical differences are no more and no less than different formations of natural life energies.

Taoist First Recover Their Own True Nature as Virtuous
Heavens and earths are the dispersion and collection of energy. Beings and things exist through the dispersion and collection of energy. The astral worlds are the extension and display of the Heavenly shiens, the original energy. To cultivate Tao, to become a shien, it is first necessary to recover one's true nature by recovering one's virtues, in the sense of collecting

> power. [Virtue means true gain in life. By realizing virtue, one reunites with Tao. In order to restore virtue, one must restore the purity and clarity of one's mind. Taoist purity and clarity means the normal energy of an original, undistorted true being.

No acceptance is given to the external bending of true nature and virtue. True virtue is not based upon vulgar worldly beliefs and constructions, unnatural moral codes or false virtues held by small communities, parties or religions. Good deeds are doubtlessly the correct virtuous expression of good people. Virtuous behavior and spiritual merit can bring good opportunities for yourself as a response, but if you hope to become a shien and to verify the eternal truth merely through the accumulation of external credits, you are still a great distance from your goal.

Cultivating Pure Chi

The vital constitution of everything depends on the one integral pure chi for its stability and well-being. For the purpose of cultivation, one should not deviate or deflect this true original chi. More than anything, the true chi should be protected and nurtured. This chi must be embraced and cultivated. It is a supporting power for living in this world. Taoists are aware of this, thus, cultivation becomes the vocational mission of their lives. This achievement becomes the principal method for eliminating difficulties and bitterness in life. The ability to gain new energy from the universal source is the goal. It is true that the ease or difficulty of dealing with problems depends on how you arrange your energy.

The exhibition of Heavenly scenes, shiens' realms and all kinds of beauty appear to those who refine their energy. Parades in full rank and colorful celebrations all show the wonders of magnificent energy. You will then be the master of your life on some level in this world, with or without glorious colors.

The accumulation of good energy is like the moon becoming full. Your breath will become light, and the vastness of pure sky will be brightened by your body of high purity. You will see that all things and beings are merely the collection and dispersion of this energy. At this point you will have already realized that the master is the pure energy and not the contaminated ego. When there is no Heaven for you to rely on and no hell to fall into, then you will have already become a true original being of the Heavenly realm.

The Energy of the Host and of the Guest of the Universe

In the practical application of our self-cultivation, the true energy may be differentiated into the energy of the host and the energy of the guest according to the ancient distinction. The host energy is the eternal pure chi of the universe in a broad sense. Transient phenomena are the guest of the universe, for their energy is only temporary. It is important to understand the way of the host energy as distinct from the way of the guest energy in our cultivation. If you do not make this distinction, you might mistake thieves for your host and you will be controlled by the wrong energy.

The everlasting energy of the center never changes. This core energy is the natural purity of one's mind. This natural purity becomes disturbed and obscured by self-created turmoil. By keeping calm, the energy of the center appears. Overreaction to external stimulation will only destroy the calmness of the true mind. By following harmony, one follows the directing energy of the host. When people are over ambitious, they just invite harm and turmoil. They must blame their own actions. By blaming circumstances, one will gain nothing and further dishearten oneself, as well as lose the kindness of the host.

The misfortune and pain of all worldly activities comes from the dreaming patterns of the human mind. If these dreaming tendencies are not removed, they will become the origin of one's own destruction. Therefore, the basic principle of Taoist cultivation is to break the dreaming patterns of the lower mind, which are created by confrontation with daily life. How can this be done? Because the human mind contains impure chi, it contains dreaming qualities as well as purity and clarity. Purity and clarity help pave the developing road in a person's life to escape alternating patterns of influence by sadness and joy, prosperity and decline, order and confusion.

The roughness of human history and the evolution of all cultures and civilizations are just the reflections of the dream pattern of the composite mind. It is as easy to observe human success today as it is to observe how failure followed human success in past events. It is easy to find something newly established by humankind, and just as easy to observe its rapid elimination. The movements of almost all the inferior worlds of the universe follow this melodramatic pattern.

The activity of dreaming tendencies takes place at the edge of the mind, not far from its connection with the sensory organs. Most people never discover their minds completely, and by employing only a part of it, stumble along the route of their lives.

> The center of the mind is the residence of the pure chi. The unchanging eternal Tao dwells there. In the postnatal dualistic world, most superficial activities of life take place far away from the pure chi of the center. Thus, favorable and unfavorable, beneficial and harmful interact on the edge of the vast ocean.

Many ancient cultures and civilizations have already become mere traces in human history. Some have left stone ruins standing, but most are just totally destroyed cities which are now under the ground. Their vanity and glory were created and destroyed in their dreams. Such undertakings cannot progress beyond the dream patterns of the human mind of the past or future.

Tao in Individuals Creates Tao in Nations

If one connects with the harmony of the great Tao, then one already has hold of the greatness of life. When such people become the majority of this world, then the world will become healthy and peaceful. Consider a family, village, town, city, country, or a nation. If the majority of individuals of these populations become healthy in mind and body, then those who decide, implement and follow their policies will respond to the great harmony of Tao.

All far-reaching affairs begin with the individual's self-cultivation. The world's peace and well being is only possible through self-cultivation. This is the fundamental policy of Taoists toward saving the planet.

In the human realm in places where the energy is pure, Heavenly beings as well as wandering shiens appear. Where the energy is impure, the inferior spirits of "ghosts," "goblins," "specters" and "evil genie" gather and create misfortune, disease and death. Where the energy is average, people enjoy their normal activities.

Chapter 9

The Virtues of the Universe

The Formation of the Universe

The universe is not formed by time and space, but by energy. This is the inner view of the universe as recognized by the ancient Taoists. The energy creating the universe multiplies itself on many levels.

The original chi or energy of the universe is the primal productive energy. It is also called the Mysterious Mother of all existence. All phenomena are merely one state of the great transformation of this primal mysterious energy.

Outwardly, the universe has form, color, size, etc. However, in its essence, the universe is intangible, uncontrollable energy of subtle constitution. There are clearly distinguishable differences among the energies of the universe. Some energies are essential or central, some are less essential or marginal, some are delicate, and some are gross or coarse. Gross energies are easily recognized through their form, color, capacity and dimension, but energies on the subtle level evade perception by the rigid intellectual mind and can only be known intuitively.

As the primal energy extends itself, phenomena and beings manifest on the tangible level. As it retreats, phenomena and beings also disappear. The primal energy exercises itself through the interplay of yin and yang, a movement which resembles the game of hide and seek. All phenomena and beings, with their different dances and costumes, become apparent with the movement or silent music of the primal energy.

A human soul can attain spiritual freedom on the different subtle levels because the subtle levels are more stable. Everything on the gross levels die. Only the subtle essence endures. Therefore, people of high awareness simplify themselves in order to harbor the essence of their eternal being.

The most exquisite energy of the multi-universe is called the Jade Emperor. Jade symbolizes purity, incorruptibility, dignity and many other high qualities. Thus the ancient Taoists used it as the symbol for the subtle essence of the multi-universe. The Jade Emperor functions as the subtle connection, the subtle responsive energy and the subtle ruler of the multi-universe.

The Heavenly divine sovereign governs the physical sphere of the universe through the five basic types of energy: the energy of productivity, symbolized by wood; the energy of expansion, symbolized by fire; the energy of harmonization, symbolized by earth; the energy of change, symbolized by metal; and the energy of circulation, symbolized by water.

> The five types of energy manifest as strong or weak, positive or negative, and thus create the division of yin and yang categories. In this way, the energies of the Ten Heavenly Stems and the Twelve Earthly Branches evolve. All of these are basic elements widely used in Taoist philosophy and holistic sciences. Their functions must be clearly understood by the student.

The Virtues: the Various Describable Attainments, Attributes and Qualities from the Manifestations of the Primal Chi

The macrocosm comes from the original chi. This primal chi transforms itself into multiple variations, following the order that "Tao gives birth to one, the principle of singularity, neutrality and harmony. One gives birth to two, the principle of duality. Two gives birth to three, the principle of multiplication. Three gives birth to all things and all beings."

After the original oneness became divided and Heaven and earth were born, the primal mysterious energy began to manifest. The particular qualities of different states of this energy which manifest in people are called "virtues." One can accumulate either positive or negative energies as elements of one's personality. The original chi manifests in numerous forms, in as many forms as there are phenomena found in the evolution of the external world. Physical evolution parallels spiritual evolution. Numerous virtues (attributes) originate from the one natural virtue (Teh), just as forms come from the original chi.

This means that the development of the physical and mental world is the observable reality of the one original chi. These worlds are the primal chi projected into many variations. Therefore, the one chi is not limited to mind or matter, but mind and matter are the main manifestations of the one chi. One may say that the chi is able to transform itself into mind or matter.

The Tao is the indescribable ultimate moral nature of the universe, while Teh (virtue) is the describable varied virtue of the universe. The ultimate moral nature cannot be conceptualized by isolating it from any single thing in the universe, but the various virtues as special attributes of a thing can be described in many ways. When we look at the various virtues of things and the numberless manifestations of the universe, we are puzzled and perplexed about the source of all lives and things. We wonder about the real authority of all matters. When we retrace all virtues and manifestations, we find the inseparable ultimate moral nature of the universe, the mother of all.

The Virtues of the "Five Starry Oceans" of the Universe

The Three Original Virtues of the "Central Starry Ocean"
The Original Simplicity contains all the variations of the natural positive virtues found in the universe and is the highest virtue of all. From this Original Simplicity developed the three original virtues: original truth, original beauty and original goodness. These three virtues are the first three divisions from the one chi, manifesting as the three virtues or powers of the "Central Starry Ocean," the main supporter or the direct source of all astral worlds. Thus, all things and all beings which come from this "Central Starry Ocean" also individually contain all three original virtues.

The Four Uniting Virtues of the "West Starry Ocean"
Producing the four powers of the "West Starry Ocean," the multiple primal chi manifests as the uniting virtues of the universe. These are helpfulness, practicality, activity and service.

The Five Virtues of Beauty from the "East Starry Ocean"
The five powers from the "East Starry Ocean" manifest the original beauty and produce the five virtues of beauty. These are intelligence, grace, delicacy, attractiveness and dexterity.

The Six Virtues of Goodness from the "South Starry Ocean"
The original goodness of the universe manifests as the multiple primal chi and develops into the six powers of the "South Starry Ocean." These six virtues of goodness are gentleness, talent, intelligence, maturity, abundance and optimism.

The Seven Virtues of Truth from the "North Starry Ocean"
The seven powers of the "North Starry Ocean" manifest as the original truth. They create the seven virtues of nobility, wisdom, dignity, decisiveness, leadership, beneficent powers and

courage. At the same time they create time, space and energy manifestations.

The Separation of High and Low Virtues

These virtues complements each other as yin and yang in the interaction of creation, and also distinguish themselves as high virtues and low virtues. The beings with high virtues do not consider themselves as virtuous, but only know to follow the ultimate universal nature of simplicity. The beings with low virtue emphasize individual personal virtue because they lost their true vision by holding onto the deceptive concepts created by their isolated mental attitudes.

The people of inferior virtue are not satisfied with themselves. They are continually reforming and remaking themselves in the hope of becoming good, beautiful or holy. Their personality manifestations multiply and expand; their personal energy contracts. Endless confusion is the result.

When one has learned to harmonize with the ultimate moral nature of the universe, one knows this truth: that mind is matter and matter is mind. The differences between the two are only in appearance and are based on external observation. In reality, they are one. We thus summarize all various activities as stemming from the Original Simplicity. By adhering to the Original Simplicity, one can integrate oneself with the entirety of the universe. When one maintains simplicity in one's life, one fulfills the true goodness, beauty and sacredness of life.

The Interaction of Yin and Yang

The energy flow of nature is cyclical. In the creative order, the energy is transformed from the phase of fire to metal to water to wood. In the destructive order, energy is transformed from the phase of fire to metal to wood to water. Because there is resistance to creative transition and conflict between the two conquering phases, fire and metal or summer to autumn, an abrupt transition would cause radical change and thus be too strong. Therefore, earth forms a transitional phase during the change from one phase to another. It functions as a harmonizing and balancing power between the other phases.

As energy transforms itself, the differences between the Twelve Earthly Branches appear. They express the low sphere of energy which cooperates with the high sphere, the energies of the Ten Heavenly Stems. Coming together, these two energy spheres form sixty different new sub-energies which are used to mark yearly, monthly and daily energy cycles and the energies of the different directions.

This system is widely used in Chinese medicine, personal energy analysis (astrology) and geographical energy analysis (geomancy). It can also be used as a tool to predict the future when the present energy formation is known. It is also applied in Taoist internal alchemy and mystical cultivation. It is as precise as mathematics. In this book, I can give only a general understanding of it.[1]

The Energies of the Ten Heavenly Stems

The original energy creating Heaven and earth is the energy Jia - masculine, productive Heavenly energy.

The energy giving form and detail to all creation is the energy Yi (pronounced e) - feminine, productive Heavenly energy.

The energy cultivating and illuminating all aspects of life is the energy Bien - masculine, reinforcing Heavenly energy.

The energy that assists and improves all aspects of life is the energy Ding - feminine, reinforcing Heavenly energy.

The energy establishing and protecting all beings and things as individual integral energy fields is the energy Wuh - masculine, balancing Heavenly energy.

The energy inherent in and supporting all life is the energy Ji - feminine, balancing Heavenly energy.

The energy eliminating corruption and restoring freshness is the energy Geng - masculine, reforming Heavenly energy.

The energy consistently maintaining the creation's perfection is the energy Hsin - feminine, reforming Heavenly energy.

The energy circumfusing and encompassing all creation is the energy Ren - masculine, circulating Heavenly energy.

The energy connecting the beginning and the end of creation is the energy Quei - feminine, circulating Heavenly energy.

The Energies of the Twelve Earthly Branches

The energy reviving the seeds and multiplying the rats is the energy Tze - masculine, reproductive earthly energy.

---

[1]For further information on the Heavenly Stems and the Earthly Branches, see *The Book of Changes and the Unchanging Truth.*

The energy supplying nourishment like the cow is the energy Chui - feminine supportive earthly energy.

The energy sprouting vigorously and striding forward like the tiger is Ein - masculine, progressing earthly energy.

The energy growing rapidly like the rabbit is the energy Mao - feminine, self-accomplishing earthly energy.

The energy strong as the dragon is the energy Ch'en - masculine, active earthly energy.

The energy moving hidden like the snake is the energy Sze - the feminine, maturing earthly energy.

The energy striving toward the peak of prosperity like the running horse is the energy Wu - masculine, expansive earthly energy.

The energy amiable like the sheep is the energy Wei - feminine, tranquil earthly energy.

The energy effecting change like the restless monkey is the energy Shen - masculine, flexible earthly energy.

The energy receptive like the hen is the energy Yu - feminine, receptive earthly energy.

The energy possessive and watchful like the dog is the energy Shu - masculine, dominant earthly energy.

The energy enriching itself like the swine is the energy Hai - feminine, storing earthly energy.

The Subdivisions of Power

The subdivisions of power from the original One Nature manifests in different formations of virtues with positive, negative, or combined effect in the human world.

The Thirty-six Distinct Characteristic Powers of the High Sphere

The Positive Category of Distinct Personality Projections:

1. *emergent leadership*	10. *strength*
2. *the witness*	11. *ingenuity*
3. *intelligence*	12. *activity*
4. *bravery*	13. *penetration*
5. *majesty*	14. *richness*
6. *heroism*	15. *longevity*
7. *firmness*	16. *resourcefulness*
8. *tolerance*	17. *speediness*
9. *agility*	18. *levelness*

The Negative Category of Distinct Personality Projections:

1. *inertia and uncooperativeness*
2. *dissipation*
3. *vulnerability*
4. *ineffectiveness*
5. *wastefulness*
6. *unclarity*
7. *unproductiveness*
8. *lowliness*
9. *loftiness*
10. *impatience*
11. *boastfulness*
12. *solicitation*
13. *jealousy*
14. *wildness*
15. *negligence*
16. *aimlessness*
17. *selfishness*
18. *roughness*

The Seventy-two Distinct Characteristic Powers of the Low Sphere

The Distinct Personality Projections:

1. *viciousness*
2. *savageness*
3. *the darkness of hatred*
4. *cruel wisdom*
5. *vanity*
6. *stagnancy*
7. *ferocity*
8. *pride*
9. *guile*
10. *ignorance*
11. *distortion*
12. *aggression*
13. *unrighteousness*
14. *deviation*
15. *going astray*
16. *evil associations*
17. *dwarfing of virtue*
18. *negativity*
19. *uselessness*
20. *hopelessness*
21. *stupidity*
22. *barbarity*
23. *parasitic behavior*
24. *greediness*
25. *blamefulness*
26. *unmercifulness*
27. *fury*
28. *wandering*
29. *cunningness*
30. *uncleanliness*
31. *blind forwardness*
32. *fullness*
33. *unfaithfulness*
34. *incompleteness*
35. *sinfulness*
36. *peculiarity*
37. *injustice*
38. *arrogance*
39. *disharmony*
40. *hastiness*
41. *suppression*
42. *cessation*
43. *devilishness*
44. *performing black magic*
45. *obscurity*
46. *emptiness*
47. *inadaptability*
48. *insensitivity*
49. *inconsiderateness*
50. *disfavor*

51. *scheming*
52. *corruption*
53. *insufficiency*
54. *sharpness*
55. *irresponsibility*
56. *hoarding*
57. *troublesomeness*
58. *harmfulness*
59. *undeservedness*
60. *crankiness*
61. *sneakiness*

62. *shadowiness*
63. *avenging*
64. *stubbornness*
65. *inferiority*
66. *mightiness*
67. *filthiness*
68. *thievishness*
69. *narrowness*
70. *ruthlessness*
71. *manipulation*
72. *indignity*

The Difference Below the Three Realms of Purity

The energy of the beings outside the three Realms of Purity (Heavenly, astral, earthly) differs from the energy of the beings within these pure realms. Impure beings move forcibly through the world. Their movement is overly strong or overly weak rather than natural. Their behavior is conspicuous and sometimes violent. These beings are classified according to their many varied levels.

In these levels below the three Realms of Purity we find the beings with partly pure and partly impure energy. Because their energy is incomplete, these beings have a specialized and, therefore, only a partial nature. The strong energy of the astral worlds manifests as rays with differences in brightness and darkness, lightness and heaviness. When the qualities of the rays are different, their energies are different. When their energies are different, their function will also be different.

To live in harmony with the pure illimitable Tao, one needs to simplify one's behavior and activities of life so that one may accumulate positive energy. Internally, one must cultivate one's positive and high energy by the same principle of simplification. Thus, by following the Tao, one can become self-achieved and restore one's connection with the Heavenly source.

The energy levels closest to Heaven are the purest, and those farther away are less pure. Human beings can be classified in a similar manner. Hence, some can become achieved and connect themselves with Heaven and make it their shelter. Others have difficulty lifting themselves above the troubled waters.

The farther away from the three Realms of Purity one's energy is, the more impurities and the less freedom one has.

The stronger the bond of one's impurities, the greater is one's unhappiness. People generally give this realm the name "hell." The reason for the existence of Heaven and hell is found in the different kinds of energy. Without virtue, one cannot endure. With complete virtue, one can be united with Heaven, and one's search for divinity can become a reality.

The Flexibility of Virtue and Non-Virtue

The material world of non-virtue and the spiritual world of virtue must find unification. So must the materialistic and spiritualistic characteristics of human beings. Separation contains the original unity and must continually return to it. Any movement in a single direction must come to its end, but if the movement is cyclical, then going is returning and returning is going.

The simple primary energy performance of contraction and expansion brings about all things in the universe, with all kinds of attributes and virtues. If one is confused by this, it is because one has lost the view of the Original Primal Simplicity. By returning to simplicity, one may find the ultimate moral nature of the universe. The entire universe will then maintain its productivity and creativeness within you, and you can give support to your own life. Then you can continually regenerate your life without exhausting yourself early.

The Unification of Internal and External Worlds

From the above, it becomes apparent that we can perceive the multi-universe as a multifold development of the original chi. If we act directly from our moral nature, there is no need to try to distinguish our motives and incentives with our minds. Our life's straight, sincere activities cannot be separated from the inexhaustible source. The connection with universal life can then be restored in our inner order. Thus, we simply accomplish unification of our internal and external worlds. There is no need for complicated ideologies or profound theological processes.

The subtle divine energy of justice is the secret factor in the endeavor of human life and death. It becomes apparent in an ordinary life that the opportunity to obtain support from the divine energy is easy. Virtuous individuals can commune with Heaven and keep their roots there with incorruptibility. The high, self-aware ones are able to pre-experience Heaven through their daily self-cultivation and self-purification. Their energy stretches into the three great pure realms by remaining stable, constant, original and free from worry. Whoever adheres to one's pure nature is able to attain support from the universal divinity without paying any price.

Completeness in Simplicity

Whether of religious nature or social purpose, any teaching which requires that one develop in an unnatural manner in order to achieve a goal leads one away from one's true nature. By taking a particular standpoint and thus becoming polarized, one loses one's originally well-balanced nature.

This approach causes people to become sharp-edged and acute, and brings about spiritual, psychological and social conflict. It creates endless trouble and prevents real social and individual growth.

Ancient Taoism teaches that returning to the Original Simplicity is to embrace one's own nature. When this is achieved, one leads a life of fullness and truth. Nothing external needs to be added to one's own nature. Life, Tao and everything is formed with one true nature. There is nothing to achieve and nothing to sacrifice, for all truth is here and now.

Chapter 10

The Subtle and Human Realms of Earth

Basic Understanding

The earth is where people reside, and although people are familiar with its superficial and concrete aspects, they are still not knowledgeable about its more subtle and profound reality. People know its contour, but not its inner truth. Few people can achieve such understanding, and only those with completely developed spiritual power can understand the entire truth. In my tradition, the testimony of the ancient Taoist Masters' knowledge of the subtle realms is true knowledge. Most people are ignorant of it until some unknowable trouble occurs which makes them puzzled at the subtle influence.

Besides the many human beings who live in the physical realm of earth, there also exist many different energies and spiritual beings in the spiritual realm of earth. We can also use the divisions of the three categories which were discussed in previous chapters to describe the earth. When discussing the "Heaven" of earth, we mean the pure energy of earth which includes the spirits of mountains, lakes and lands, and also the shiens who have ascended to some subtle energy spots above the earth. The "earth" of the earth is the sphere where the energy is impure. Here, many kinds of "genie" and certain animal spirits like cow spirits, snake ghosts, goblins and specters exist as transformed unhealthy energies. These energies diffuse to become special viruses, which become the cause of different diseases and troublesome subtle influences for worldly people. Especially when people are weak and confused, these energies can brew common diseases or unusual troubles. This is part of the reason that a practitioner of the shien tradition may prefer to live in solitude. And of course, the "man" of the earth is the sphere where normal human beings live.

Dwelling Places of High and Low Spirits

In the vast universe extending to the entire multi-universe, there are many big holes. Traditionally Taoists call them "Heavenly Caves." The "Thirty-Six Heavenly Caves" are famous for being the paradise of the shiens, the immortal divine beings. Among the many holes in the multi-universe, some are big, bright holes with a positive manifestation where eternal life really happens. Others are black holes with a negative manifestation which are the home of death and the shadowy beings. In addition to the big holes, there are numerous smaller ones. Among these smaller holes, the bright ones are the abode of the shiens and other beautiful beings, birds, animals, trees and flowers. Even an ordinary thing, once it has had the chance to touch these positive energy spots, is immediately transformed from being mortal to being immortal and from death to life. Heaven, caves and holes are terms which describe different dimensions of existence. The thirty-six caves in the universe are ❮ 36 spiritual dimensions or the development of the reality of beingness.

In Chinese literature, there are popular records of the experiences of certain historical characters who had the unusual luck to come upon some unimaginable places where the shiens lived. One such story is "The Wonderful Happenings of Lew and Yeum, the Wood-cutters." They mistakenly went to the Heavenly Terrace, which is generally called Tien Tai Mountain and is the abode of many immortals. They were transformed there by their contact with the high energy. After many generations, Tien Tai Mountain became a Taoist and Chinese Buddhist center where the famous Han-shan and Shih-Teh enjoyed their hermetic life during the Tang dynasty. The story "Upstream of the Perch" by Tao Yun Ming in the Chen Dynasty is another account of a wonderful land in Chekiang province.

❯ Black holes exist throughout all space. These are the dimensions which belong to demons who enslave innocent but ignorant souls. Sometimes these black holes are simply "soul-swallowers." All kinds of immature and unnatural deaths may be the result of the summons of a Demon. Innocent people have more chance of running into these black holes and becoming really lost. The reality of the existence of these black holes forces spiritually aware people to work on self-cultivation for their actual protection and salvation. In the teaching of Tao, what is termed black holes are different than what modern physics calls black holes. In the teaching of Tao, they are negative dimensions of being rather than positive ones. It is a different conception of the term "cave," "the universe in caves" or "the caves in the universe" which describe the different dimensions where various high beings live. The universe is an existence of multiple dimensions.

From the t'ai chi principle: where there is the universe, there is also the anti-universe. Where there are particles, there are also anti-particles, etc. Thus, you have the cave-universe of the immortals, and the black holes for the demons. It could be conceptual development. The central learning of life is the healthy nature of life. That is the goal of learning Tao.

The three spheres or treasures of the universe are Heaven, Earth and Humankind. Heaven is the creative energy of the universe. Earth is the supportive and receptive energy of the universe. Human beings are the harmonization of the positive yang energy of Heaven and the negative yin energy of earth. With achievement in self-cultivation, one can advance to the pure yang of Heaven as a shien with absolute freedom. With failure in self-cultivation, one becomes a heavy soul of earth. Ordinary death is the result of failure to maintain one's bright vitality, thus after leaving the sphere of harmonized life, one becomes a shadowy being. However, having refined their earthly energies, shiens take their bright, subtle essence with them. They leave their gross physical form and enjoy immortality.

The Phenomenon of Spirits on the Earthly Level

The Green Spirit
The green spirit is transformed from vapors of the hot, cool and wet weathers, the energy of the trees and grass, or the frightened, intimidated human souls or any other soul.

The White Spirit
The white spirit is the transformation of remorse and sorrow. This group includes the white animal spirits, various kinds of subtle energies, the energy related to silver, snow, and especially old exposed skeletons in the wilderness.

The Red Spirit
The red spirits are confused, angry souls, and the spirit of fire. When fire accidents happen without obvious causes, it may be that fire energy incited them.

The Black Spirit
The black souls are wronged or persecuted souls. This group also includes animal souls, especially those of black color.

Men and women who sleep nude or face up, either during the night or day, allow the black souls to suck their energy from the spot between the breasts. Other spirits, like white and yellow ones, do the same.

All these parasitic energies may be external reasons for nightmares. However, nightmares also have many internal causes like emotional disturbance or shock, tension, general fatigue or a combination of these.

The Yellow Spirit

The yellow spirits are kind spirits, religious ghosts and the spirits related to the earth. This group also includes animal souls of yellow color.

The General View on Souls

The spirits mentioned above can accumulate energy and with it form themselves, touch, attack and move things. They are usually a weak force with little strength and energy in general. It is a completely different energy category than the gross energy of the human world, but under certain conditions, they can possess people and create much trouble. If one has high spiritual energy, one either cannot be attacked or will be less influenced than if one has low spiritual energy and a weak vital condition.

In general, an ordinary soul is black, white or yellow, and of no harm. Souls with high energy can accumulate light to fortify their light forms. These souls with high energy acquire this energy through self-discipline. Other souls, like righteous heroes, martyrs and sages, gain righteous energy and become spiritual beings and deities by their confirmed virtue. They do not attack people, but halt evil in order to protect the good. Some of them are able to ride light and gather other kinds of energy to disperse evil, as well as kill demons.

Because of the subtle background of human life, spiritual practice is as important and effective as self-protection. The performance of exorcism, if practiced property, is of therapeutic value.

For those adept in Tao and who are self-disciplined, the refinement of their good qualities, virtues and way of life, including the knowledge of nature's cyclic energy movements, are all helpful in safeguarding them and their surroundings.

People who have heavy contamination of their soul throughout many lives will generally be more troubled than others. The monastic way of life would be more suitable as a safeguard for them, if they truly understand its significance for their lives. Such a lifestyle means full-time discipline.

A fundamental attitude of trained Taoists toward spiritual phenomena is that "the virtuous can dissolve ghosts, and the righteous can break evil." This means that one must really be of high virtue or else one is still vulnerable to the energy of ordinary people. The most important understanding is that, as the *Tao Teh Ching* says, "When the Tao permeates one's being, all ghosts and demons become inactive."

The Central Sphere of Earth: The Human Sphere

In the center of the earth is the sphere of humankind which receives the harmonious middle energy. In it are the human tribes, which are many and prosperous. The life and behavior of a person dwelling in the middle energy level is greatly influenced by the energy sphere above and below. These spheres may influence a person in different ways. If one cultivates the Tao with high sincerity, then one receives only the pure energy from above and rejects the evil influence from below. On the other hand, an ordinary person would rather give in to the influence of the sphere below and not accept the spiritual influence from above. We must therefore be prudent in choosing which spirit to worship, because when we approach an energy, we become influenced by it. It is of utmost importance to distinguish from where an influence comes. In order to obtain this fundamental ability, we need to cultivate a calm and pure mind.

The energy of the Heavenly sphere is totally pure, but in the human sphere there are many different energy formations with different proportions of pure and impure energy. For this reason human society is extremely complicated and diverse.

The Human Aura

A human's body mostly contains a mixture of blue, yellow, white, green and black light. Those with more black than any other color live with ghost energy, which indicates that they are sick people and that their body will soon die. Those who have more yellow light are kind and merciful. Those who have more blue light have greater wisdom. Those with more red light are easily angered and easily create conflict with others. They are also very adventurous physically. Those with more white light are skeptical and worry. Those with more green light are more egotistic. These are the colors of the bodily auras of ordinary people. They are not related to the skin color.

The Facial Color and Different Levels of Achievement

A person of cultivation can recognize the stages of a person's achievement by the color of their facial light. If the facial light is pure and white, it means that one has attained mental energy, strengthened one's lungs, and benefitted from a proper breathing system. If the facial light is radiantly black, one's kidney energy is strong and one has received benefit from the firmness of one's essences. If the facial light is yellow, one has gathered the earth energies and received benefit from the proper adjustment of one's mind. When the yellow color is strong and slightly like dye, the person may be a vegetarian and "dyed" by the color of fruit. This person also has pure chi.

If anyone who is middle aged or older still has the pink facial color of a newborn baby, and if new flesh is born to their face and they have strong dark hair, then they have received the benefits of gathering good pure energy from the special Taoist dual cultivation. These benefits are received through personal blessings and good fortune, not out of any ambition. Anyone who cultivates their own pure energy will radiate their energy's good color in their facial light. The richness and fullness of their spirit will show as a lucid light on their face.

Anyone who embraces righteousness will show the light or righteous dignity of morality on their face. They must have good behavior without going beyond their virtues, so that their body can be rich in upright energy. Those who cultivate to become earthly shiens may have a body which is slender and highly developed spiritually. Their energy is high and their light is sharp. Those who cultivate and become achieved as Heavenly shiens surpass the earthly shiens in brilliance and maintain harmony in their environment. It is difficult to fully know their depth.

Through the ways described above, one may discern the different levels of achievement in cultivation. Still, one must have good morals and virtues; firmly entrust oneself in Tao, and receive recognition from the proper tradition. Then one will receive the purple light or Heavenly honor. No title or honor from the human world is as beneficial as the true value of Heavenly honor, because with it one can enjoy the true blessings of Heaven.

The Truth of Reincarnation

When a person dies, the soul leaves the body and human realm, but it may be born again or reincarnate into human life. The soul follows a natural cycle in an almost endless process of transformation and evolution. The cycles may be compared to different versions of a work of art. Each new version is undertaken with the expectation of improving the previous one.

During the first several lives in the human realm, a person may make many mistakes and accumulate much dissatisfaction. This accumulation will affect the present and future lives of the individual. It is like making a sculpture. Every application of the chisel leaves its mark in the statue. In the same way, everything one says and does is an exact projection of one's energy. When the inner being leaves the body, it carries with it the accumulation of internal and external behavior of the previous lives, which in turn form the actual energy basis of the present life. By the same principle, the behavior one projects in the present life will continually bring reformation.

Although all human beings begin with the same original nature, what each individual says and does creates wide differences. Our actions determine whether we distinguish or degrade ourselves. By cultivating self-awareness, we have the possibility of living according to our original nature rather than according to the pressures of society or one's own emotional disposition.

Through the subtle law of energy response, we know that all actions are an exact expression of one's energy. All human beings reveal their most intimate secrets through the expression of their energy, whether it is high, low, positive, negative, creative, destructive, inert, concentrated, moral or vicious. There is no way to hide this from the intuition of a developed or undistorted human being. Such a person can tell intuitively how far the inner being has evolved throughout its many lives.

Life itself is a continuing evolutionary process. A soul, whether it is well shaped or not, is subject to this process every second, minute, hour, day, month and year. It is also possible that stagnation may slow down the process of evolution due to deviation of the soul. Normally, a soul evolves through the pattern of incarnation, but it is possible for the abnormal "devolution" of a soul to occur through the same pattern. Normally, the process of evolution moves from the gross to the subtle level; from the physical to the spiritual realm; from dependence on the biological basis of life to independence. At this point, the long journey of the soul is finished and a shien, or divine immortal being, is completed by the process of refinement of ordinary life.

Taoist internal alchemy is a process for actualizing the development of the inner being from a mechanical pattern of life to a life of absolute freedom. The final refinement of energy is only possible for one who has reached a developed state of being. Some degree of self-discipline is necessary for this process, but it is totally different from external disciplines such as the rigid practices exemplified by most religious disciplines.

Reincarnation of a soul into a new life always occurs at the precise level of evolution or reality of that soul. It is an illusion to think that one can achieve a better next life than one's evolution of consciousness and awareness of the range of spiritual life actually merits. Although the goal of reincarnation is to become a more refined being, refinement does not happen at the moment of reincarnation, but during all the minutes, hours, days, months and years of one's present life, right here and now. Just as the fruit we enjoy in the present life is the result of the achievements of our past lives, whatever we do in this present moment will affect our life situation from now on. Whatever we suffer from - troubles and sickness, or good fortune - is an accumulation from the past. All apparent accidents have hidden causes.

The cause of suffering is the distortion from the right way of life. The unnatural situation of human society creates more difficulties for individuals than they do themselves. Personal well-being is acutely affected by the social environment, but self-cultivation is individually based. All people are aware of the troubles in the world, but few are aware of the source of their own problems.

All lives spring from the creative nature of the universe. If a new formation of universal energy, as a life, cannot agree with the peaceful core of universal life, it naturally deviates from the main flow of the universe. Surely we can see that what a person says and does in ordinary life is for the most part marginal activity. It does not seem connected with the deep mind. But the center is nevertheless affected by the totality of these marginal activities.

The cycle of incarnation occurs through the pattern of life and death. Life does not mean a start and death does not mean an end. People who consider a human life as only existing from birth to death are misled. Some people with a partial understanding of incarnation take the physical appearance and disappearance of life as being one life. This is also inaccurate. Life itself is a continual process of transformation and evolution. When slow physical transformation takes place as a person grows older, we still identify the person through the old traces. But in reality, the person is not the same, because of conscious and unconscious internal changes. If others ignore the interior change and treat the person exactly the same as before, it can create difficulty. It is like putting wine in an old whiskey bottle; people may think the contents are whiskey, but they are not. What is inside the bottle has changed.

Once when I was young, I had just come back from my rough Kung-Fu practice. I was thirsty and there happened to be a cup of water on the table in our house. With my brisk Kung-Fu movement I hastily put the cup to my mouth and drank it with great satisfaction. When I was almost finished, I made the late and unhappy discovery that I had drunk gasoline that had been left out for the purpose of cleaning some oil spots. It caused me great discomfort afterwards. To me, the kitchen table, the cup, the fresh clear look of water, and the mind which decided it was water, together cause me to neglect that the interior of the cup had changed.

Names, appearances, and other superficial identification only convey a symbol to a person. The human world is not like the world of vegetation. The color of the maple tree varies with the seasonal changes, but it is still a good maple tree. That is because the interior of the tree does not change too much. In the human realm, every individual has the same biological basis, but the conceptual interior of individuals varies widely. The exterior form does not reveal the interior, although the world of common sense believes in appearances. The inner being of an individual is continually changing despite the appearance of the exterior. At a more developed level, a human being cultivates the interior and lets the form follow.

The reincarnation cycle of human beings usually takes place over a period of 240 years. Half the cycle is in the manifest sphere and half the cycle is in the unmanifest sphere. This does not mean that when people come into the world they automatically have 120 years allotted to them. In most cases, the normal span is shortened by a person's obsession to live a happier, better, longer life. Both parts of the cycle can be relatively lengthened or shortened by the quality of a person's life activities. The duration of the cycle might also differ greatly from ancient to modern times because of the change in lifestyle.

The second part of the cycle begins when the soul of a person passes into the invisible or yin realm, generally termed the shadow world. After 120 years of dwelling in the invisible realm, one then has the opportunity to return to the visible world. One will usually return as a human being, unless one has been deformed by abuse of the body or mind through the use of drugs or due to other unnatural means or behavior.

If one dies young without having reached the end of one's natural energy, one will come back again quickly to finish one's cycle of 120 years in the visible realm. The number of years that is allotted depends on one's vital energy. In Taoist terms, life can exist if the life chi exists. When the life chi expires, then life expires also.

There are several laws which determine if a person will reincarnate into a particular family or nation. The first priority is the law of kinship. Members of the same family frequently come back to their sons, daughters and grandchildren. The second priority is the law of passion. If you love or hate a person very much, your mental energy will respond to them, and it is likely that you will be reborn as their son or daughter. If your are strongly attached to a particular community or nation during your lifetime, it is certain that you will be reborn in that same community or nation. Suppose, for example, you were a soldier who had been killed by a soldier of the enemy nation. Because of the hatred you felt for the person who killed you, the intensity of the emotion is like the attraction of a magnet, causing you to be reborn into your enemy's family. Emotion causes a tremendous amount of almost unending internal conflicts. Thus, it is important to detach oneself from one's passions in order to avoid being reborn into an unhealthy environment. A healthy opportunity is given to an individual who has a well-developed mind and who is free of the encumbrances of strong love, hostility or antagonism.

In Taoism, we value the virtue of being. This means that life itself is the virtue of the universe. The virtue of life is to be positive, creative and constructive. To realize the nature of life is to keep to the true center of our being. The purpose and direction of the life force should be to carry out the virtue of life. In our work and in our relationships, let us not follow the law of emotion, but rather, follow only virtue. Virtue means function. Thus whatever position or stage of life we are in, we faithfully carry out our function. We cannot run away from the reality of life. It is the nature of life to live, not escape.

To raise oneself up so as not to be susceptible to the power of reincarnation is the creative goal. It is easy for people to know about life in this world, the visible half of the cycle, but few have the expanded awareness and knowledge of the invisible half of the cycle. The two halves are like the day and night of life. They could be compared to a tree in winter, whose total energy has been withdrawn deeply into the roots to quietly await the next spring. Only for humankind, is a new life given.

The shadows of life, ordinarily called ghosts, may be perceived by the sensitive vision of certain people. In most cases, these visions are only psychic traces of the past and not true clairvoyance of what is occurring in the present. But beyond our speculation about what occurs in the shadow side of the life cycle, there is one irrefutable law that applies to the whole cycle: the content of mind is equal to the content of life. This means that the manner in which one forms or cultivates one's mind will determine what kind of soul-life one will have. The decisive factor is internal, not external. The subtle power of one's subjective effort in self-cultivation and self-discipline can also overcome any negative external situation.

The passions of love and hate play an important role in the reincarnation of a soul as well as in forming a person's interior. The stronger one's passion, the more solidified are one's habitual tendencies. Thus, the manifested mental tendency determines what kind of new life and destiny one will have. To dissolve one's "contamination," as it is called in Taoist terminology, is to dissolve one's passions in order to prevent them from molding the next life. Reincarnation is just like making a new pair of shoes for yourself: you make them, and then you have to wear them.

In Taoist cultivation, we aim at dissolving the framework of the mind and following the unstained purity of life. We do not wait for a better reincarnation or improved next life; rather, in the present life we do not allow any accumulation of worldly contamination. We do not evade the cycle of life, yet we avoid getting trapped in any part of the cycle.

My Masters, who evolved to become shiens, do not follow any mechanical cycle. They are Immortals. They are not affected by any natural physical forces, and are always aware. They do not "sleep" in any one corner or place, once they have passed away from the ordinary senses. Yet they awaken in the subtle, flexible, immortal realm. They respond to my refined spiritual energy and are concerned with my work of keeping up the divine way in the human world from which they have lifted themselves.

We are not followers of the law of reincarnation, but of the law of spiritual renewal. To lift oneself up means to raise oneself above the unwished-for reincarnation which is the result of the heaviness of one's energy. If the energy is too heavy, then one remains under the big wheel of reincarnation. If the energy is light and refined, then it provides a vehicle to transport one anywhere one wishes to go.

Life is just a manifestation of energy. If you have complete energy, you have a fuller life. If your energy is incomplete, you only enjoy part of life. It does not matter whether you are rich or poor, noble or ignoble. What matters is the virtue found inside of you which manifest in ways such as honestly, sincerity, patience and courage. It is particularly important to cultivate these basic virtues with a positive attitude. The more you worry, the more you darken your soul and weaken you power. The virtue of life is by no means external or artificially contrived. It is deeply rooted within your soul.

Chapter 11

The Nature of Human Beings

Tao and the Universe Within Our Body

Because the integral energy of the universe forms man's individual energy, humanity is a microcosm of the universe. This entity is comprised of three spheres: "Heaven" as one's spirit, the gross "earth" as one's body, and the mind of "the human being" which makes one either superior or troublesome. The human body is a small but exact model of the universe, and as such, contains the same principles of law, number, energy and phenomena which manifest throughout the universe as a whole. It is a matter of the quality of energy which differentiates between the human body and other individualized manifestations; that is, whether the energy is gross or fine, partial or complete, subtle or organic. The other individualized manifestations may or may not have a complete awareness of the universal principles which govern their existence. When a human being achieves true self-awareness, or enlightenment, one becomes one's own "Jade Emperor," the authority of one's own being.

Because the human physical body is a small model of the universe, it is an integral t'ai chi. The laws that apply to the universe also apply to the human body and mind. Thus by knowing the law, one can know the nature of the body and the mind itself. Pure law is not a single isolated phenomenon. Rather, it is omnipresent within the nature of all Heavens, earths, and universal manifestations. The nature of this law is not to restrain, but its influence is inescapable. Thus it is called the subtle law.

The nature of the entire universe is revealed to the mind which has a fully developed intuition. The ancient Taoists intuited a vision of the beginning of all life, which they communicated in images of water and fire as the regenerative forces of life. In the *I Ching*, they used signs instead of language to illustrate their knowledge. The system of Taoist alchemy, which deals with the transformation of life within the human body, follows the principle of the *I Ching*. The universal process as well as that of the body and mind is "hidden" within the lines of all the signs and changes in the *I Ching*. Through knowing this system and its transformations, one is able not only to understand and regenerate oneself, but also to become one with the perpetual flow of the universe.

The Three "Bodies" of an Unrefined Human Being

The Physical or Sensory Body

This body is obviously visible and everyone accepts its existence. It has eyes which respond to color, ears which respond to sound, nose which responds to smell, tongue which responds to taste, and tactile senses which respond to texture, hardness or softness, and temperature. These all combine to provide a sensory life. Yet this is the shallow layer of life. It lasts only for the span of one's physical life. If a mind has a strong attachment to the sensory body, one's development will be confined to that. If a soul has a deep attachment to sensory habits, it can actually retain this attachment after death. Of course, the sensory abilities themselves are lost after death. However, the soul who remains attached to the senses and to sensory stimulation has a different experience after death than the person who has developed his or her spiritual root of life. The latter is able to function and remain effectively independent from the physical body, in other words, this person attains a more enduring life.

The Intellectual Body

The five sense organs and the objects being sensed function together as the sensory world. The underdeveloped mind is limited to the scope of its sensory perceptions and its reactions to an array of varying stimuli.

The function of the self as the conceptual center is almost as shallow in its perception and narrow in its reach as the sensory organs. It is the inflexible, rigid mental constitution of the lower sphere. This intellectual body resides in a position between the five senses and their objects. When the intellectual body becomes active, either in a creative or destructive manner, it is limited to its abilities of inference, deduction, generalization, analysis and summarizing. Such intellectual abilities are merely the markers behind the stage of the sensory world. Although this part is deeper than sensory reaction to the outer world, it is still a more shallow layer than the spiritual center of life.

THREE ASPECTS OF AN UNDEVELOPED PERSON

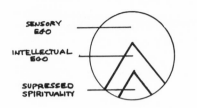

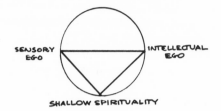

THREE ASPECTS OF A PERSON DURING SELF-CULTIVATION

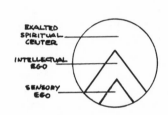

THREE ASPECTS OF A NORMALLY DEVELOPED PERSON

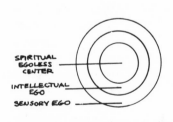

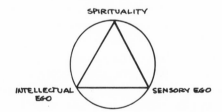

THE STATE OF AN ACHIEVED INTEGRATED PERSON

After a person dies, the five outer senses also die, and intellectual effort and achievement are also cut off. The intellectual body ceases its functioning after death, although the attachment to the sensory world can still remain in the form of memory. To the person who seeks spiritual truth, the reliance on the five senses can be a barrier and, on most occasions, the intellectual body can rob one's integrity of being.

The Spiritual Body
The core of spirit is separate from most mental activity, but self-awareness as a higher function of the mind is one way to approach the spirit. Subconscious mental activity, as in dreams, is in most cases a leakage and loss of spiritual energy. Of course there are some positive benefits from such activities, such as enlightening insights and foreknowledge. In a lifetime, the spirit is the last faculty to develop, and at death it carries forward the root of life forward. In a sense, spirit is not the same as the soul. Spirit is impersonal energy, whereas the soul is personified.

Correct spiritual practices of detachment from sensory and intellectual barriers can reinforce the soul. The spirit itself is infinite so that it may also appear in personal form. It is free of definition and it does not need any conceptual doctrine. The spiritual body can live independently since it contains all seeds of developing possibilities within itself. It cannot be seen with eyes or heard with ears, but it can only be perceived spiritually. If one's gross layers have been unravelled, it is a great blessing to become conscious of one's spiritual body.

Cultivation of Body, Mind and Spirit
When practicing Taoism, one must develop one's physical and mental capabilities as well as one's spiritual abilities in order to cultivate oneself completely. One's life will then be full of balance and righteousness. Just as when one speaks of the great manifestation of the universe as law, energy and phenomenon, the three human partners of body, mind and spirit are also one complete whole.

Intellectual Mind is a Partial Faculty of Universal Mind
Human cultural achievements, although minute in relative terms, represent the essence of humankind's experience and painstaking efforts at self-refinement over centuries. Cultural

achievement involves the intellectual facet of the mind. When the intellect, being only a part of the whole, is allowed to dominate the total mind, a situation is fostered which can be disastrous to both humanity and the environment. Humanity struggles to produce multiple intellectual creations, often only to create bondage, confining individuals to transient, limited and material lives. In such a case, intellectual development has become a hindrance to healthy integral development.

Life becomes a tragedy for individuals of intellectual development who lack awareness of the subtle truth of universal energy. Riches, academic honor, power, fame and affection - if not obtained together with refinement and improvement of one's entire being - represent merely a partial achievement which can destroy the balance and wholeness necessary for true well being. Any of good things of the world can too easily become poison.

The ancient Taoist Masters, foreseeing the trouble of future human society, made themselves models for the attainment of high awareness, setting up the goal of integration of their own lives with the universal integral flow. Only in this way could they participate in the reality of universal infinity.

The Original Pristine Nature of the Mind

When the mind is full of distorted images and confused concepts, it experiences deviation from the true nature of mind. Taoist sages value the mind in its original state of pure integrity. They consider the mind that has been developed only intellectually to be deformed. Such a partially developed mind needs to be rebalanced in order to reach its state of original health.

In an unconscious effort to rebalance their minds, intellectuals suffer from ceaselessly subjecting themselves to new ideas and new stimulations in an effort to reach a balancing point or to make an external attachment. Such dualistic intellectual development really only pacifies the psychological component of mind, and is an addiction to mental buttresses. Having developed in this way, one can no longer enjoy the simplicity and integrity of the pure mind.

A partially developed mind resembles the architecture of a poorly designed building, which uses elaborate patterns for the secondary part of the building while lacking a strong main structure. This approach repudiates the Way of appropriateness described in ancient Taoism. The Taoist Way is for the form to follow the function, not for the function to follow the form.

Living in this modern society of specialization, one may not be able to avoid creating imbalances while preparing for one's career. Therefore, to restore one's balance, new effort eventually becomes necessary. This task is like adding adhesive structures to save a poorly designed building; it may finally be successful, but is still awkward and inexpedient. Such a technique is more a wastage than a necessity in one's mental development, and the process can form a vicious cycle in the growth of personality.

As a basic principle of one's personal psychological life, the ancient Taoists recommend Wu Wei, "non-deviation," "non-making," "not pretending to be," "non-establishment" or "non-partial development." They do not advise that, in one's psychological life, one use "water" to wash "water" in order to cleanse it, but rather they suggest letting the "dirt" in the water settle to the bottom by itself, then letting the water flow as good water.

In this way, the Taoist approach varies from common religious methods which emphasize the psychological practice of repentance and confession. Likewise, modern techniques used in psychoanalysis and related methods release a person's deep emotions by stirring up one's problems. But in the Taoist view, this attempt at restoring psychological balance can rob the person's inner peace even further, causing more disturbance. Certainly there can be some beneficial results from these techniques, especially for the extremely dependent person. But it should be remembered that the need to talk about one's problems can become an end in itself or a crutch which can create further psychological imbalance.

There is a widely quoted Taoist saying that "there are no disturbing events occurring the world - only foolish people who create confusion and disorder." This is close to the wise western saying that "no news is good news." The Taoist approach takes this attitude toward worldly affairs, whether they be minor emotional frictions in one's family and neighborhood or international conflicts.

It is obvious that a completely balanced and serene mind cannot be obtained by forcefully working on it, but by letting go of one's tense hold on the issue causing the disturbance. One cannot help a horse that has been overstrained for a long time by making it work harder. It must be allowed to return to its pasture or stable. By following false expectations as to the horse's capacity for work, one can ruin it altogether.

A valuable suggestion from ancient Taoism is that adding something new to our knowledge of life is excellent, but it is also helpful each day to take away some of our old mental attitudes and habits. This is the simple Way of maintaining health and integrity for the novice as well as for the Taoist adept.

The Intuitive Faculty of the Mind

Concentrate on the "nothingness" of the mind. Through this practice, the mind will attain clarity instead of expending energy in negative or wasteful thinking. One's intuition revives when one does not abuse the mind. Once the intuitive faculty of the mind is revived, one is less dependent on the senses.

For instance, fire burns and is hot; if one depends on one's senses and experience to gather information about it, one must get burned in order to know its qualities. This is the way in which the ordinary system of knowledge was obtained, composed and tested, even though modern science sometime uses laboratory animals in place of humans. However, by using the intuitive faculty of the mind, one does not need to experience touching fire nor set up a series of elaborate experiments to know that it burns and is hot. The intuitive approach can be applied similarly in many other instances.

Our conditioning in favor of the empirical method may often cause us to become rigid and uncreative in problem-solving situations. For example, a young mother may become annoyed and nervous from her baby's restlessness during the night. From many past experiences, she concludes that her baby cries when it is hungry and that nursing usually stops its crying. But on this particular night, the restlessness may be from another cause and the baby may be trying to refuse the nipple. If the mother nevertheless nurses her baby repeatedly during that night, she only makes the situation worse. Because her mind is conditioned and has lost its flexibility, she may insist on her prior correlation regarding crying and hunger, and actually refuse to notice the baby's rejection of her breast. If instead she tries intuitively to understand why the baby is crying, she might find out that the baby was overfed and is therefore crying out of nervousness and discomfort.

Acquiring knowledge through experience usually requires a high price from the one who is learning. But this is not the case when one uses the intuitive mind. If we do not create problematic circumstances, then there are no events to be experienced and no experiments and pieces of information to be collected. One may then fulfill one's life following the straight Way without losing oneself in events and excitement. This describes the simple life exemplified by the ancient Taoist sages. For them, the many sources of experiment and the enormous system of knowledge as in the establishment of modern science did not exist. Actually, modern people are not often aware of the fact that much of the ordinary knowledge system is gained through partial use of the mind. In many cases, experience is created, then the intellectual part of the mind is applied to establish knowledge about the experience. In this way, more foolish events are experienced, more information accumulated, and more intellectual burdens forced upon the mind, gradually causing it to become imbalanced and deformed. All of this is unnecessary when people learn to effectively use their intuition.

When using the intuitive mind, the foreknowing faculty tells one what will happen and what can be done at the moment of subtle contact with the matter. Therefore, all problems are solved in the instant they appear. No enormous knowledge needs to be learned before one may act. No hypothesis needs to be engaged in to cognize reality beforehand or to find the supposed way out. Many modern developments give rise to much waste, making people work hard at learning and then applying what they have learned.

Sometimes we make the mistake of compromising our insight. We give up what we intuitively know to be right because of insistence from those who rely on past experience to guide their current actions. Throughout my life during the fulfillment of my duties as a healer and teacher, or in my personal involvements, some bad experiences and wastage have occurred, simply because people have insisted strongly on their experiential knowledge about matters. To take an example on a rather trivial level, several days ago, a student of mine suggested taking me to eat salad in a Mexican foodstand somewhere in a nearby town. Though my intuition told me to prepare food at home since we were both already hungry, it was hard to refuse such a friendly invitation. And even though I feel that eating at home is usually best, I went with her on her strong insistence. On our way, we got lost and I suggested again that we should forget the adventure and return home. But she maintained the image of her past experience and pressed forward. We finally arrived there, but to her surprise, on that particular afternoon all the foodstands in that building were open except that one. This was not really a serious case; we spent a little more time and searched a little more, that was all. But the same principle holds true, that we should never neglect the best part of ourselves, our intuitive mind. We should never allow reliance on the empirical method to lead us astray by ignoring our deeper insights.

To prevent unnecessary trouble and waste, most ancient Taoists avoided situations of potential conflict with people of the world. I myself am a modern Taoist with a worldly mission. In my life, I allow subtle messages to decide my activities, no matter how big or small the decision. Trouble arises only when I begin to compromise with the laymen in my surroundings. Compromise usually costs a price. In compromising with the world, or even with one's own family members, one is automatically required to diversify one's way in order to balance new emotional input. The resulting fragmentation causes backward development of the mind, moving it towards a more dualistic attitude.

When I was younger, I was hasty and impulsive. This attribute of my personality taught me many lessons. I gradually had to recognize that the subtle power is much more effective than mere force.

The nature of the simple intuitive mind of a Taoist is difficult to show. The present world is dominated by modern science, but the truly bright future of human society needs both the intuitive and the intellectual mind employed parallel and in cooperation with each other. Once two people lived together in a house. One was blind and the other was lame. Under ordinary circumstances both were able to function well. One night, a cinder flew out of the fireplace and within a short while the entire dwelling caught fire. Each of them individually tried to rush out of the house, but neither was able to succeed. Finally the blind man said: "It seems that we will both die here if we struggle each on our own to get out. How about if you get upon my shoulders, so that I can carry you? This way, you can be my eyes and I can be your legs. "The lame man agreed, and at last both of them, with some effort, were safely away from the house. In the case of the present human crisis it will be the same way: either we come out of it together or we will perish.

Practical Applications of Intuition

The development of modern science depends upon the sensory organs and on devices which extend the capability of the senses. Laboratory experiment is the foundation upon which modern science is built. Contrary to this method, in the Taoist science of medicine, it is unnecessary to cut the body open in order to know about it and gather information regarding the organs. Rather, the intuitive mind fulfills the function of the surgical knives in gathering knowledge or understanding. Similarly, the profound and practical system of Taoist herbal medicine is comprised of ancient knowledge attained through the subtle use of intuition about the properties and benefits of individual herbs.

Taoism in all its aspects may be recognized as the sacred practice of sound health. Acupuncture, herbal medicine and other aspects of Taoist healing were developed and are practiced through the use of the trained, accurate intuitive mind. Taoist healing may also be used to prevent illness through applying insight as to how one can remain healthy. Taoist medicine values preventative methods more than remedies and compensating efforts. The Su-wen (the upper section of the Yellow Emperor's *Book of Internal Medicine*, a fundamental classic of Taoist Medicine) tells us that "the ancient sages emphasized not the treatment of disease, but rather the prevention of its occurrence. To administer medicines to diseases which have already begun is comparable to the behavior of one who begins to forge his weapons after he has already engaged in battle. Would these actions not be too late?" Again, the important role of intuition is emphasized so that one may keep in tune with the internal condition of one's body on a daily basis, not waiting for obvious signs of serious and complicated conditions to appear.

The wide scope of ancient Taoist medicine includes many daily preventative approaches such as breathing techniques, energy guidance exercises (Dao-in), gathering energy through moving and sitting meditations, spiritual practices and other methods. The ancient science of health also includes the science of environmental health, as, for example, the science of Taoist geomancy. Geomancy focuses on using geographical energy as good support for human health and on the environment's subtle energy rays as support for one's descendants.

Besides the effects of geographical location on one's health, there are many subtle influences from the astral environment. People's daily fortunes consisting of their happy and unhappy experiences, strongly affect their health. Thus, the Taoist science of accurate prediction of an individual's development through the use of the *I Ching*, the system of the five subtle elemental forces, and the other predictive methods are also highly beneficial.

The food one eats as well as the way in which one's food is grown and prepared influence one's health. These subjects are dealt with in Taoist agriculture and cooking. In addition, there are many influential factors inherited from one's parents at the outset of one's life.

Life is the center of Taoism. All aspects of Taoist knowledge and techniques serve the function of improving the quality of life. The complete system of Taoism combines much diversity in its broad latitude, all aimed at helping the individual lead a whole, integrated and happy life. According to Chinese understanding, a shien is a happy being. A truly happy being must be a healthy being; an absolute being cannot be unhappy in some area. Thus a totally happy, healthy individual must be a transcendent integral being. The knowledge and practice of becoming a shien, passed down through my tradition, was attained essentially by the intuitive mind.

Taoists have made some valuable contributions in the development of modern science in addition to metaphysics and internal alchemy. Yet these subjects still do not invite the widespread attention of serious modern scholars. Perhaps these areas will become the new direction for a younger generation of researchers. A Taoist knows the universe but not through the intellect nor based upon fragmentary information. Because intuitive discovery reaches the vastness of the universe, its whole view and scope cannot be put into words. Still, the task of modern cognitive systems is to explain, and though merely partial, these explanations can bring the various facets of Taoism into modern awareness. So, there is a valuable place for the intellectual, explanatory, fragmentary approach. But, as always, we must remember not to lose the view of the whole from focusing too exclusively upon its parts.

Chapter 12

Reuniting with Tao

The Separation of Tao and Man

The pure law manifests within human life. The Tao is always present in our ordinary life; the separation between an individual and Tao is caused only by oneself. Why must one either become too materialistic or too idealistic? Either way represents a separation between the eternal Way and the human effort. Instead of finding peace within their innate, divine nature, human beings create external worship through the religions they have made. People inadvertently lose themselves in worldly life by taking a competitive, aggressive attitude. In all these deviations from the Tao, duality replaces integrity and the relative replaces the absolute. Then human nature cannot remain coherent with the nature of the unborn realm; the integrity of its wholeness is lost. The Taoist tradition imparts a profound truth in the saying that "Tao is internal but reaches the external. Heaven is inside life but salvation is found on the sharp edge of life."

How to Reunite with Tao

The fragmentation of an integral being caused by abusing the sense organs' capabilities, overdeveloping the intellectual part of the mind, and neglecting and ignoring our spiritual root deforms the modern human being. In order to reunite all elements as an integral being to serve the spiritual center, one must completely dissolve one's ego, formed through the sensory apparatus and intellectual concepts held in one's mind. Through the growth of spiritual awareness comes dissolution of the ego. Then one may unravel all knots which bind one to illusions, thereby attaining transcendental consciousness of the totality.

Instead of worshipping an external object or being, Taoists practice cultivation of the inner, Integral Way in order to reintegrate their beings with the eternal flow of the universe. By fully dissolving the individual ego, one unites with the entire universe. Realization, therefore, of the divine, pure universal law is not beyond one's being, and one's being is not beyond pure law. Through self-cultivation and discipline of one's lifestyle in the world, one may grow into an integral consciousness which will be fully actualized rather than become trapped in the dualistic framework of external worship.

Rather than searching for external support only, the student of the Integral Way of Tao must first attain the awareness of the omnipresence of pure law. Through experiencing the enlightenment of the subtle truth, one will discover that the law, though it is without, is also within. Having achieved this important understanding, one may then be contented with a simple life formed of two elements; integrity and serenity.

Therefore, learning Tao and dissolving the ego is the starting point of the refining process in the cultivation of the Integral Way. An important goal of self-cultivation is the complete evolution from the substantial, limited energy level to the pure and completely unlimited true yang energy, which is the immortal energy of the universe.

Do It Yourself, Be It Yourself

Spiritual development follows an absolute principle, which is to do it by yourself and be it by yourself. Spirituality is an art and a science of life. No one can share one's spiritual profundity, and it can never be fulfilled merely by belonging to a group. It is spiritual law that when one follows the true eternal nature of life, returning to the realm of the true origin of universal vitality and filling oneself with high energy, one will be able to make connection with the deep universal root, thus living without an actual terminal death. The ancient Taoists called this Way "refining the elixir of immortality." Through self-cultivation, one eventually becomes skillful enough to reach a state of freedom wherein one may enter or exit the Subtle Origin at will. At this level of achievement, as in the case of achieved Taoists or practitioners of Ch'an (Zen in Chinese Buddhism), one is no longer concerned with life or death.

One may reform oneself with the refined energy and continue to live in the world or ascend into the subtle divine realm of pure energy. After preparing oneself through virtuous and meritorious deeds, one may retreat as a hermit to enjoy nature in a place full of positive energy, continuing one's cultivation and self-dissolution.

Chapter 13

Virtue - The Foundation
Of All Self-Cultivation

The Common Foundation for All Kinds of Cultivation

The common foundation for all true methods of cultivation is the opening of the energy channels, breaking through the energy blocks within the body and opening all the cerebral compartments in the head. This process will fully develop and fill you. You will then have the opportunity to become highly achieved.

There are some people whose energy meridians are not complete, although they take human form. Do they have the opportunity to prove Tao? There is a way for these people who are born with incomplete energy meridians - not by following the method, but by following the virtues.

For these people the virtues are the method, and with them the value of the method can be proven. Without them the method is groundless. Moreover, if those who cultivate energy neglect their own behavior, good merits[1] and spiritual credits, then their energy channels and blocks will not be opened. Therefore, all Taoists must follow their own virtues to aid their self-achievement, or else obstacles will constantly be interfering with their progress.

On Self-Development

All of the Heavens, planets, stars and beings of the universe are composed solely of energy in various states of pure and impure combinations. A human being with self-awareness may enjoy the blessings of life, become an integral person and spontaneously achieve being of everlasting quality. Intellect and other learned abilities are the branches and flowers. However, their origin is the root and spring which feeds them. Thus, the first Taoist principle of self-cultivation recommends that while it is good to enjoy the tree and flowers, one must never neglect nurturing the root and tending its growth at the source.

---

[1]Merits are socially useful, selfless acts.

The energies of the universal order interweave into a net which comprises the subtle connecting system and operates as the subtle regulator. If one ignores the power of the subtle energy network, with behavior either too strong or too weak, one will fail to channel oneself well enough in the normal flow of life. It is preferable to act and react to things gently. Any harsh movement tends to cause damage to oneself and others. For example, when one takes an aggressive action, one becomes bound by the restriction created by one's own energy. Thus, before one attempts to employ any kind of strong movement, it is necessary to understand the subtle law of energy response. This cosmic law warns people of the danger of abusing the energy allotted to them by blindly or forcibly trying to obtain their own temporal desires. Each person's degree of spiritual protection is created by one's own actions operating continuously within the universal energy net.

Eliminating Wrong Habits and Unravelling Blocks
If one has seriously followed a worldly religion or any other spiritual practice, one must, after becoming a Taoist, thoroughly cleanse oneself of all the previously gathered energies. After the inferior energies are removed, divine energy enters one's body and one begins to communicate with it. If such experiences occur in dreams they have the same significance.

These are the signs showing one's change: after practicing Taoist cultivation for some time, if someone converts to another teaching, this person will also experience some signs announcing their loss of divine energy. This is one proof which verifies the change. Because cultivation is a matter of energy development, anyone who cultivates Tao must experience change, whether obvious or subtle. If the experience of the change is strong and intense, it means that the person's past poisonous roots were deep and the effect is clear. If the experience is subtle and slight, it means this person's past was normal, or it also may indicate that their involvement and commitment is shallow and superficial. However, both cases do not mean that the obstacles in the journey to total liberation and refinement will fewer.

The Way of learning Tao, the obstacles and the new communication will be described in the following subchapters.

Using the Virtues to Open the Blocks

Tao is the door for virtuous people. By becoming virtuous you can become Tao. The most important virtue is to be simple. Tao and virtue are an undivided one, because good virtue itself is the manifestation of the nature of the universe. Humankind evolved out of the nature of this universe; therefore, humanity fully contains all its virtues. Here, humanity's nature is considered the same as Heaven's nature and also the same as the universal nature.

This is the prenatal nature of humankind without any pollution from postnatal civilization. Within our pure, true nature can be found all the good virtues and the Original Simplicity of the universe. Humankind and Heaven have the same root in Tao. By following this original nature according to your own circumstances, by not violating this nature but instead developing it, this nature will become virtue and will manifest in whatever the environment might be.

If you act against your true nature, you become negative. You depart from the true virtue, and you also lose the Tao. Following the Tao really means to be plain. In order to cultivate the highest purity, one needs to follow the essential principle of adhering to one's true nature and the original virtue of life, and maintaining one's Original Simplicity. If this is accomplished your life will succeed in being fulfilled.

Even without social acknowledgement for good merits, one can still live fully within the ultimate truth of life. But for Taoists who live in the manifested world, it must be precisely understood that Tao and virtue are one body. Tao becomes virtue in the stages of manifestation in which life is formed and individualized, and virtue returns to its root in Tao.

We cannot say that we only need to keep the root, and neglect to realize the virtue of being useful and helpful in our daily lives. If one does not follow virtue, one's cultivation will become like a dry well, just as is the case with some religious cults which use beautiful churches or temples as their dark hidden corner. There must be a sweet fountain springing forth from the bottom of the well to benefit anyone who comes to it. This is the virtue of being a well.

Your cultivation must become a true fountain in both helping yourself and benefitting others; to be sweet is best, to be pure is necessary. Becoming just like a tree of life, one radiates and fills one's surrounding atmosphere with a special sweet and beautiful scent, or at least one does not emit a disturbing odor. Then the internal self-cultivation and the external good merits will interweave to become the Taoist way of life. Fulfilling one's personality, beautifying and lightening one's own life, flowing with one's nature, and not violating it in exchange for reputation or deceptive pleasures is the only correct way for a Taoist to live.

The Difference Between True Virtue and Common Virtue

All good behavior can please Heaven and humankind, but there are differences between true virtues with roots deep in Tao and occasional good behavior, or common virtues. Because the true virtues of achieved Taoists have their roots in the nature of the Subtle Origin, their lives are not separated from the Tao. However, ordinary good behavior is like a dry well which occasionally gathers some water from the rainfall, but eventually dries out again because it is cut off from the origin of the water fountain.

Ordinary good behavior and merits are socially useful, selfless acts. This behavior changes one's energy, dispersing contamination and gathering good energy. All good behavior and merits have a direct and parallel response. This means that because of one's good merits and behavior, one automatically calls the positive and productive energy to come to aid one's life and to make it one creative and productive. It is not necessary to be rewarded by any external sovereign.

True virtue is not something one does deliberately. It is simply a spontaneous expression of one's pure being. Virtuous and simple behavior is first formed by a motive. Then it becomes the conduct and also the result at the same time. At their roots, both conduct and result are the same kind of energy. This energy attracts the same frequency vibration of energy from the source of the great nature. Good attracts good. Bad attracts bad. Everything responds directly as cause and effect. How things happen is not the result of interference from any third person or entity.

Therefore, through one's own good and simple virtue, one can gather beneficial energy by drawing it to oneself, which in turn builds one's body and enlightens one's life. If one's energy is negative, one causes pain and suffering to be drawn to oneself.

These are direct reactions to actions of one's virtues. This is the truth of the Heavenly law.[2]

Deviation is not True Virtue

The formation of any behavior which comes from nature is virtuous, unless it is unwittingly twisted. Any behavior is the nature of the acting person manifesting at any given moment. Thus, by looking at someone's behavior, one may know what kind of energy the person embodies and which energy is manifesting to create a certain behavior. The energy itself is the source because the user, the used, and also the whole resulting series of events are all one and the same.

The following is a story about a man in Asia who cultivated himself in the woods:

Once a Heavenly being decided to find out if a man was really achieved. Thus he transformed himself into a troubled young man and appeared in the woods displaying great difficulty and helplessness. He paced back and forth in a small area which was not far away from where the achieved man meditated. His behavior finally caught the attention of the highly achieved man, and so he left his meditation and approached the young man asking, "Son, you look like you must be having great difficulty. Would you like to tell me about it?"

"No," the young man said, "I don't think I will tell you or anybody. Please let me be with my own trouble!"

The achieved man said, "This is not the way to solve your problem. Together we can find a solution for you. Sometimes a talk can at least relax you."

"It is not talk that will make me better," the young man said," why should I tell you? I think that under Heaven there is nobody that can help me. Please leave me alone."

The achieved man was a caring person and so he said, "Don't be like this. There is always a way. I am concerned about your difficulty. Because of my many years of cultivation I vow to help you."

---

[2]The reader may find more explanation of the importance and the details of the universal subtle law of energy response in Master Ni's book *Tao - The Subtle Universal Law and the Integral Way of Life.*

The troubled one stared at the achieved man with doubt and finally with some hesitation said: "Just so you can understand I will tell you. My mother has a serious disease. The best doctor I could find wrote her a prescription, but it added only more difficulty. Besides the herbs in this formula it needs an eye of a man of meditation to strengthen the herb soup. How can I find an eye from a man like that? I have become so helpless and miserable. Please! I don't want to talk anymore."

After a second the achieved one said, "Please wait a moment. Am I not a man of meditation?" The young man said, "Yes, you are. You have stayed in these woods cultivating yourself for more than my years. You have never touched worldly things and you keep yourself pure. We all respect you."

Then the achieved one said, "Look! There is someone coming."

The young one turned his head to look in that direction but found nothing. When he turned his head back, to his great astonishment he found the achieved man's face bleeding and in his palm was one of his eyes. "No! No!," he said, "you can't do that. How can I take the eye? I cannot accept it for my problem."

The achieved one said calmly, "Go ahead, young man, and take this eye. Go home and use it to make a soup with the herbs for your sick mother. I do not depend on my physical eyes anymore. Go ahead and take this eye."

The young man painfully hesitated, but because of the virtue of the achieved man he decided to accept, and thanked him many times before quickly disappearing.

The next morning, to the astonishment of the achieved one, the young man was there again walking and circling as on the day before. "Good morning," he said, "how is your mother? Is everything well?" The young man kept quiet. But the achieved one continued to question him. Finally the young man answered, "The doctor said it should have been a left eye, but you gave me a right eye."

Then the achieved one ordered him to close his eyes. The young man was too tired to argue, so he closed his eyes for just a moment. When he reopened them, to his great fright he found the old man's face full of blood and the other eye in his palm. The achieved one made the young man receive the eye and went back to his meditation. Later he received a Heavenly reward for his conduct.

This is a beautiful and striking story from the influential work of Dragon-Tree, who was the reformer of the destiny of Buddhism and changed it from a small, philosophical practice called the "small vehicle," to becoming a large religion called the "big vehicle." He taught selfless sacrifice through this story.

When I stayed in Taiwan, I learned of another similar great example. During the Ching dynasty under the reign of Chen Lung (1736-1796 A.D.), lived the scholar Wu Fung. He was assigned to be a civil officer for the "Ali Mountain" tribe on the island that is now known as Taiwan. At the time, this island was for the most part inhabited by aborigines. Once a year, the aborigines had a custom of hunting a head from a stranger passing through their territory. Then they would offer it to the spirits in order to receive abundant harvest. When Wu Fung took over the administration of the tribe, he forbade them to kill people for their offerings. He taught them morality and kindness, civilizing them with the great teaching of ancient China and with his own great patience.

The aborigines obeyed him and loved him for many years, but then there was a serious drought. The aborigines suspected that the cause of the drought was that they had offended the deities by not making their offering. Therefore, they urged Wu Fung to agree with the restoration of the head-offering custom. At this time Wu Fung faced the real difficulty presented by the drought. However, he refused to give his consent and demanded patience and order instead.

The people respected him and also his good teachings, but they felt the threat to their survival became heavier and heavier as the days and months passed on. During the three years of the drought, the aborigines lived on their stored food, and now, as it was coming to an end, their appeals became more urgent and a rebellious attitude began to spread among them.

At last Wu Fung realized that his good teaching had not invited the Heavenly response. Under the critical circumstances, he was forced to grant them their wish. He permitted them to kill any person who would walk along a certain path during the twilight of the early morning hours, if the person was wearing a red hood.

The aborigines were reluctantly content with this because the terms were difficult. However, they went out on ambush the next morning. When no one passed by, they complained to Wu Fung once more. Resolutely, he would not allow them to look for someone during the daytime. On the third morning, finally, someone with a red hood appeared in the distance. The aborigines were excited and shot him with their spears and arrows and went to behead him. Curious about who the person was, they lifted the hood and found that Wu Fung had given his own head for their offering. Thereafter, the aborigines of Taiwan abandoned their customary offering entirely and built a beautiful temple in his honor in Ya Ji. The whole tribe venerated him as a real god. Throughout the nation at the time, whoever heard this story titled him as the "Sage of Benevolence."

To Be Plain is to Be Virtuous

It may be to your surprise that these two beautiful ethical attitudes above seem to have little in agreement with Taoist teachings. Once, when I was a Taoist student, I retold the first story to my elder brother in Tao and expressed how I was impressed with it. He said to me that he would act differently if he received this trial from the high realm. Then I asked him what he would do.

He said: "I would tell the vexed young man that may mother too, is old, weak and sick, and that she needs the head of a divine being from the higher realm, who is disguised in plain clothes and is concealing his true self from others. See, since your cultivated yourself many years, how can you still have the ego to be proud of how high and how holy you are?"

When I was working on this book, I asked one of my students to take note of the second story. She seemed to love it. She was anxious to know if Wu Fung was a Taoist. To her disappointment, Wu Fung was a good Confucianist. Then she was more anxious to know what a Taoist would do in Wu Fung's situation. The truth I gave to her is simple. A Taoist would make rain actually come. This was a Taoist occupation in ancient times, and I myself was rainmaker in my twenties, thirties and forties. That is doubtlessly what a Taoist would do.

As a response to the first story, if I were the achieved practitioner of meditation living in the woods, I would offer the young man a good new formula without eyes according to my knowledge of healing. For the young man himself, today I would advise him to see a psychologist and save my breath!

Dear readers, you can see how different the Taoist ethic is. We teach people to be normal, rather than to be distinguished. We exalt the principle of usualness higher than extraordinariness. We do not teach people the artificial and external law of cause and effect which states that if you do good, you will receive good. To Taoists, this equals putting the cart in front of the horse. In reality, the beautiful behavior of a person is the flower displaying the beautiful nature within this person. People can develop in this way no matter what the outside environment might be.

In the logic of most religious, a person has to act a certain way in order to become holy. They are not aware of the true nature which exists before it becomes spoiled and distorted by worldly life. We do not have to do anything to be pure, for our original nature is already pure in and of itself. Even if it does not become anything else, nature remains holy on its own. Once true nature is restored, it can be considered the highest accomplishment of one's cultivation. This pure nature in people reveals the basic root of all conduct.

To Taoists, the realization of their true nature in daily life is more important than any special outstanding temporal action. Behavior and conduct in life are just like the twigs and small branches of a tree. They are only one part of life - a fragmented manifestation of the root from which a healthy and decent life grows.

Any enlightened being knows that retribution is not practiced by any external spiritual sovereign or being. It happens only by your own energy self-responding and interacting with the universe. Nothing can escape this true law of nature. By understanding this truth, one can decide which types of behavior are positive and which are negative.

Those with "Heavenly eyes" can see that all positive behavior comes from the same origin, i.e., the pure and wonderful light of the Heavenly shiens. Both good and simple conduct contain the same high value. All daily activities contain this great light and fragrance. This light can reach far to brighten all of Heaven and earth, and make all the high spiritual beings praise the greatness of your proper conduct in daily life.

This light of good conduct can save one from disasters and remove one's difficulties. The conduct itself is both the cause and the retribution. Without any barriers, one can penetrate directly to become Tao, true virtue, spirit, holy, immortal and in addition, transcend the great transformation. This truth has been proven by Taoist Masters as a fact of life. But it may become enlightenment for the latecomers.

The Self-commandments to Enhance One's Spiritual Life as a Disciple of the Shiens

Sincerely follow Tao, the path to eternal life.
To turn one's back on the universal origin
    is to face darkness and degeneration of the soul.
Experience and cherish the pure happiness
    within your own soul.
It is eternal and constant.

The treasures of the world are deceptive and fleeting,
    causing the progressive erosion of one's subtle,
    spiritual essence.
Be plain, simple, honest and practical
    when dealing with the world.
It is better to be naive than cunning,
    better to be fooled than suspicious.
To sacrifice one's sincerity is to pay too much for
    too little.
Consider righteousness before profit.
To gain profit and lose virtue
    is no bargain.
Pay attention to the laws of the world.
Behave with conscience and maintain dignity.
In this way, you protect the freedom for self-cultivation.
Plant yourself firmly in Tao.
As the tide ebbs and flows,
    so does the great transformation of the myriad things
    sweep away all but the firmly rooted.
Become familiar with the relation between cause and effect,
    and deeply penetrate the truth of the universal
    response of energy.

To sow is to reap. To do is to be.
Energies of the same frequencies always attract each other.
Therefore, blind desires lead to blind alleys
*   and righteousness leads to eternality.*

Share happiness with others.
By extending ourselves to other we enlarge our being.
Selfless service is our sacred vow.
Receiving by giving is the universal law of supply.

Unite yourself with Heaven and earth.
Be unconcerned with life and death.
With clarity and self-awareness developed through
*   self-cultivation, transform your being,*
*   and thus end your bondage to the law of the*
*   great transformation.*
Clearly and completely discern the heart
*   of these unadorned teachings.*
Passed down through generations,
*   they have come from our ancient masters.*
Our way is the gathering of the greatest simple truths.
The wellspring of eternal life
*   is the infinite simplicity of Tao.*

Chapter 14

The Way of Learning Tao

The Four Stages
THE SEARCH: Only by earnestly searching can you find a truly enlightened one who will help you to begin your spiritual journey on a pathway that is right for you.

THE FIND: After finding a truly achieved Taoist Master and obtaining instruction, you must unceasingly dedicate yourself to your practices. If you accurately follow the method of strengthening through softening, you will be able to share more fully in your master's harmonious, spiritual light as it is absorbed into your soul.

CULTIVATION: Only through constant self-discipline and cultivation can the goal of your own true enlightenment be realized. Any occasion or circumstance can be a useful and beneficial opportunity in which to creatively express your cultivation. When living a worldly life, every day people strive to acquire more things of the world. When living a spiritual life, each day Taoists cast off some of their worldly acquisitions.

ACHIEVEMENT: By holding peace and calmness within and having complete dedication to truth, the way is accomplished and the highest fulfillment of spirit is achieved.

Milestones in One's Development
RIGHT MOTIVE: Right aspiration with a humble spirit, wholeheartedness, and open-minded trust in the broad pathway of naturalness will ensure a good beginning.

FIRM COMMITMENT: In order to achieve your spiritual goal, you must be willing to discipline and refine yourself according to the instructions of the truly achieved Taoist Master, who is the embodiment of simplicity, truth and quietude.

COMPLETE DEDICATION: Only total dedication and selflessness will bring the highest achievement. Any reservations or hesitation will retard your growth.

REGULAR CULTIVATION: In order to make true progress, regular cultivation is absolutely essential. Steady determination and boundless patience will bring results. Impatience and hastiness are stumbling blocks.

VERIFICATION OF PROGRESS: Transformation of behavior and attitudes, decreased desires, increased wisdom and understanding, communication with the subtle worlds and sensitivity to natural law as it miraculously manifests in daily life, all confirm your progress.

CONSOLIDATION OF SUBTLE ENERGIES: Following your true nature, you solidify your Taoist character and personality while allowing the refined subtle energy of your spiritual fetus to form.

ACHIEVEMENT: Through diligent self-cultivation, achieve the complete integration of body, mind and spirit and dissolve all illusions.

COMPLETE FULFILLMENT: The spiritual fetus, or the diamond body as it is sometimes called, has matured and exists in complete freedom, independent of physical restrictions.

SACRED WORKS: Selfless service to humanity consummates the process of self-cultivation and restores the complete reunion of Tao and humanity.

Difficulties and Obstacles Caused Through Inappropriate Cultivation

Impatience in trying to succeed with self-discipline, and carelessness in handling the difficulties you encounter.

To compare yourself to others, to be jealous of others' gain, and to complain about your own lack of accomplishment rather than to realize that spiritual growth is an individual experience and each person develops at his or her own pace.

To not empty your mind and straighten your thinking.

To have great expectations and not consistently follow the Master.

To not have sincerity and respect for the Sacred Method when it is passed on to you by your Master.

To be skeptical and doubt self-cultivation will bear fruit.

To compete with your fellow student, try to be "one up" on them, or always want to be a winner.

To show off your virtue and achievements.

To be a "big talker and little doer."

To be positive in speech but negative in mind; to have discrepancies between what you say and what you do.

To discuss your spiritual experiences, making yourself seem important in order to attract attention.

To have no self-discipline and yet be critical of others.

To work only for immediate personal gain, thereby losing the long-range spiritual benefits of self-cultivation.

To selfishly abuse the abilities gained from practicing the sacred method by using them for your own convenience or self-aggrandizement.

To be greedy for psychic powers and experiences while neglecting true spiritual evolution.

To linger with and try to hold on to any kind of ecstatic visions or experiences.

To place too much emphasis on or actively seek visions and other such mental or spiritual phenomena.

To think you do not need a teacher; to show pride in having a famous teacher; to seek too many teachers; or to rely on your teacher to do everything for you.

To display pride in front of your teacher by building yourself up, or to devalue what progress has been made by falsely putting yourself down in front of her or him, or any other attempt to manipulate the teacher.

To be unwilling to inconvenience yourself for the benefit of others, or to be unwilling to selflessly serve your Master or fellow men and women.

To place too much emphasis on external things such as dress, food, drink, music, dancing, etc.

To be greedy for material pleasure or indulge in sensual desires.

To scatter your energy and have a restless mind because of too many interests and diversions.

To quote the Masters and classics in order to put others down.

To use self-cultivation and self-discipline as an escape from the reality of your life or to avoid facing problems.

To become proud or conceited because of your knowledge or abilities.

Normal and Auspicious Responses from Appropriate Self-cultivation

The following mysterious communications are signs of correct efforts in self-cultivation to verify spiritual progress in Tao:

While practicing the self-discipline of the sacred method there is a wind, but the fragrant smoke of the incense still rises straight up.

Sometimes without burning incense and also without any fragrant flowers nearby, a rare fragrance suddenly comes to your nostrils. This scent does not belong to this world. It is a message from the mysterious world responding to your self-cultivation and verifying your spiritual growth.

A strange or auspicious light suddenly enters your room and fills it with a rare brilliance. Or in an empty room where you are meditating, there comes a wonderful brightness that continues even throughout the whole day. Or you may see the earth radiate light. These are all messages from the mysterious world to verify your spiritual achievement.

Some strange but strong chi approaches your senses and makes you feel as if you are taking a bath in a spring breeze or a shower with the warmth and clarity of winter sunshine.

In meditation or in the tranquility of your daily life, you suddenly feel a kind of wonderful milk-like liquid flowing from your top down your whole body, making you feel wonderfully cool.

Sometimes your mouth becomes filled with the taste of sweet dew (beyond anything you have ever experienced), or like thousand-year-old Chinese amber wine.

In your ears you hear the Heavenly drums, Heavenly music or the Heavenly calling.

Sometimes in your meditation or in daily life, your body suddenly shakes like a big earthquake from bottom to top.

In your shrine or your meditation room there is a rain of flowers from Heaven spread all over your body and beside you, which suddenly disappears. Sometimes a rain of gems and pearls or five-colored stones comes from Heaven to your altar during the night and can still be seen in the morning.

Auspicious clouds or bright light always stay above the roof of your home, or you see pure, bright clouds with many beautiful colors in your meditation.

Your meditation room or shrine sprouts a beautiful cloud-like mushroom which continues to grow there.

Above the roof of your home there is an auspicious star or stars which stay for a short or long period of time.

The white crane or wonderful birds soar over your home or stop there.

The flame of your candle which burns in the shrine becomes a flower or a wonderful creature or sign.

Angels personally come directly down into your room while you are meditating.

Your evolved soul, through your self-discipline, makes tours to the highly evolved shiens' caves and fairylands, and you have many interesting experiences there.

On certain occasions, you have the luck to gain secret Taoist books which are left by the ancient shiens, or other kinds of valuables or instruments of the Sacred Method, or the Holy Medicine, or the precious sword for the Sacred Method.

Your garden or court naturally grows an unusually beautiful flower or special plants. Moreover, sometimes a group of wonderful birds or animals surround these special plants.

Suddenly during your meditation you see the Heavenly door open and a true Heavenly scene is shown before you.

Suddenly in your meditation you see a white light rush into Heaven. This is a message to say that there are some fellow Taoists who have achieved Tao and are ascending to Heaven.

In your "cloud traveling" or pilgrimages to certain holy mountains, it suddenly rains but you do not get wet.

When you are hungry, delicious foods are supplied to you. When you are thirsty, a fountain comes out from the earth. When you are sick, some useful herbs are given to you.

When you meet danger, you find safety. When you have difficulty, things become easy. When you meet death, there is life for you. When you meet failure, there is success.

Sometimes during or after you meditation, your face produces jade light, your body becomes light, and all your old diseases disappear.

When practicing the Sacred Method, you gain the signs from the mysterious world which you expected.

Every sign comes to you without your intention. You need only to keep your mind in proper meditation.

Sometimes you make peaceful and steady progress in self-cultivation, but without the appearance of any special signs. This is also a sign of correct efforts in self-discipline to show your achievement of Tao.

Chapter 15

The Way of Cultivating Tao

The Direction

We dedicate ourselves to the Tao. To follow Tao is to follow the eternal "cosmic law of life." To turn from Tao is to follow the path of self-destruction.

We dedicate ourselves to the Taoist Sacred Method. This Taoist method of self-transcendence is the absolute method. With it, one can go beyond one's own mental and physical limitations and surpass all temptations and confusion.

We dedicate ourselves to our Taoist Master. He or she is the outer manifestation of our own inner spiritual process.

The Final Harbor

Tao is the absolute.
It is the origin of life
It is the source of all that is created,
And all that remains yet uncreated.

We dedicate ourselves to the Tao through dedication to the Subtle Origin of the universe, and to the three Heavenly Realms of Purity, where all supreme beings reside.

We live in harmony with all spiritual beings, regardless of their mental or physical references.

All names are only titles and are ultimately left by the gate to the subtle realms.

All spiritual beings share the same sublime essence. In our tradition, subtle, spiritual beings are referred to as shiens.

This title designates the subtle beings of purest and highest spiritual energy; it is also conferred upon the most natural, complete, and balanced human individuals.

Shiens are the Tao manifested as beings in time and space.

The True Way

All spiritual methods are either temporal or eternal in nature.

Temporal methods are artificial and reinforce the ego by offering psychological consolation or appealing to mental vanity.

Eternal methods, however, reveal the light of plain and simple truth which shines from within one's own true nature.

Rather than separate the three aspects of an individual's being or focus on only partial development, the purpose of the Taoist Sacred Method is to harmonize, complete and integrate body, mind and spirit.

Only through cultivating and balancing all three can there be true evolution of beingness.

Through this Sacred Method, one's physical, mental and spiritual impurities can be burned away and refined.

In the process of our own spiritualization, we can reform and refine our gross energy to become high subtle energy. Then we can transcend our bondage to the universal laws which govern the physical plane.

Refinement of our gross and impure energy to higher and higher states is the only way to guarantee the effectiveness of one's "Sacred Immortal Medicine."

With this true clarity, harmony with the entire universe will be achieved.

The Divine Teachers

We dedicate our lives to the Taoist Masters of the natural and eternal way of the universe.

True Masters preserve and continue the pure lineage of Tao and are the vehicles of our rebirth.

Through their subtle influence and inspiration, we are reborn into our original state of clarity and purity, and become the sacred fruits of their complete cultivation.

Because their spirit is right, their method is true.

Their mastery is not only external, but also internal.

Therefore, they are true Masters.

If the spirit is not right, then the method is harmful and unnatural. Such teachers must also be unnatural.

The true Master benefits all, while the false teacher leads them astray.

Because we live in ignorance and suffering, and know nothing of the sacred culture and methods of the eternal Tao, our Masters patiently and kindly open our eyes so that we may experience that the perceiver and the perceived are truly one.

Although it is impossible to repay our Masters for the grace they bestow upon us, the best we can do is to offer ourselves to them in whole-hearted dedication.

To serve a true Master with passion rather than virtue is to make one's path short and incorrect.

The correct manner in which one should offer oneself to the Master is with faithfulness and devotion to the truth.

En Route to Eternity

The creative energy of Heaven is the paternal source of our being.

The receptive energy of earth is the maternal source of our being.

Receptive and creative energies are combined in order to give birth to all beings and potential beings.

The Tao is the true origin of life.

Heaven, earth and the Tao are to be found dwelling in all humanity. Thus, the Way to serve Heaven, earth and the Tao is to serve one's fellow men and women.

In Tao, we have life as well as life's virtues.

Living in a temple or a church does not necessarily mean a person is spiritual or virtuous. Temples, churches and statues are merely symbols and images.

We are not misled by external appearances, but instead focus on the true, inner spiritual source.

The worship of force and the suggestion of conquering is the way of worldly deviation. The worldly point of view states that might is right.

To the Taoist Way, righteousness is might. Subtlety and gentleness is this tradition's Way of cultivating eternality.

When we worship, we do not distinguish between the internal and external or indulge in the creation of spectacular visions.

With gentleness, we always maintain the spirit of creativity.

When the creative spirit sings in our hearts, our surroundings benefit from the compassion we radiate.

We use gentle means to educate people and nurture their spiritual growth.

We care not for profit, but are interested only in serving the eternal Tao.

There are many spiritual paths. Objectively evaluate all of the choices before becoming a younger brother or sister of this Taoist tradition.

Once we have dedicated ourselves to this sacred tradition, we stay with the Tao and never go astray.

So-called saints, gods and buddhas are the objects of worship of the ordinary mind.

Followers of Tao dedicate themselves to self-discovery, self-discipline and self-mastery.

What We Offer

We offer our spirit to the teacher. His spirit is the manifestation of the subtle realm of the eternal Tao.

We offer our energy to his divine work.

We offer our support to his spiritual purpose.

We make money righteously and in turn spend it righteously. If it is used to assist the refinement of our true nature, it is a precious thing. If it is used to support our desires, it is a poison to our spirit.

Three Virtues to Use

COMPASSION

Compassion is the extension of our true nature. We do not contrive artificial compassion, but extend true compassion developed from the treasure of our deep nature.

MODERATION

Through moderation we can have endurance of life. When we are born, we are true to our nature, but as we grow older, we attempt to imitate other members of society by chasing after fashion. Thus we must develop moderation to free ourselves from social vanity.

HUMILITY

Through humility we can gain enlightenment from the wonders of great nature. When we lose humility, we stray from the energy channel of our true nature. When we reestablish humility, we bond together spirit and mind.

Compassion is the first virtue of a supreme being.

With moderation we can live a balanced life free of vanity.

With humility we can empty the mind of its accumulated false knowledge and become receptive to the true consciousness that all things have the same Subtle Origin.

This understanding is the foundation of our companion for others and moderation with ourselves.

With these virtues we refine our spirit, mind and body so as to become the embodiment of the Tao.

By living a compassionate life, we can touch the creative origin of the universe. Creativity is the essence of our nature.

Mind and our nature can produce many wonders.

To realize the true nature of life is the purpose of following the path of Tao.

The Observances

First, purify your heart by simplifying your mind and spirit.

Thinking, speaking, doing and not doing all come forth from the origin of simplicity.

To simplify the spirit is to achieve all else.

The Tao is elusive, but spiritual energy can become tangible through a sincere and true way of thinking and acting.

By seeing things only partially, we miss the target of complete uplifting of life.

Diligently cultivate and deepen your roots in Tao.

Deep roots in the eternal Tao are the foundation of our immortality and freshness of spirit.

To be honest in self-cultivation and make advancement step by step is the Way to achieve "non-self" realization.

Your spiritual evolution depends mainly on your own daily self-inspection and self-examination.

Stay on the right path and avoid self-destructive patterns. Keep away from behavior harmful to oneself and to others.

Mundane burdens obstruct our hearts and prevent success in the achievement of our spiritual actualization.

It takes three years to form a good habit and only one day to destroy it. One moment of negligence can cause a lifetime of cultivation to become deteriorated.

Selfishness hardens the heart, while selflessness allows it to blossom.

Unrighteous means will destroy good intentions. With pure energy we move forward; with impure we digress.

In all matters, the eternal Tao is our final measurement in choosing and determining our own life and behavior, both mentally and practically.

On the Road of Taoist Cultivation

THE ORIGIN
Before Heaven and Earth come into being
and Tai Chi is not yet manifest
There is the Great Silence,
the source of life.
It has no form - no name - and is made of no-thing
and yet as the Eternal Breath of Tao
it contains all.
It is, in its creative subtle energy,
continuously manifesting.
We call it the Mysterious Mother.
In her divine embrace
she nurtures all life.
We call it Tao.
It is the Subtle Origin.
All life depends on this.

From the Eternal Breath of Tao came forth
spontaneity as universal law.
Movement and change,
Tai Chi revolving in time and space
and the yang and yin interacting its energies
form all manifestations in relative order.
This is the fundamental principle of the universe.
The knowledge has been handed down to us
by our revered Grandmaster.

THE LAW OF THE GREAT ENERGY TRANSFORMATION

All manifestations of life with its changing events
depend on the Heavenly order of energy transformation.
The subtle workings of the universe
cannot be fully understood by the mind.
But to help you in your self-cultivation,
our Grandmaster formed the subtle truth
into words and images
as a tool to reach the depth of true understanding.
He handed down to us
the esoteric knowledge of the Heavenly order.

ENERGY FORMATION MANIFESTED AS BEINGS

In the center of the universe
    nourished by the divine energy of the Mysterious Mother
    resides the Jade Emperor,
    the Undecayed One, (Self So),
    named the Te in ancient times.
Its energy is most supreme.
Its light illuminates the universe.
Its brilliance is all-encompassing.
This is the core of all manifested life.
From this center, radiating out to its circumference
    from the most subtle to the coarse,
    all spiritual beings receive this light.
All natural and supernatural deities, sovereigns
    and spirits surround it.
They are very subtle beings.
The most subtle of all are the shiens.
Their energy is highly refined and pure.
They can be with or without form,
    and have reached perfection and self-mastery in life.
They are immortal through continuous self-renewal.
They are, together with the living Master,
    our guides in self-cultivation.
To evolve to this high and pure manifestation of being
    is the goal of one who follows Tao.

YIN AND YANG, THE FIVE BASIC TYPES OF ENERGY TRANSFORMATION AND THE LAW OF CHANGE

From the interaction of the Subtle Origin in the
    Mysterious Mother
    and the balanced energy of yin and yang,
    all phenomena of life came forth.
Yang energy is subtle and spiritual.
It is positive and has action as its nature.
Yin is coarse and physical
    and is referred to as earth.
It is negative, and receptiveness is its nature.
Both energies are equal, and support
    each other in perfect harmony.

THE FIVE ELEMENTARY PHASES OF ENERGY TRANSFORMATION

The five basic types of energy are symbolized by
fire, metal, water, wood and earth.
The earthly energy has a balancing function.
They manifest the relationship between all universal energies.
They penetrate sub-energies
and have their own main function.
Each phase of transformation has a positive and negative,
a yang and a yin, and within each phase
is contained the five energy transformations.
They work in perfect order and embody harmony.
When the natural order is disturbed, disharmony results.

THE LAW OF CHANGE

All universal laws are under the governing law of change.
In daily life the five phases of transformation
are present in every event.
There are five kinds of relative situations
existing at the same time
and every change can manifest the aspect
of one of the phases.
The law of relativity is illustrated
by the five basic types of energy.
The Book of Changes is the tool
to fully understand this universal law.
Under the Law of Great Transformation,
the energies are constantly changing,
never static.
Their movement in change is constant.
Therefore, the future of a person has several possibilities,
but nothing is certain,
until the person makes it so.

THE THREE REALMS OF THE UNIVERSE

To have some understanding
of the subtle workings of the universe,
we categorize the different energies as "realms."

There are three realms of existence:
The spiritual realm, referred to as "Heaven"
or the Realm of Utmost Purity
containing spiritual power.
The mental realm referred to as "human"
or Realm of Crystal Purity
containing rational power.
The physical realm, referred to as earth,
or the Realm of Great Purity
containing organic power.
Those realms also exist in the physical body:
The spiritual realm resides in the head.
The mental realm resides in the heart.
The physical realm below the navel.
These are the three Tan Tien.
Since one within oneself is a miniature universe,
all cosmic laws apply to us as well.
Gathering the coarse and subtle in one's form,
one stands between Heaven and Earth.
One's mind is the instrument
to unite the spirit with the physical body.

GUIDELINES TO SELF-CULTIVATION: THE UNDERSTANDING OF MIND IN MACROCOSMS AND MICROCOSMS

Behind all phenomena is a universal mind.
The origin of humankind in universal existence is very subtle,
and is brought forth by this universal mind.
Our mind, in this physical body, is also very subtle
and was formed in this universal mind-energy.
Through the mind, we manifest our function in life;
depending on the use of our mental energy,
we weave the pattern of our life.
One has received one's mind as an instrument
to unite the spirit with the physical body.
One has the ability to move one's mind
to the direction of one's choice.
One can follow one's instincts and desires
and move downward into more physical realms,
or bend one's desires to positive, constructive actions;

*thus allowing oneself to move into higher energy vibrations
and evolve to spiritualization,
which gives true joy and eternal life.
One can become an instrument to help humankind
understand its true nature
and free itself from blind suffering and ignorance.
Your evolution or devolution depends on the subtle movement
of the mind.
Respect this divine instrument and use it well.
After refining the mind to more subtle levels,
one can experience the Subtle Origin of the universe
and thus the origin of one's own existence.*

*The Subtle Origin is formless.
It is made of no-thing.
But from this no-thing all existence comes into being.
This no-thing of the universe is creative and constructive energy.
If you keep your mind in this nothing
which in its very nature is being,
you imitate the process of the universe.
You will flow on the stream of creative and constructive energy
and all your positive thoughts will come true.
This energy will flow from the origin of the universe,
from the origin of your true mind.
Keep your mind still without coming or going
and you will be one with Tao.
You will know that your own energy
is the energy of the universe;
that the universal spirit is your own true spirit.
This spirit is all-powerful, all-creative,
and can penetrate the material world.
Since it is formless and has no substance,
there are no obstacles in its way.
Nothing can harm it.
It can come or go as it wishes.
This spirit, as your true nature, can float in space.
In the morning it can roam over the earth
and at night sleep in the Heavenly realms.
Boundless space is its home, your home.*

THE REALIZATION OF ETERNAL EXISTENCE

Follow the method of self-cultivation
  and connect yourself with the supreme sovereign
  of the universe.
The divine spirits will then authorize your
  self cultivation
  and help you on the path of Tao.
When you can combine your energy with their subtle energy
  you imitate Heaven and all your deeds become pure.
You will spread your spiritual energy
  as a spiritual strategy to help humanity.
Your positive energy can permeate all Heavens and Earth.
All divine energies are in their correct position
  and communicate their magnificence to your cultivation.
They will pass down the highest wisdom
  when you have attained your self-realization,
  then your true nature will shine forth.
You will have sovereignty over nature
  and complete dominion over the physical world
  and your own life.
Refine your physical body,
  until and coarse energy becomes exquisite spiritual energy.
In this way you will reach eternal life.

The Way of Self-Channelling for a Taoist

The life channel of a Taoist is the reunification of one's body, mind and spirit with the universal, eternal oneness which we call Tao. In order to achieve the goal of reunification of body, mind and spirit with the eternal Tao, and to be receptive to the subtle energy of the universe, a Taoist must adhere to the Integral Way of Life in the following simple manner:

1. First, Taoists must make the effort to dissolve the concealed, individual ego in order to unite with the eternal universe and embrace all humanity.

2. Taoists are not overly attentive to their physical necessities, at the expense of nurturing the spiritual essence of one's life.

3. Taoists strive to comprehend deeply and follow strictly the universal laws of life, rather than to allow themselves to be controlled by blind impulse, which invariably leads to confusion and suffering.

4. Taoists endeavor to achieve moderation and regularity in their lives.

5. Taoists maintain their freshness of spirit by having an optimistic attitude, by striving to be above the frustrations of life, and by rejuvenation through self-cultivation.

6. Taoists spiritually offer themselves in service to the world without demanding compensation.

7. Taoists cultivate a kind nature and a tolerant attitude toward others.

8. Taoists remain true to their divine nature, which inherently embodies goodness, truth and beauty, by endeavoring only to participate in positive, creative and constructive activities.

9. Taoists do not allow their mind or soul to be corrupted by external pressures or internal impulses.

10. Taoists never display their achievements or take advantage of another's shortcomings.

11. Taoists wholeheartedly pursue the perfection and total completeness of their true nature. Rather than limiting themselves to the standard concept of relative morals and ethics by being virtuous for the purpose of personal gain, Taoists strive to transcend themselves by embodying absolute virtue and truth, thereby fulfilling the ultimate goals of the universe.

12. Taoists decrease the luxuries of their material life and eliminate the burdens of the intellect in order to realize the fullness of spirit.

13. Taoists do not conduct themselves frivolously, but deal with their worldly activities clear-mindedly, following the wisdom and example of the Taoists sages.

14. Taoists strive to become aware of difficulties in their unformed stage, thereby controlling or avoiding problems before they manifest.

15. Taoists practice the principle of universal love by becoming involved in worldly affairs but not indulging in competition.

16. Taoists do not allow themselves to be in bondage to their old bad habits, nor do they acquire new ones.

17. Taoists learn to take it easy under pressure. This makes them better off in such a circumstance.

18. Taoists keep the minimum standard for maintaining their lives, rather than over-indulging in physical pleasure.

19. Taoists restore themselves to their true, simple nature and faithfully fulfill the divine nature with which they are endowed.

20. Taoists value the simple reality of integral spirit, never the superficial and overwhelming ocean of descriptive words.

21. There are six main Taoist classics which contain the foundation and principles upon which the understanding and practical disciplines of Taoism are based. They are as follows:

The *I Ching* or *Book of Changes*[1],
The *Tao Teh Ching* by Lao Tzu,[2]
The *Nan Hwa Ching* by Chuang Tzu,[3]

---

[1]Translated and elucidated by Master Ni as *The Book of Changes and the Unchanging Truth*.

[2]Translated and elucidated by Master Ni in *The Complete Works of Lao Tzu*.

[3]Translated and elucidated by Master Ni as *Attaining Unlimited Life*.

The *Hung Lei Ching* by Hui Nan Tzu,[4]
The *Lieh Tzu* by Lieh Tzu,[5] and
The *Pao Po Tzu* by Kou Hong.[6]

Most of the other essential Taoist texts have been compiled into what is known as the *Taoist Canon* which is an abundant accumulation of knowledge about natural life pertaining to the achievement of spiritual, mental and physical harmony, and the continual development and evolution of self. In addition to these are numerous excellent works by the Ch'an Masters in a branch of Buddhism which is also called Zen.

---

[4]The story of Hui Nan Tzu and his teachings are absorbed in all of Master Ni's work.

[5]The teachings of Lieh Tzu are given in the book, *Tao, the Subtle Law and the Integral Way of Life* in quotations.

[6]His teachings will be introduced in a future work by Master Ni about two Taoist masters.

Chapter 16

The Integral Way of Tao

Integral Beings in the World

The Heavenly shiens are immortal, holy beings who exist in realms transcendent to time and space. They are the first beings to conglomerate from the divine, pure yang energy of the universe and have existed since long before the formation of Heaven and earth. They have continuously exerted a subtle influence, not only on humankind and earthly events, but also on the entire universe. Since the beginning of time, all things have been constantly changing under the universal law of great transformation. Only the immeasurable Heavenly shiens never grow old because of their continuous, instantaneous renewal through self-mastery.

In the beginning, the earth was uninhabited by any beings. The shiens descended from another space of the universe and combined themselves with the yin energy of earth, thus giving birth to humanity. Naturally, they became the earliest, true ancestors of the human race. Because the first inhabitants of earth were true to their divine nature, it was not necessary for them to cultivate or discipline themselves. They spontaneously enjoyed full, effective lives without needing to use their intellects. Even though they did not require self-refinement, they still lived good, long lives. However, after many generations, humanity began to degenerate and its subtle divine energy (the ling) gradually dissipated. Consequently, it became necessary for them to develop their intellects. They became more concerned about the flavor of food than whether it contained happiness and health. All kinds of excitements to stimulate their worn minds became their way of life.

As a result of this, it was necessary for them to rely on religions to rectify their negative behavior and thinking. Many religions appeared and many doctrines were produced. It is no wonder that people's minds became confused. The more the mischievous intellect developed, the less effective humanity became, until people could no longer maintain harmony and balance. So there were endless calamities which became the side-product of the overdeveloped mind. Unfortunate events happened, like waves in a stormy sea, entangling humanity more and more in negativity.

During the early stages when humanity was still uncorrupted, shiens frequently descended to earth and made its inhabitants their company. But after some time, the human mind became spoiled and worn out by the loss of its naturalness. Therefore, the shiens only make brief visits to earth during times of peace because humanity has now become tainted. The shiens do not like to see this beautiful world being destroyed by humanity. In a bad year, perhaps there are only a few Heavenly shiens who come to earth to rescue humanity in the hope that they might subtly change the destiny of the world. They come to the world and take human form in order to openly teach the most virtuous people the way back to their divine nature. They try to protect all people from the negativity which has arisen as result of the loss of their subtle, divine energy (ling chi).

The Heavenly beings who were our first ancestors are the divine origin of humanity. Even though their examples and teachings have been scattered through the ages, their tradition has not been entirely lost. Through the tradition of the Heavenly lineage of the "Union of Tao and Man," we can now still obtain the most precious enlightenment. This enables us to free ourselves from the bondage and attraction to our illusions, and at the same time restore in ourselves the simplicity and integrity of our natural being. The shiens' teachings are left in the world as a ferry to help people cross their own troubled waters. The choosing of disciples in this lineage is strict. Only those with the highest degree of sincerity and willingness to accept the Heavenly responsibility of being wise can receive the sacred tradition. Only through purification and self-cultivation can one hope to attain self-transcendence and completely unite with Tao.

Every level of existence contains its own particular nature as a result of the specific energy formation it expresses. Some beings are suited to live in air, some in water, and so forth. But all beings are produced from the creative, generating energy of the universe which is generally referred to as "Heaven." All manifestations are the offspring of this prime energy, the "Mysterious Mother" of the universe. Each classification of energy formation stands as a universe unto itself, with its own measurement and awareness or unawareness of time and space. The principal classifications of energy formation are the spiritual realm, the mental realm and the physical realm, referred to as "Heaven," "humanity" and "earth," all of which comprise the thirty-three categories of the universe. The first eleven categories express more yang energy and are spiritual; the second eleven are the intermediaries of yin and yang and are mental, and the last eleven express more yin energy and are physical.

Within each category there are many sub-categories, all of which comprise the vast universe. The human body, as a microcosm of the universe, contains and thereby is connected with all three principal classifications of energy formation: the head embodying "Heaven" or spirit, the middle part of the chest embodying "the human" or mind, and the lower part of the trunk embodying "earth" or physical energy. Another way of describing this would be to say that spirit is the core, mind is the undergarment, and physical body is the overcoat.

The Heavenly tradition of the "Union of Tao and Integral Person" reveres the divine primacy, the creative energy of the universe, which is associated with the head. This energy is the highest in all Heavens and is the originator of the universal Heavenly order. It is Heavenly law itself and is divine nature. It is Tao. There are many forms of energy in the universe. The original primal energy has twisted and distorted itself into many different reflections, none of which are the Tao. It is only the Tao which this divine tradition reveres. All phenomena are offspring of this subtle, generating energy, which in ancient times was revered and titled "ti," the stem or stalk of the universal total existence, and later "the Jade Emperor," or Undecayed One.

From the original divine substance came all the variations of the universe. The Heavenly shiens were the first manifestations of this original, creative energy to become beings. They are the most essential and respected of all beings, and are the most noble in the universe. The number of shiens is unknowable. According to the law of energy correspondence, if there is a difficulty, the shiens pave the way to the solution. However, the frequency of one's energy must be the same frequency as that of the Heavenly shiens in order to obtain a response from them. This stream of eternal spirit responds to the divine method of self-cultivation whereby one can refine one's energy to become the same quality as that of the Heavenly shiens.

Humankind has within itself the divine essence from above, but its divinity has been covered over by many layers of mental creations, acquisitions and confusions. At first, the mind, as the intermediary of the spirit and the physical body, offers its appropriate service. However, after some time, because its role has been overplayed, it overpowers the main pillar of human existence, which is spirit and then the physical body.

The Author's Tradition: Union of Tao and Integral Person

The spiritual roots of the "Union of Tao and Integral Person" can be traced to prehistoric times. The Chinese believe that during the time before Emperor Fu Hsi, who is said to have reigned around 8,000 years ago, the earth was inhabited by gods. These supernatural beings came into existence as the result of the combination of subtle, creative universal energy with pure, physical energy of the earth. These gods lived spontaneously and intuitively in perfect harmony with nature and had no need of any method of self-cultivation or restoration. Their lives were the manifestation of pure natural law.

The period after Fu Hsi until the end of the reign of the great Emperor Yu (2205-2125 B.C.) was known as the age of the semi-gods. During this period, emperors were profoundly wise, spiritual people deeply involved in researching and practicing esoteric methods to restore their divine quality. Fu Hsi, to whom is attributed the discovery of the eight manifestations of the *I Ching*; the Yellow Emperor, Huang Ti (2697-2597 B.C.), who was the author of the classic on internal medicine; and the great Emperors Niao (2357-2258 B.C.) and Shun (2255-2208 B.C.) all practiced and handed down the Taoist Sacred Method until the reign of Emperor Yu's son (2205-2125 B.C.), who was Emperor Chieh (2125-2116 B.C.). Emperor Chieh was the first to inherit the throne through family succession, whereas before the rule had been passed only to sages. Those who succeeded Emperor Chieh were unable to attain the Heavenly qualities of the sages and so the age of the semi-gods came to an end.

> *In the tenth moon, plum blossoms bloom,*
> *Awaiting the early arrival of spring.*
> *If inanimate things can predict nature's Way,*
> *It would be folly for us not to follow the Tao.*
> Lu, Tung Ping

Then came an era of leaders who were not spiritually developed. In this era, the Taoist Sacred Method was no longer handed down through the Emperors but was transmitted generation after generation by inspired sages called shiens who lived in the high mountains as hermits, apart from the masses who abused themselves through their lifestyle. These enlightened people live simply in harmony with nature, and enjoyed the unceasing regenerative power of the universe. Sometimes the shiens would come to live among the people, but they generally went unrecognized because they hid their great wisdom and miraculous powers. Sometimes they would travel throughout the countryside helping people in need. Most of them, however, chose to reside quietly in the remote mountains far from the tumult of the worldly populace.

> *To attain Tao,*
> *It is not necessary*
> *To go to the mountains.*
> *Stay right here.*
> *In the red dust, riding a golden horse -*
> *There is a great practitioner of Tao.*
> *Thus it is said*
> *The mountains only provide quietude.*
> Lu, Tung Ping

Prior to the Han dynasty (206 B.C.-219 A.D.), Taoism was a pure spiritual tradition involved with the restoration of human beings' divine nature through the cultivation of Tao, and was studied and practiced only in the high mountains by the shiens and their disciples. These shiens were the forefathers of my tradition, the "Union of Tao and Man." At the end of the Han dynasty (C. 184 A.D.) a local religious cult, "The Yellow Hood," appeared and also called itself Taoism. Several such cults existed in different ages. However, those religious movements should not be confused with the pure, spiritual tradition of ancient Taoism. They should never be mistaken for the ancient teaching of the Taoist shiens.

> *What is Tao?*
> *It is just this.*
> *It cannot be rendered into speech.*
> *If you insist on an explanation,*
> *This means exactly this.*
> Lu, Tung Ping

One of the most famous shiens at the end of the Han dynasty was Kou Hong (205 A.D.). Inspired by his shien grandfather, he went to Tien Tai Mountain in Chekiang Province to practice the secret formula of sublimation and refinement. He authored the book *Pao Po Tzu*, a collection of all the Taoist methods of self-cultivation in existence at the time. The theoretical part of his work has been translated into English. He succeeded in his cultivation and became an Immortal. In the same mountains, but in the Tang dynasty (618-906 A.D.), Master Sz Ma Chung Jen, the author of "The Theory of Sitting, Forgetting and Uniting," and his teacher, known as "The Son of Invisible Heaven," who authored a book of this title, both cultivated themselves and practiced the Taoist Sacred Method.

> *The elixir of immortality:*
> *There is no need to beg from others.*
> *The eight trigrams,*
> *The nine colors,*
> *Are all on your palms.*
> *The five elementary formations,*
> *The four figures of the diagrams,*
> *Are all within you.*
> *Understanding this*
> *You can communicate with the spirits.*
> Lu, Tung Ping

All of the famous Eight Immortals are descendants of the sacred tradition of the "Union of Tao and Man." The most famous of them is Lu, Tung Ping, who lived during the Tang dynasty and whose poems are quoted herein. The story of Lu's enlightenment is contained in the famous play of the Yuan dynasty entitled the "Yellow Millet Dream." This play depicts Lu as a scholar travelling to the capital to take the Court Examination in hope of becoming appointed to a governmental position. He stopped one evening at a road-side inn, where, while he was waiting for his supper of yellow millet to be cooked, he fell asleep. He dreamt that he went through many distressing circumstances until he finally met Chung-Li Ch'uan, who opened his eyes to the truth. Upon his awakening from the dream, eighteen years had already passed.

Master Lu lived during the period of Chinese history when Buddhism was starting to flourish in China. He departed from the Taoist custom of avoiding people of the world and traveled around the country teaching the truth of immortal life.

People sit until the cushion is worn through,
But never quite know the real Truth;
Let me tell you about the ultimate Tao:
It is here, enshrined within us.
                                        Lu, Tung Ping

Master Lu's Disciple, Leao Hai Chan, was the premier to Emperor Yen (c. 911 A.D.). Leao Hai Chan passed the Sacred Method to Shueh Bau Guan, who passed it to Shih Sing Ling, who passed it to Bai Yu Chan. These five shiens are called the Five Forefathers of the Southern Branch.

Close your eyes to seek for the Truth
And Truth comes naturally.
The pearl of Tao emits liveliness.
Play with it day and night,
And never throw it away
Lest the God of the Netherworld
Send his underlings after you.
                                        Lu, Tung Ping

I, myself, am a descendant of the shiens of Tien Tai Mountain, where Kou Hong refined his elixir of immortality. The Taoist Temple in Tien Tai Mountain was built in memory of the enlightenment of the Taoist Prince Tung Pa, the son of Emperor Ling Wang (571-543 B.C.) of the Chou dynasty. Master Sz Ma Chung Jen of the Tang dynasty (618-906 A.D.) is the remote spiritual heir of Master Dao Hong-Cheng of the Chen dynasty (265-588 A.D.). Both he and Master Jang Tse Yang of the Sung dynasty (960-1276 A.D.) cultivated in Tien Tai Mountain and were part of the Southern Branch.

The Northern, Western and Eastern Branches were all formed separately. The Northern Branch started during the Yuan dynasty (1277-1367 A.D.) with Wang Jung Yang, who tried to preserve the Chinese heritage from destruction by the invading Mongols. The most striking difference between this branch and the others is their strict practice of independent cultivation, with celibacy for the novice. The Western and Eastern Branches were formed during the Ming dynasty (1368-1644 A.D.) and Ching dynasty (1644-1912 A.D.), respectively. Both schools share the same truths; the only difference being in a few secret techniques of cultivation.

Some of the Masters of the sacred family of shiens which constitute my lineage are:

Master Shigh Ga or "Stone Drum." His name comes from the practice of engraving mystical pictographs in stone. He lived in the Da Lu Mountains in Shueh-An County of Chekiang Province.

Master Shih Je or "Stone Disaster." His name comes from his liking to break stones with his forehead. He lived in the South Yen Tang Mountains in Ping Yang County of Chekiang Province.

Master Tai Huang or "Great Wilderness." He lived in the Da Lu Mountains.

Master Weh Feng or "Revolving Peak." His name comes from the fact that the wild geese on their journey south or north would circle around the peak of the mountain on which he lived. He lived in the North Yen Tang Mountains.

Master Teah Yuhn or "Crown of Strength." His name depicts his strong virtue. He lived in the Mao Mountains in Chu Yung County of Kuansu Province.

Master Tung Yuhn or "Purple Clouds." His name came from purple clouds appearing in the sky at the time he achieved enlightenment. He is the author's father and lived in Chekiang province, practicing Taoism and traditional Chinese medicine.

Master Yen Tang Yin Jung or the "Hermit of Yen Tang," Master Tai Ruh Yin Yung or the "Hermit of Tai Ruh," Master Da Tao Tsu or the "Son of the Eternal Tao." He is the author, Ni, Hua-Ching.

> *Sojourning in the Tau-yu Mountains,*
> *Who converses with the white crane*
> *that comes flying?*
> *How many times have the mountain people*
> *seen the winter plum-flowers blossoming?*

Spring comes and goes,
deep in fallen flowers and streams.
People are not aware
of the many immortals around them.
Lu, Tung Ping

Non-integrated Spiritual Practices Can Be Harmful

Certain practices of some sects are not only not beneficial for one's self-cultivation, but can be dangerous as well. Several patients have come to me with spiritual damage due to the unnatural and premature "raising of their Kundalini." Certain sects place too much emphasis on a specific area of cultivation. Some emphasize sitting too much, and even some Yoga postures are unhealthy. Others have weakened themselves through extreme so-called spiritual diets consisting mostly of brown rice. There are even a few sects that insert a piece of glass into the soft spot on top of the head in order to open up that center to communicate with Heaven. These practices are never as beneficial as true cultivation. By making an effort to reform the energy formation of the entire body, the brain and the skull become soft naturally, and open and close in their due time. It is true that if the energy channel on the top of the head does not open naturally, all the mysteries of the universe will never become lucid. Real spiritual progress is not achieved by inserting glass, or forcing energy in any way, but only through continuous daily self-cultivation.

Position for Cultivation

Meditating in a sitting position is not the only correct method for cultivating higher energy. On the contrary, you may weaken yourself by using solely the sitting position. To refine coarse energy to become fine and to change from the visible to the subtle, it is better to also practice various standing positions. The true knowledge of energy is deep and profound, and can be learned only through actual training from a Taoist Master.

After breaking through all the blocked channels of energy in your body, you can then single-mindedly cultivate yourself towards one destination. If the true energy channel which connects with the Heaven in your body cannot be opened, then your cultivation will be in vain and your harvest will be empty.

The human body seems limited, yet through the body, Taoists actually practice the responsive subtle law of the universe.

Eliminating the Gloomy Body
The gloomy body of a soul is the low sphere of one's inner being. It is the yin sphere of the energy in a living being. When an ordinary human life is over, there is no energy left in the yang sphere. If one has already exhausted the yang sphere of energy, and also during one's lifetime one did not develop the upper or high sphere of one's inner being, then during one's lifetime the gloomy body keeps growing, and when one dies, this is the part that becomes a ghost. If one hopes to achieve divine immortality without thoroughly eliminating the growth of the gloomy body in one's lifetime, then one's cultivation is inaccurate.

Actually, the gloomy body is the real source of obstacles which block your cultivation of divine immortality. This is because the three negative parts of energy have not yet been removed. They will cause many signs of disharmony in your new subtle integration. Oneness normally manifests as quietude or silence. However, unless you efface the gloomy body, you will still have many dreams in your sleep and a hidden flow of distracting consciousness in your mind. These three negatives are mental blocks, uncontrolled passions and desires, and harmful sex.

They become the actual destructive energies living in the upper, middle and lower parts of your body. They are traditionally named as pong chu, pong chi and pong chia. These three destructive sources undermine your well-being. They continuously grow without your knowledge. They are the enemies of a good, virtuous life. They must be restrained and destroyed. When they become active, they enslave your soul and disintegrate your entire being. They are the root of the dark ghostly world within you. Those who cultivate themselves must entirely remove these bad roots. One must extinguish the three death spirits within oneself from the three parts of one's body, and then attain the great harmonious body as the correct strong foundation for the attainment of the crystal and subtle bodies.

Cultivation of the Light Heavenly Energy
It is much better for a person's energy to be light than heavy, and is preferable than it be pure rather than mixed up and cloudy. Some people are born with contamination from the pre-natal stage or from past lives while others have added new

contamination from their post-natal lives. In the Taoist view, these situations can be reformed by the refinement of one's personal energy through self-cultivation. In this way one can reform the "deterministic" destiny of one's life.

The light energy in the human mind is respected as the energy of Heaven because this energy connects with the high energy sphere of nature. If this light energy is nurtured and developed, the mental faculties become clearer and more effective. However, if this light energy is wasted and ignored, the mental faculties become dulled and deranged. The full maturation of our daily lives cannot be realized without the utilization of this light energy or spiritual energy. No valuable scientific achievement can be accomplished without it. No great artistic work can be created without it. All beneficial industry, all high academic studies, all wisely formed political policies and institutions and all highly valued civilizations evolve through the connection with higher energy. Through the high subtle light energy, all beneficial and creative manifestations appear. These manifestations take form in the "born" stage of the world through the endeavors of mankind, but are originally inspired in the "unborn" realm through the operation of the spiritual light.

The practice of Self-Transformation within the Alchemical Furnace

The ancient Masters of the Integral Way were aware that the entire universe is an enormous alchemical furnace in which the transformation of the universe takes place. All phenomena come from the nature of transformation. Transformation generates from the one subtle energy embodied in the pure law. For precise understanding of this "big furnace," the ancients invented the system of the *I Ching* as a tool for the subtle practice of controlling all phenomena in the natural process of transformation and in the internal subtle practice of self-transformation. After one has achieved a high and profound development of one's mental capabilities, one will come to understand intuitively how all being and things are molded by this great "furnace" of transformation.

One will find the true knowledge of life and also an effective way of self-discipline and self-refinement through the basic and intensive study of the *I Ching*. It is precious to those who brush away their impurities and the contamination accumulated throughout the years of their lives and return upstream to the realm of purity. One unites with and enjoys the one chi of divine immortal energy. When one succeeds in cleansing one's impurities and retaining one's essence, and finally achieves the refinement of the "Medicine of Immortality," then it becomes difficult to distinguish which is the part being refined and which is engaging in the refinement; which part is the Immortal and which is the immortal medicine. At this point the need for any division vanishes.

The Senses Have No Reality in the Absolute Realm of Integration

When one has freed oneself from the bondage of sensory perception, one can see through the impressions of the five senses as though bubbles. Suffering, thinking, doing and knowing are only empty bubbles in the sensory world.

Things with form are not really any different from emptiness. The formed is empty, the empty is formed. The high beings form themselves with emptiness. In the higher spiritual realm, there is nothing which can be augmented and there is nothing which can be diminished. There is nothing to be brought about and there is nothing to be thrown away.

In the empty eternality, there is nothing which can be called form, suffering, thinking, doing or knowing. There is nothing which may be thought of as clean, nothing which can be thought of as not clean. There is nothing to be witnessed by eyes, ears, nose, tongues, bodies, feelings and thinking because there are no colors, sounds, odors, flavors, configurations or approaches. There is no room for eyes. There is no darkness. There is nothing that can be called the elimination of darkness. Furthermore, there is no age and death or salvation from old age and death. There is no such thing as troublemindedness, calming down, total liberation or the path.

The person connected with high awareness, following one's own true wisdom, has no obstacles in one's mind. Therefore, one has nothing to be afraid of. One can leave any troubles and nightmares far behind and reach for the final completeness. The high beings of the past, of the future, and the present follow their own true wisdom to gain the highest awareness and achieve the highest clarity. Hence one may know that true wisdom itself is the great spiritual key to liberation. It is the most enlightening doctrine that exists. It is the all-encompassing word with most power. But, it cannot be mentioned or described by words, colors, volume, shape or anything else involved with the senses or thinking.

The Subtle Body of Tao

The true source is beyond description.
Pure law is formless and unspeakable.
Though appearing as two,
in essence there is only one.
For want of a better word,
the ancients called it Tao.

This primal mystery is the Mother of all.
All phenomena proceed from it.
All phenomena journey back to it.
Through phenomena, we also return
to the great mystery.

Existing - yet not existing.
Doing nothing - yet leaving nothing undone.
While remaining eternally free,
it masters all through selfless activity.

Although Tao is one,
the shiens are many.
Residing in the true Heaven of sublime energy,
they are pure reflections of Tao.
Through them, the great oneness can be known.

Their lives are subtle and deep.
They appear to be born with and without form.
Self-formed and self-denying,
they are the most mysterious of all beings.

For a long time we are trapped
in this earthly net of life.
We lose ourselves behind a soiled veil
and appear separated from the truth.

Through enlightenment by the shiens,
the way of release is known.
In no time, the veil is lifted,
and we are free of all bondage.

When we receive the power of the true source,
we are free and never lose the Way.
Centuries of guilt are washed away
and the accumulated evil of many lives
is cleansed.

The influence of pure law is everywhere.
Our body is the shrine where we worship it.
Our light and its light merge into one.
In this way, no part of reality is missed.

If you see only life and death,
you will become confused and misdirected.
If you accept one thing and reject another,
you will isolate yourself.
If you think the calculating mind can know Tao,
you are far indeed from the ultimate truth.
With a pure heart and clear mind only,
can one regain the power of Tao.

Without regarding this as being the only truth,
we worship the subtle body of Tao.
From the beginning, the Tao serves us,
and in return, we humbly serve the Tao.

The uncountable stars have their number.
The unfathomable seas have their limit.
The void can be captured and the wind tied,
but the subtle body of Tao is beyond all knowing.

O mystery of mysteries, heart of hearts,
you are the most revered of all.
Dwelling in the depth of the deep,
you are the universal essence of all.

Chapter 17

Cultivating to be a Shien

The Individual Human Being as a Microcosm of the Universe
The human body contains all the virtues and spirits of the universe. However, if we are only partially developed, we violate the completeness of nature, which was originally formed in us during the prenatal existence of all our lives. Through proper self-cultivation, we can regain self-enlightenment. After the restoration of self-enlightenment, one can experience one's divinity beyond all doubt.

This is because human beings are the offspring and diffused energy of the Jade Emperor. If they adhere to Heaven, they keep the subtle essence as their being and spirit. If they combine with earth, they become life with form. Within the human body all the universal treasures are contained.

Without leaving the earth, people can ascend into Heaven. The ancient Taoists said that "the human body is a universe and the universe is not beyond the body." They proved this within their own bodies. The sacred cultivation method of Taoism considers the head of a human being as Heaven, the abdomen as earth, and the body as the whole universe. All three sections of the body, or tan tien (upper, middle, and lower alchemical energy factories), have ten Heavenly stem energies and twelve earthly branch energies for their communication with the energies of Heaven and earth.

Each tan tien has its own vibration and three responding points. These nine points have nine different rays corresponding to the rays of the Jade Emperor, and also nine different vibrations. These valuable discoveries formed the Taoist method of self-cultivation and are for general use in our daily lives.

Cultivation to Become an Earthly Shien
At the extremity of the physical earthly level, the "lower alchemical field" is the main workshop where one can refine one's essence to be superior energy. Then one lets the energy of earth ascend and meet with the energy of the astral Heavens. This energy can be found responding to the point in the middle of the chest which the Taoists call the "middle alchemical field," or the workshop for cultivation to the level of an astral shien. Here one receives the harmonious energy of the earth and astral

Heavens. With this energy, one can experience a harmonious body and enjoy a long life. One will then become an earthly shien with the earth as a companion throughout many years.

Cultivation to Become an Astral Shien

For those who cultivate the physical astral Heaven, the "middle altar" or "middle alchemical field" is also a main responding point. Taoists use this point to gather the energy of the astral Heavens and transform it to highly developed mental power. Then the astral Heavenly energy is led to ascend and combine with the energy of the high Heaven. Here one receives the energy of astral Heavens and experiences the existence of the crystal or lucid body. With this achievement, one will definitely ascend to the astral Heavens and become a new starry shien, a relative of the supernatural beings of the five Starry Oceans.

Cultivation to Become a Heavenly Shien

Now one refines the energy which was gained from the astral world to become true spirit. The point in the front of the head for cultivating the Heavenly shien is called the "upper alchemical field." When one achieves Tao and the divine subtle level, one's inner being is lifted from the body like a cicada removing its old shell. Transformation of the subtle body is then accomplished and one rises up in bright daylight.

Or, one cultivates oneself through the whole proceeding of refinement and finally dissolves one's body, thus achieving the subtle body which can then ascend. Many Taoists throughout the ages experienced this. For those who cultivate the true Heaven, the "Mysterious Dome" becomes the main responding point which can gather spirit and unite one with Tao.

When the pure energy can go through the "Mystical Pass," then one can gain the subtle energy and experience the subtle body. Then Heaven will become one's companion throughout one's long life. At this stage one becomes a Heavenly shien.

The Meaning of Integration in Self-cultivation

Without earth there cannot be Heaven in the relative sphere. All three alchemical fields are located in the human body. One must first gather the true energy from the yin chiao at the bottom of the "mysterious sea." Then the energy must be raised from the extremity of earth to the extremity of Heaven. Those who cultivate themselves to become earthly shiens must cultivate the pure energy in the area of the lower abdomen. Those who cultivate themselves to become astral shiens must cultivate the harmonious energy in the area of the chest and upper belly. Those who cultivate themselves to become Heavenly shiens must cultivate the integral area of the head in order to strongly mold their inner being. If one is successful in cultivating the pure, harmonious, and complete energy in the three areas of the lower, middle and upper alchemical fields, then one will achieve the bodily experience of being the Jade Emperor. Reaping these kinds of fruit depends solely upon the achievement of the purification of one's energy. The pure energy is the foundation and the key for attaining Tao and becoming a shien.

The Mysterious Way of Three Becoming One

This discussion is about the true knowledge which has been passed down from the ancients as "The Mysterious Way of Three Becoming One." Besides the cultivation of the three alchemical fields, there is another requirement in directing one's cultivation to become a shien. It is purification. Fundamentally speaking, the pure energy is Tao itself. You must gather together and store the pure energy. You must purify daily, and also achieve three other things in order to build your good foundation. First, you must be highly enlightened; second, you must be well self-regulated and have good discipline; and third, you must stay mentally and spiritually detached from the vulgar world of impurities and turmoil. Then you can easily reach achievement of Tao. There are many obstacles on the road of cultivation. Spiritual achievement is the main emphasis, which depends upon your mental and physical cultivation. True cultivation cannot be partial achievement. Taoists use different ways to achieve one purpose; this allows you to follow the true nature of life and unite yourself with the great oneness. In this way you will become the subtle body of Tao.

The Practical Requirement of Being a Shien

Crystal self-enlightenment is the first proof of true achievement and success in the spiritual shien's cultivation. You must first succeed in breaking through your blocks which present obstacles to your spiritual eyes. After you open your Heavenly eyes, you will be able to see the view of Heaven, the noble lights of the high beings, and have foreknowledge concerning all human affairs and worldly historical changes.

How can this be done? It is possible because the subtle form of energy precedes a person's actions. By being aware of the patterns of energy, you can know the possibilities that exist in each situation and thereby gain foreknowledge of the events.

Often people mistake "dream eyes" as Heavenly eyes. Dream eyes are dim because dream energy is impure. Those with dream eyes might see spirits of ghosts and have many visions, but these are mostly illusions caused by the weakness of their own spirit. It is difficult to see the truth. To attain Heavenly eyes, one must develop one's true chi through the process of energy refinement and then send the refined energy to the appropriate location. If you can achieve calmness in your daily life, then your Heavenly eyes will open and become active, allowing you to directly see or pre-experience facts before they actually take form in the physical world.

If the Heavenly eye is active in your dreams, what you sometimes receive is the mind's interpretation of the facts. These visions must be investigated, explained and understood properly. If one can see the vision, but does not understand its meaning, one has an incomplete Heavenly eye. Only if one understands what one sees, can one be considered to have perfect and true Heavenly eyes. Then the wonders of the perfected Heavenly eyes can fully develop under the guidance of careful and conscientious cultivation.

Some Taoists not only attain a breakthrough of the limitation of the eyes, but at the same time dissolve all the blocks of the ears and mental faculties. This achievement is called "Crystal Awareness." After full development of crystal awareness one can see into anything, no matter what the obstacles to one's awareness are. There is practically nothing one cannot know. The subtle contact of energy is perceived with one's crystal clarity, and in this way one gains knowledge of all the facts.

If you are determined to cultivate and to become a shien, you must daily follow the Taoist methods of managing and exercising your mind and body. Then evidence which helps you to be aware of your own achievement will become obvious.

If your determination is to be a spiritual shien, the secret is the opening of the Heavenly eyes, the complete Heavenly awareness and the accurate response from practicing the Sacred

Method of mystical cultivation. Day and night, you and the mystical world will mutually respond, and it will offer you encouragement regarding the correctness of your achievement.

If you cultivate yourself to be a Heavenly shien, you must develop Heavenly awareness, effective Heavenly response and subtle Heavenly capability. After developing all of these, you must stop communicating through all the windows of your organs. You must follow the high teachings which say that you must give up your so-called intelligence, forget your wisdom and return to nature, to the Original Simplicity and the simple truth of Tao. To embrace the Tao and keep your undecorated nature is the acknowledgement of being highly achieved.

The great and wise person is like a fool. One who possesses the most prefers to own nothing. The greatest breakthrough is like being completely empty. The greatest achievement is like not yet having learned. All the absolute wonders of a Heavenly shien are not something ordinary people can easily understand or recognize. It is not necessary for the ordinary person to understand or know how you achieved the understanding that your true nature is quite sufficient to experience a complete universe and a world full of beauty, truth and goodness.

After your achievement, you may leave society and be independent in isolation, or you may shade your light and serve the people of the colorful, dusty world. Your work may be tedious or amusing, depending on your cultivation and achievement. Either way, it no longer affects your completed awareness. If you make up your mind to achieve the full knowledge and abilities of an astral shien, you should not struggle to gain ordinary information and skills. Only a small amount of true energy is needed to lightly touch you, and you will immediately be inspired with multiple knowledge and skills.

In the ordinary world, sometimes a ghost or animal spirit comes to a person's body. Such people can then temporarily go beyond their usual knowledge to say and do things beyond their normal ability. However, this is only a one-time, temporary spiritual phenomenon. It may be considered a personal spiritual disaster. It has nothing to do with a true breakthrough, which requires the right kind of energy to open all the channels in the body, especially in certain positions of the cerebral area. In this way, full knowledge and greater abilities develop.

Taoist knowledge and skills like literature, painting, calligraphy, music, military strategy, practical policies, the management of human life; the secrets of Heaven, earth, medicine, and divination; the knowledge of the stars, palm and face reading, and so forth, are all developed by energy breaking through first in the mind and then in the body. After this, one receives the knowledge and skills. These are the accumulation of Taoist cultivation for the convenience of worldly life.

If you have the ability, you must concentrate on the important knowledge of life and, more importantly, on the achievement of spiritual life. Be sincere, one-minded and diligent. Then you will have the opportunity to go higher and experience much more beyond your present knowledge, and experience the existence of Heaven. For this you must have Masters to pass you the secrets. You must also have teachers to point out the secret points in your body. But most of the details, techniques and methods of cultivation depend mainly on yourself. After many different important breakthroughs, you can understand three things at one time, even if the teacher teaches you only one thing. This seems to happen of itself and does not become self-aggrandizement, because now you are close to becoming a spiritual shien. You must start as an ordinary person and refine your gross energy to become the golden immortal medicine. This depends entirely on yourself.

The Simple Way of Purification I Practiced as a Novice

If you aspire to be a shien or a healthy person, you must keep yourself pure, righteous and high-spirited, because Heavenly shiens hold the highest position among all spiritual beings. You must also maintain the following disciplines as I learned them:

Eye Purification

Do not look at the dead. This hurts your chi and makes you morbid. Do not look at pornographic pictures and shows, and you will have less difficulty keeping peace of mind and bearing good fruit in the self-cultivation of your divine nature. These sights will not damage the already dissipated.

Mouth Purification

Do not eat raw or half-raw meat or stimulating spices, or drink stimulating drinks. Do not use stimulating or addictive drugs, and eat only pure and clean food.

Do not use profanity or speak harmful words. In general, do not speak too much so that you may nourish your vital chi, the pure energy used in self-cultivation.

Body Purification
Keep yourself physically and mentally clean. For an adult novice, anyone with whom you have sexual intercourse must also be physically and mentally clean because sleeping with a person whose energy is impure will strain your energy. This also applies to general contact with people. For a young novice, starting sexual life is like hurting the root of a young tree.

Nose Purification
Avoid decayed and strong smelling odors. They hurt your chi. In order to maintain your clarity, purity and sensitivity, avoid inhaling drugs.

Ear Purification
Avoid jarring noise, low-class music and listening to excessive talking, because this will disturb your mind and your chi.

Mental Purification
Do not have unrighteous or excessive ambition. Too much ambition will stir up your mind, while good motives will sanctify your mind. Calmness can unite your soul with the root of the universe and can make you effective, thus helping you to become a shien.

In general, clean yourself externally and purify yourself internally in order to protect your precious chi. Depend on your pure energy to ascend into the Heavenly realm. Your return to the "Heaven of Great Purity," the "Heaven of Crystal Purity" or the "Heaven of Utmost Purity" depends on the quality of your energy. Your Heavenly attainment will be clear, because it will not allow for the slightest injustice. If you go against these prohibitions or commit errors, you will ruin your chances of becoming a shien, or even a healthy person. If your cultivation is incomplete, how can you expect to achieve the three realms of spiritual purity? Because of the impurity and heaviness of their energy, most souls cannot ascend. The law of the shien is just and clear. If you follow this sacred method of self-cultivation, you may begin with these purifications. If you practice them conscientiously, you will surely attain Tao.

Conclusion

Although the earthly shiens are admirable for their long life, the worldly environment is not always equally good and supportive. Therefore, the earthly shien has less chance to experience peace and happiness.

The spiritual shiens are more alert and carry more responsibility for the world. Thus, they must work harder to face the problems of the inferior world. It is not difficult to have the perseverance of virtue. It is difficult to attain wisdom, a continuously happy life and longevity all at once in one's life.

The only way to develop oneself into a Heavenly shien is to let the pure subtle law appear in one's body-mind-spirit. Then one's mind will be truly enlightened and never need search for blessings, because the blessings will come effortlessly to the enlightened one. Enlightened ones will never ask for wisdom, but the wisdom will reveal itself to them. Through doing nothing and keeping no partial connection, they embody themselves with the great nature. They never only partially develop themselves and therefore achieve the wholeness of the universe.

Sublimate your essence and store this refined energy at the top of your head. Keep your mind peaceful and retain your "fire" in your middle abdomen. If it is in your head, it manifests as anger; if it is in your lower abdomen, as strong sexual desire. The subtle energy transformation will take place within until your realization. Never become stubbornly attached to worldly attractions or let your mental energy stagnate in your thinking and ideas. Keep your mind righteous, just and whole, and await the reappearance of the original simplicity, your true nature. After restoring the true simplicity, you will become one with Heaven naturally. You will achieve the magnificence of life, and truly become a Heavenly shien, a divine immortal. After uniting oneself with Tao, one will reside in the three realms of purity.

On Being an Immortal

Master Gnawholes asked Master Wrapper about being an Immortal, and he answered:

"Set your body straight and unify your gaze; then great, natural harmony will be yours. Extract your know-how and unify your measures, then the divine, immortal energy will take up its abode in you. Perfect, natural behavior will then be your beauty and divine energy your abode. The pupils of your eyes will then be pure like the new-born baby's and will seek no why's and wherefore's."

After this reply, Master Gnawholes came into a deep, quiescent sleep. Much pleased, Master Wrapper went away singing. His body was like the strong trunk of an old, old tree and his heart and mind like cold ashes of an unquenchable fire. He knows only the truth and he does not maintain himself with specious reasoning. Dissolving his identity and merging with the totality, he is without mind and is not to be schemed with. Who like this is not a man of immortality?

**Ensuring that Your Own Jade Emperor
is Firmly Seated in its Throne**
The divine immortal medicine is within you.
It is composed of three elements:
  Sen, the spirit and mind; chi, the general vitality;
  and ching, the sexual energy.
Do not employ them singly.
The positive effects come with the whole.
Remain intangible and natural, and return to the subtle breath
  which existed before you were born.
After one hundred days of practice in concentration,
  one will have an effective foundation of mystical cultivation.

Do not become attached to all kinds of spiritual phenomena.
But only commune face to face with the crowned Jade Emperor.
You will hold the reign with him to rule
  the entire spiritual empire.
You will ride with him on the nature wheel
  comfortably making the royal patrol.
This is easy for a wise person to practice.
It is hard to make the ignorant understand.

Follow only the Heavenly subtle light.
Inhale the pure and exhale the impure.
Visit often the palace of the primal mysterious mother.
Keep your mind regulated and at the same time free.
Repose deeply in the root of eternal life.

Gather essence by undoing.
Combine your ching with your chi,
and your chi with your sen.

Connect your life with the subtle truth of the divine origin.
Then every minute of your life is new.
You will find the truth of immortality effortlessly.
Detach yourself from the things with only temporary names.
Enjoy only the one integral reality.

Powers depend on your refined spirit.
Your refined spirit is able to penetrate the hardest stones.
Spirit can fly to reach the high and dive into the deep.
Spirit cannot be drowned in water,
nor can it be burned by fire.
Spirit must integrate with form.
Subtle essence adheres to the vital chi.
Undecaying and unwithering, your true life shall last
like the ever-green pine tree.

The three elements obey only one lord
who keeps the one mystical law of life.
When the elements come together,
you have the sacred immortal medicine and subtle power.
When they are separated, then you have none.

The seven orifices of your face communicate with each other.
Each orifice gives its own light.
The sacred sun and moon are always shining in the golden court
within you.
Once you come here, you will never lose yourself again.
Your body is light, your bones are full of elixir.
and your life is giving out auspicious light.

As a human being you are powerful
when you receive the sacred immortal medicine.
Otherwise, you must struggle for your balance and well-being.
The sacred immortal medicine cannot be bought.
It has no color, and is neither white nor black.
Persist in penetrating,
then the wonderful secret will be self-evident.

Chapter 18

Cultivating the Three "Bodies"

Requirements for Attaining Yang Energy

In the multi-universe, Tao is the ultimate truth. One must abide in sincerity in one's own life cultivation, because one who aspires to prove the truth of life and transcend vulgarity must gradually remove all layers of bondage which one accumulated throughout one's life, until one restores one's true whole soul. One has to strip off the many outer layers of the "multifold body" to reach the final immortal "one body."

Retreat from all the attachments of the physical body of flesh and blood, and return to the everlasting body of pure law. Gather and enforce the pure yang energy, which is what the Heavens are made of. When you establish your new everlasting life, it is important to break through the shell of your ego, self-deception and stubbornness. At the same time, you become the great universal soul.

Before this happens, you must also make an effort to unravel your form, which is composed of a confused mixture of energies, and keep only the pure energy. You must break through the body's blocks and connect all the physical energy channels. There are four practical requirements to attaining the undecaying pure yang energy: 1) untying the muscles and tendons; (2) untying all the systems and organs; (3) untying all thoughts; and (4) untying the consciousness. These achievements assure your complete liberation, with the possibility of living as pure energy with or without form, enjoying absolute freedom and the happiness of divine immorality.

Mentally you may follow the instructions for the unfolding of your spirit from the traditional advice which helps you attain liberation through breaking the nutshell of your ego. You may also attain spiritual highness of Heavenly freedom by reading and learning the spiritual truths in all my various works. With all these instructions you can reform your body, mind and spirit. Then your mind can rise above its old structures, and your spirit above your pure mind. Thus, you gain final fulfillment, both internally and externally.

After success in your emotional achievement, the journey of your cultivation will become easy, and the fruit ripe and sweet. Through mental achievement, you may strengthen your body, and likewise your physical achievement will reinforce your mind. Then you will embrace the Tao and unite yourself with the eternal truth.

Refining the Three "Bodies"

All your cultivation leads to real proof of your achievement in this lifetime. Your original spirit of life, the true being of your soul, has a real possibility of transcending the many layers of worldly entanglement. The beings of high self-awareness in all dimensions will accept you. Then you will really become one of them and live in the Heavenly paradise as you actualize it. This is all based on the true work of refinement of your body, mind and spirit, to distill their essences as the true medicine of immortality.

Help yourself to leave behind the old patterns of thought and behavior and renew yourself. Your body must comprise only the pure yang energy. Your mind must become one with universal reason. Your spirit must embody itself with the Jade Emperor, the true law. This is the correct route to safeguard your precious soul to return to its Heavenly home. This road is easy, simple, straight and without any obstacles, but you may have created difficulties or detours for yourself. Your real attainment comes through unravelling the tight knots which bind you to the heavy coverings of your present body, mind and spirit. As previously mentioned, the enlightened one has reached total liberation.

To summarize the route map once again, from your present situation you may begin with the disharmonious or partly harmonious body and cultivate to achieve the ordinary balanced body. Then you will have attained normal health and the being of the normal body-mind-spirit. Then again you move forward to refine the ordinary balanced body to reach the great harmonious body. At this stage you will become internally and externally harmonious and balanced. Because you harmonize with the great nature of the universe, you will be true body-mind-spirit. After this you may again reach out to attain the "crystal or lucid body."

With the attainment of spiritual communication and Heavenly awareness, and the virtuous capability to display supernatural powers, you will be able to perceive all the subtle changes of the human world where you live; the events of the past, present and future. With the tolerance and perseverance of your highly developed virtue, you may brighten the world of the people around you. Through your spiritual merits you will achieve the being of the sacred body-mind-spirit.

Attaining the Three "Bodies"

For your complete liberation, you attain the great harmonious body. For the achievement of clarity, wisdom and enlightenment you realize the crystal body. For your virtuous realization and the foundation for the integration of yin and yang, you attain the subtle body. Now all illusions have been eliminated, deviation has been corrected, and you return to the original simplicity, which is the eternal breath of the subtle origin. Only when the foundation od cultivation becomes firm will your spirit become strong. The right mind will appear and the illusions disappear. When you continue the purification, you reach the body of Tao.

At this level you have already forsaken the sense of the body and completely become the body of pure law living as eternal wholeness. Then you will not follow the mental patterns you used to have, and will not struggle with great nature and make it a different entity. You leave no trace of your cultivation to be followed because you will have already achieved the "integral being of great nature." You will have become really omnipresent in all space and everlasting in all time. You will be a being of fullness and truth. When you have this form you will have become the eternal Tao. Retreat to the beginning of the great transformation. Return to the original chi of the universe. Embrace the wholeness in your spirit.

Tao is the whole. One should not insist on keeping the concept of the "body." Once you attain the knowledge of the subtle body of Tao which provides you with absolute freedom, the gathering and the dispersion of form become just as simple as your utterance. It is never a problem to be or not to be.

Return to the Pure Chi

The most important thing for you is to become the pure law of the universe and to gain the eternal original chi. Through developing the being of the body of balance, body of great harmony, crystal body, subtle body, and body of pure law, one can return to the great one chi through self-evolution. It is this one chi which manifests as evolution and devolution. When the gross physical chi retreats from being the dominant force, the subtle law reveals itself. When the chi moves forward to the visible level, then phenomena manifest.

Subtle chi is the creative, pure yang energy. When this leading energy spreads, the law prevails. In one's self-cultivation of immortality, one holds the portion of yang chi within oneself. It must not be misused, but instead must be reintegrated with the universal pure yang energy as the pure law. This means to break through the confinement of individualized bodily life. The immortality of life comes with spontaneity. With spontaneity, one reverts to the true chi of eternal life with nature. Then, the pure law appears in one's enlightenment. One's enlightenment appears in the refinement of one's mind. The refinement of the mind takes place in the body. High awareness is the root of life, and life is the realization of high self-awareness.

Three Kinds of Meridian Systems that Communicate with the Universal Energy System

The energy of the ordinary body is mentally and physically stagnant and blocked because of unhealthy experiences. However, there are common meridians in all human bodies which function as channels for communication with the universal energy system, if they are fully developed. We have three kinds of such meridians. The first is of rationality, the second is of sensitivity, and the third is of the organic. We are all born with these three kinds of meridians to be evolved and developed. Thus, we can extend our life experience to all the wonders of the supreme subtle realms through the development of the superior energy of our own lives on a high level. Through exercising your high level mental faculties with sincerity in Taoist science, full development can be obtained. Sincerity is the highest power of the mind. It is the connecting point with the natural high energy. When we embrace sincerity within, it is simply the Jade Emperor is enthroned in our being. Thus by maintaining sincerity within ourselves, we come close to the nature of the universe, which is Tao. We come close to everlasting, divine immortality.

The Body of Great Harmony and the Eight Extra Meridians

In order to achieve the body of great harmony to be an earthly shien, an earthly integral being, one needs to open the "eight extra energy channels," each of which is connected to one of the "eight trigrams" or eight natural manifestations. These eight channels are:

tu mo - the directing channel as chyan
jen mo - the receptive channel as k'un
chung mo - the generating or reproductive channel as chen
yang wei mo - the yang connecting channel as sun
yin wei mo - the yin connecting channel as k'an
yang chia mo - the yang supportive channel as ken
yin chiao mo - the yin supportive channel as li
tai mo - the yin supportive channel as tui

At first you must restore a healthy flow of energy throughout all the channels to obtain the general balanced body. Through the refinement of one's energy one receives more chi, and the quantity of one's blood decreases. Then one may reform the flow of the energy and even rechannel it to break through to the energy centers and the Mystical Pass. When this is accomplished, one can enjoy high frequency communication with all spheres of the world and within one's own energy system.

The Crystal Body and the Meridians or the Law
THE HEAVENLY STEMS AND EARTHLY BRANCHES
If one aspires to achieve the body of crystal purity to become an astral shien of efficaciousness, one must connect all related channels of universal law in one's body and develop their sensitivity to high frequencies. Among these are the ten channels which connect one with Heavenly energy, the "Heavenly energy stems," and the twelve channels which communicate with the energy of the earth, the "earthly energy branches."

The energies of Heaven and earth have intercourse in our bodies, thus becoming our physical energy channels of universal law. The Heavenly energy stems and earthly energy branches are connected vertically and diagonally to form sixty sub-channels. All energy channels are subjected to polarization as yin and yang, which assist each other and check each other. There are 36,000 main points in our bodies which are interconnected and interwoven by the sub-channels. The sub-channels consist of the Heavenly stems and earthly branches, and meet at two different ends of the body, at the top of the head and at the tip of the tail bone. Both together form the central channel which connects the internal and external energies correctly as in a fully developed human being, a shien.

The Heavenly stems are divided into groups of yin and yang. The five Yang stems are jia, bien, wuh, geng and ren. The five yin Heavenly stems are yi, ding, ji, hsin, and quei.

The earthly branches are also divided into yin and yang, and are associated with the twelve meridians in our body. The six Yang branches are tze, ein, ch'en, wu, shen and shu. The six Yin are chui, mao, sze, wei, yu and hai.

The Heavenly Eye

The Heavenly eye as the organless organ in the middle of the forehead becomes the pilot for all of these efficacious sub-channels and points. After succeeding in opening this Heavenly eye and obtaining full use of the organless organ, you will have natural high self-awareness and thus truly prove the objective truth contained in this subjective instrument. The ability to use this Heavenly eye results from breaking through the energy blocks and barricades which exist in an unrefined entity.

The Subtle Body

If you aspire to achieve the subtle body of pure yang energy, you must enforce your connection with universal law and dissolve the tremendous mental block of the ego or the self. One must have combined Heaven and earth in one's body, and must harmonize oneself with both the internal and external worlds. Once one's individualized desire for all kinds of possessions is eliminated, one's true nature is unveiled. One opens to the unnameable Tao, the non-active action of collecting the pure, immortal and indestructible universal yang energy. The non-active accumulation of yang energy enlightens your internal world and brightens your external world, and is the path to maintaining good control and poise in one's life. The knowledge and method of being a Heavenly shien and dealing with the body-mind-spirit has reached its high peak at this stage.

Refining the Elixir of Immortality: The Three Bodies of Transcendence

Under ordinary circumstances, people have one form with three different aspects - physical, intellectual and spiritual.

Transcendence of these segmented bodies can surpass all difficulties and even the great transformation between life and death. Once one is connected at different levels with the subtle root of the universe, three bodies of transcendence gain immanence: the harmonious body, subtle body, and crystal body. These three become imperishable after having been attained through self-cultivation.

Chapter 19

Cultivating Pure Mind

**Refining the Subtle Energy in Our Pure Mind
as the Connecting Link to the Subtle Origin**

The subtle energy of our intuitive mind is the pure law of the universal life within us. It can be recognized as the subtle integrator of the universe practicing its function in the individual mind and spirit. It is helpful to embrace this original purity, following the innocence of our spiritual origin firmly in all the activities of daily life. Then the problems of life will settle down like sediment in pure water, and spiritual uplifting will ensue. But if one is impatient and disturbs this subtle process with intellectual suspicion and judgment, one will lose the ability to properly guide oneself in a balanced way.

Therefore, it is helpful to keep the intellectual mind still and passive in all circumstances. It is only when troublesome intellectual activity is stopped that the peaceful flow of the intuitive spirit will manifest. If the intellectual faculties are active in scheming, planning, judging or worrying, the intuitive spiritual faculties will be impeded. When the intellectual mind is strong, the intuitive spirit is hindered. This is one of the most apparent facts known to Taoists. When the intellectual disturbance is calmed, then the spirit comes to power. This is one of the most precious facts known by Taoists.

**The Restoration of the Correctly Responsive Mind Through
the Practice of the *I Ching* and Taoist Meditation**

If one concentrates while remaining receptive to one's spirit - in other words, keeps quiet within - the response received in the form of a transformed image or simple thought will be clearly meaningful. If a question arises on the level of the subtle law, then one's single-mindedness in that very moment and one's spirit at the same time will show the right answer through subtle images. However, if the mind is scattered and the attention does not return to the quiet flow of nothingness, then the spiritual response will be unclear or confused, and the individual's response will be incorrect. The omnipresence of the universal subtle energy through the individual will then become warped and twisted into a mere reflection of himself. Emotion, even in religious practice or prayer, creates separation from the real subtlety of spiritual energy.

When asking a question on the level of the subtle law, the answer is given in the very moment when one projects one's mind either in a questioning mode or in preparing to take a real action. Therefore, if a leader, for example, starts a hundred-years war with another country, the result can already be foretold in the same instant that he makes the decision to begin the war. There are both opportune and inopportune times for taking particular actions. This applies to all activities, no matter how small or seemingly insignificant, because all are governed by the same subtle law. This fact can be proven through the study and use of the *I Ching* as a gate to the wide-open mysteries of the universe.

Achievement depends on whether or not has developed one's awareness. The clarity of a responsive mind depends on purification of all mental contamination and cultivation of subtle energy. Through this practice, one may develop the necessary high-level awareness of self, becoming as essential as the Subtle Origin, eventually becoming one with the pure law. Without a thorough purification, the Subtle Origin, which is the subtle interconnection between the mind and the outside world, will not appear in one's mind. Thus, if one is without a pure mind, one cannot become responsive to the subtle communicative level.

Subtle communication between the individual mind and the real outside world is made possible by the presence of the entire subtle reality within a person. Consequently, the more firmly one connects oneself with the subtlety of the mind, the closer one will move toward the central subtle origin of the universe. One cannot make the subtle energy, the root of the universe, respond to oneself through emotional or sentimental actions. It is completely separate from any of these. Ordinary religious practices offer little to real spiritual development because overzealous engagement in religious emotions such as faith, hope and love are fatal to the spirit. If one functions heavily on the emotional level, one cannot communicate with the subtle reality. Any strong mental attitude will destroy the subtlety of the correctly responsive mind.

We reach our higher mind by keeping the mind pure, sincere, and focused with concentration on one single thing at a time. The subtle energy is evasive for the ordinary mind.

Neither the subtle energy nor the high mind, as the intuitive faculty, can be controlled by thoughts. The subtle energy is the origin of thoughts; it leads and regulates the thoughts in its normal responsive situation, and can be illustrated by foreknowledge and the ability to pre-experience. An extreme habitual reliance on physical, emotional or intellectual energy will prevent communion with one's subtle energy. Cultivation of self through the practice of ancient Taoist techniques is a good method to use for experiencing subtle energy.

The power of the Subtle Origin of the universe extends into all minds as the connection with its subtle law. This pure performance not only reaches our minds, but is also the entire composition of the universe. The subtle center performs the law of subtle energy in integrating the universe, controlling all phenomena and governing the infinite variations of existence. Not a thing or an event is beyond the control of this law. A good connection with the subtle law keeps subtle essence and rejects the gross sphere of energy.

The Subtle Origin of the subtle law manifests as the center of all Heavens, all earths, beings and things. Thus we call the performance of the Subtle Origin the "mystical womb" of the universe. Through the movement of its energy, the Subtle Origin engages in creation, evolution and progression. Destruction, devolution, and regression are side effects of the main flow of the creativity and productivity of the universe. On the gross plane, subtle energy functions as the head, the brain and the senses. The lower sphere of mind, supported by flesh and blood, has little power to manage its own processes. Wherever subtle energy is in operation, there subtle law performs.

The unravelling movement of subtle energy from the Subtle Origin is the source of infinite phenomena. In its movement, all the varied phenomena have the opportunity to come to the stage of existence, then to return to the Oneness of the origin. Subtle energy in an individual is found in the spirit or the intuitive mind. Instinct can be traced back to the brain cells as the habit of biological origin; this is not the same as the highly developed intuitive mind.

Extending beyond individual subtle energy is the oneness of chi. It is this one chi which plays many roles as subtle law, subtle energy and uncountable phenomena. This chi divides and varies itself in all phenomena as separated fragments, whereas

Tao is the oneness of chi. The intellectual mind recognizes the fragments; the integral mind knows Tao. The union of the intellect with the integral mind brings about existence and the brightness of worldly life. Life and non-life depend on the performance of the one chi. The chi is the unnameable source of the universe. It is the one energy manifesting as the subtle, supernatural and organic energies. It also manifests as universal reality, pure law and the basic types of energy of the multiple phenomenal worlds. When chi withdraws we have nothing. When there is something, nothing is implied. When there is nothing, something is implied.

In the Way of integral cultivation, we refine our chi to reach the subtle levels and to come into harmony with the chi of the high realms of the universe, which is equal to rooting ourselves deeply in the Subtle Origin. We know that working on the variations of phenomena is an endless pursuit which leads to exhaustion. Only by remaining within the one chi can one keep in harmony with the law and can all positive creations be performed. At this point, one will be beyond the ceasing of life, and will be able to transcend the superficial transformations of the apparent sphere and unite with Tao while riding gently and firmly in the subtle saddle of eternity.

Ancient Taoist Instructions on Attaining the Absolute Mind

- Adaption from Hsin Hsin Ming,
     translated by Seng-Tsan, active around 600 A.D.

The Integral Way is not difficult
     for those who have no preferences.
When love and hate are both absent
     the Way presents itself clearly.
Make the smallest distinction, however,
     and your distance from the truth
     is set apart like Heaven and earth.
If you wish to recognize the truth,
     then hold no opinions for or against anything.
To set up what you like against what you dislike
     is the disease of the mind.
When the simple reality of things is not understood,
     it is fruitless to quiet your mind forcefully.

The Subtle Origin is perfect;
  it lacks nothing and contains nothing in excess.
Indeed, it is due to our choosing to accept or reject,
  that we lose our oneness with it.
Live neither in the pursuit of outer things,
  nor become attached to the rigid practice
  of feeling emptiness.
Be serene in the oneness of things
  and all difficulties will disappear by themselves.
When you try to stop activity to achieve passivity
  your very effort fills you with activities.
As long as you remain in one extreme or the other,
  you will never know oneness.

Those who do not live in the Integral Way
  fail both in activity and passivity, assertion and denial.
To deny the reality of things is to miss their reality;
  to assert the emptiness of things
  is to miss their reality as well.
To more you talk and think about it,
  the further astray you wander from the truth.
Stop talking and thinking,
  and there is nothing separate from you.
To return to the root is to find the oneness,
  but to pursue appearances is to miss the source.
At the moment of deep reflection
  you transcend appearance and emptiness.
The superficial changes between beingness and emptiness
  can disturb only the ignorant mind.
Do not search for the truth,
  only cease to respond in a shallow way.
Do not remain in the dualistic state;
  avoid such attachment.
If there is even a trace of this and that, of right and wrong,
  the integrity of the mind will be lost in confusion.
Although all dualities come from the One,
  do not be attached even to this One.
When the mind creates no disturbance,
  nothing in the world can create difficulty.
Do not resist the difficult
  and do not welcome the Way.

The way to not give birth to difficulty
is for the mind not to perceive difficulty.

When no discriminating thoughts arise,
the old habitual traces cease to exist.
When the ability to think vanishes with the object of thinking,
the object of thinking also disappears
with the ability to think.
When the establishment of the object comes
through the ability to think,
then the ability to think is aroused by the object.
Understand the relativity of these two;
it simply returns to the original nothingness.
In this nothingness the two are indistinguishable,
the alteration of each containing itself in the whole world.
If you do not forsake the discrimination between coarse and fine,
you will be tempted to prejudgment and opinion.

To live in the Integral Way is neither easy nor difficult,
but those with limited views are fearful and irresolute.
The faster they hurry, the slower they go,
and attachment leads them astray.
Just let things be in their own Way,
in the Subtle Origin there will be neither coming nor going.
Obey the harmonizing origin of the nature of things and yourself,
and you will walk freely and undisturbed.
Binding yourself with certain concepts hides the truth
and makes the mind murky and unclear.
The burdensome practice of judging
brings annoyance and weariness.
What benefit can be derived from distinctions and separations?

If you wish to move in the Integral Way
do not reject even the world of senses and ideas.
Indeed, to keep this wholeness
is to realize the correct awareness.
The wise man strives for nothing
but the foolish man fetters himself.
The true Way is one, not many;
distinctions arise from the clinging needs of the ignorant.

To seek concepts and to neglect the Mind
  is the greatest of all mistakes.
Rest and unrest derive from illusion;
  with correct awareness there is no liking and disliking.
All dualities come from ignorant inference.
They are like dreams or flowers in the air;
  it is foolish to try to grasp them.
Gain and loss, right and wrong,
  such thoughts must finally be abolished at once.
If the "eye" never sleeps,
  all the dreams will naturally cease.
If the mind makes no discriminations,
  the ten thousand things are as they are, of single essence.
To understand the mystery of this one-essence
  is to be released from all entanglements.
When all things are seen equally.
  the timeless self-essence is reached.
No comparisons or analogies are possible
  in this causeless, relationless state.
Consider movement stationary and the stationary in motion,
  then both movement and rest disappear.
When such dualities cease to exist,
  oneness itself cannot exist.
To this ultimate finality no law or trace applies.
Abide your mind in accord with the great equality
  and all self-centered striving ceases.
Doubts and irresolutions vanish
  and life is in harmony with the simple truth.
With such non-active actions we are freed from bondage;
  nothing clings to us and we hold to nothing.
The mind is illuminated by clarity
  with no exertion of the mind's power.
Here thought, feeling, knowledge, and imagination
  are of no value.
In this world of suchness,
  there is neither self nor other-than-self.

To come directly into harmony with this reality,
  just simply do not give way to duality;
  even though it may not yet be established,
  nothing is excluded.

No matter when or where,
the truly wise enter this truth.
And this truth is beyond extension or diminution in time or space;
any single thought contains thousands of centuries.

The infinite universe stands here and there;
it is always present directly before your eyes.
Infinitely large and infinitely small;
no differences exist,
because bias vanishes in the absolute oneness.
The same is true for being and non-being.
Do not waste time in wandering;
you will miss the truth in the very moment you do so.

One is all.
All is one.
When you take no sides for the one or all,
there is nothing which cannot be dissolved
in the Subtle Origin.
Follow the absolute Way.
The universal absolute mind never separates from anyone,
but the people go astray.
When one attains absolute-mindedness,
words and concepts cease to exist.
In the great integrity,
there is no past, future or present.

Chapter 20

Breaking Through All Limitations In One's Cultivation

The Limitation of External Striving

Self-creativeness, self-mastery and self-accomplishment are natural human goals, all of which require self-cultivation. But often one may not really know what one wants or what is best, because one cultivates in the wrong manner to accommodate security, sensation and power needs. Limiting oneself only to physical instincts, one seems to constantly strive for only external things. The limitation of one's comprehension lies in the belief that external things can preserve and protect one's life.

One may have the knowledge and power to get these things, but may not necessarily possess the wisdom to use these gifts to achieve truth, peace and happiness. All efforts to fulfill one's sensual demands will result in the recognition that they are insatiable. Seeking emotional security and love, if one does not understand the true nature of love, this person is doomed to have unsatisfactory relationships. Even when one has success-fully attained any of these goals, the result at best can only be temporary satisfaction, because they are all impermanent, limited aspects of life.

In order to attain lasting happiness, we must pursue that which is everlasting and complete - the Tao. At least we need to improve our understanding of life and attain the modest wisdom which provides peace and happiness in the world. By cultivating our awareness and harmonizing with the normal flow of univer-sal energy, our self-cultivation and discipline are not futile. Remember, if you set temporal pleasures as your goal, you can receive only temporal rewards; if you set your goal for that which is lasting, your cultivation is a useful tool which can help your personal happiness, clarity and completeness. This goal is easy to attain through spiritual cultivation and discipline. Viewing it as an instrument, the integral Taoist Way of life is precise and practical. It involves the totality of our being.

The Limitation of the Ordinary World View

In the scientific Taoist understanding, the world manifests itself from the subtle spirit to the gross material level. Material or gross energy can be perceived by the five senses; spiritual and subtle energy can be perceived only through our intuitive faculties. Because these higher faculties remain unused and underdeveloped, the ordinary person perceives the world in a shallow, one-dimensional way. If, however, one becomes aware of one's limited perspective and desires sufficiently to progress spiritually, then one simply needs to follow the Integral Way of Tao. Through self-discipline, cultivation and the assistance of an awakened Master, one can discover true happiness, peace and the divinity of one's whole being.

Everything in the world exists as a manifestation of energy or energies. Energy is either yang (active energy), yin (passive or receptive energy), or a combination of both. Spirit, as represented by Heaven, is yang, and matter, as represented by earth, is yin. Human beings are a combination of spirit and matter, formed with the subtle and the gross. After death, the subtle returns to the subtle realms and the gross returns to the gross realms. Death is the final disintegration for people with ordinary development. They are reborn again into life through uncertain reincarnation. From the knowledge of those who achieve the Integral Way of Tao, the divine Immortals exist in the subtle realm above the human realm. They are the integral beings on the subtle level. Our human ancestors were taught by them to integrate the subtle energy of yin and yang, and thus to achieve divine immortality. The secret science of immortality was passed down as a reward to the virtuous. There are also those beings below the human level who have only incomplete energy. This is also the sphere of existence for people who are controlled by the mechanical laws of inanimate things.

Integral people and deities have discovered and follow the same law of integration as universal existence. To cultivate the right energy, the Integral Way of Tao is provided for the people with high self-awareness through the divine, immortal self-cultivation and self-discipline. This method, as transmitted through the Taoist Masters and recorded in hidden language in the *Taoist Canon*, is an effective way to achieve the goal of total evolution, immortality and true happiness.

The Limitation of the Five Physical Senses

As human beings, we have a physical form and five physical senses which enable us to learn about and interact with the physical world. These senses are our first and grossest connection with the external world. Our body and senses are perfectly contrived and ordered in accordance with nature. They are mechanical functions of human beings, who ultimately must serve and get their direction from the higher intellect and spirit, just as the mechanical ebb and flow of the ocean responds to the movements of the planets and other Heavenly bodies. This differentiates human beings from animals; a person is more than just a sensory, physical being.

The body and senses, when in harmony with natural law, are faithful servants of the mind and spirit, which hold higher positions in the hierarchy of the individual. Those who identify with and cling to the body forget that they are much more than just a physical entity and disregard natural order. The result is always disorder, which manifests as illness, misery, suffering and pain. Overindulgence of our physical nature keeps us dense, heavy and insecure because it attaches us to that which is impermanent and unpredictable. If we believe we are just our bodies, we become controlled by them and lose sight of anything beyond. We become servants to the body rather than the body being a servant to our higher self. We deny ourselves the exquisite, enduring pleasures of non-sensory or transcendental experiences. We limit and prohibit ourselves from experiencing the whole range of possibilities that the universe affords us.

No one is denying that the five senses are valuable. Our lives have been greatly enriched through the use of them in the arts, sciences and social life. Our error is to believe that they are almighty. Para-psychology is now enabling us to verify and develop our extra-sensory perceptions by using our instinctual and intuitional abilities. To be able to know and use our higher senses effectively, we must first become much more sensitive to the higher and more subtle vibrations through the refinement of our gross elements and the cultivation of our more subtle energies. Without self-cultivation, our higher sensitivities will remain lost and buried in the gross and ordinary energy of the physical form and the five senses.

The Limitation of the Mind
The mind, as represented by the intellect, occupies a higher level in the hierarchy of the human being than the physical body, but it too is limited, incomplete and inferior to our spiritual

being. Just as our five senses are valuable instruments of perception, so too is the mind when used properly. When used properly, it enables us to think rationally, constructively, reasonably and logically. However, the mind is one-dimensional and a person can think only one thought at a time. Life itself is a multi-dimensional, ever-changing process operating on many different levels at once. So you can actually understand something intellectually and still be ignorant.

All the education and knowledge in the world may strengthen the mind, but it does not indicate wisdom. Wisdom - seeing things completely and clearly - is a function of intuition. Intuition is the only part of our being that can fully understand the nature of things and control all of life's processes. Overusing the mind or allowing the mind to be the master of our being cuts us off from our intuitive ability. To know the totality of life, we must learn to quiet the mind and allow intuition to operate freely. Great patience and unrelenting self-discipline are required to quiet the mind so that intuition can reveal itself.

The Limitation of Psychic Powers

Once you begin to make steady progress on the spiritual pathway, you will acquire strange and wonderful psychic powers. They develop as a result of your energies becoming more refined and subtle. Your vibrations rise and become more attuned to beings of similarly high frequency. You may suddenly discover that you have knowledge of events in future times or distant places. You may hear someone speaking when no one is visible. You may project out of your body and travel to faraway lands or even to other planets and galaxies. Some are even able to fly or materialize things out of thin air. Although these fascinating phenomena really do exist, they do not guarantee happiness any more than any other talent.

In fact, these powers, like any other power, can quickly corrupt an individual. The creative use of psychic powers can be spontaneously employed for the benefit of humankind, but to spend a lot of time developing them for the purpose of self-aggrandizement will only lead to the ruination of the individual and everyone with whom they come in contact. The psychic realms are limited to time and space. Because the goal of the Taoist is to unite with the unlimited oneness, the serious students of Tao do not focus on these realms, but continue to cultivate themselves until the final goal is reached. The positive value of this is that it can improve one's confidence in going further to the ultimate truth and eternal life.

The Limitation of One's Faith

Many religions encourage or force people to believe in and follow their teachings as the truth on the basis of faith alone. Faith is believing in something that you have no knowledge of. This is ignorance, which most certainly perpetuates doubt, fear, conflict and insecurity. Faith is the antithesis of truth. Only truth can assure you of peace and happiness. Only through intuitive wisdom can you both understand life and death and have the free will to determine your destiny. The Integral Way of Tao is not a religion, but the plain truth. If people follow the Integral Way of self-discipline and cultivation, they will find truth and reality in every step.

The Limitation of Spiritual Dependence

Many people believe that it is not necessary to cultivate themselves at all. They say that all that is needed is to surrender to a savior or spiritual teacher who will take charge of their lives. While total surrender is a path towards oneness, most people are not capable of it, much less of even understanding what "surrender" means. Surrender means giving up identification with everything - the body, the mind, the heart, the environment, even the desire to be desireless must eventually go. This is arduous work and actually requires great self-discipline to be free of all desires, thoughts, preferences, feelings and prior programming. To think you can profess surrender yet live a life in which you are still attached to anything or anybody, especially to your self-image as a spiritual person, is just delusion. Surrender is a discipline of refinement and transformation which is absolutely impossible without our willing and complete participation. Then and only then can a savior or true Master manifest in our lives.

The Limitation of Philanthropy

While charitable endeavors can be good activities, most people give for all the wrong reasons: to earn a reputation as a benevolent person, to ease one's conscience or eliminate "bad karma," or gain the adoration of others. As such, philanthropy is only a gesture of self-righteousness or fear and does not denote a virtuous soul. Virtue (following the law of life) is a quality of a balanced, sacred being. Even giving or helping out of genuine concern for another does not guarantee a person immunity from, or elimination of, ignorance, unhappiness or bad habits. The only way to achieve the virtues of truth, happiness, harmony and balance in one's life is through self-discipline and cultivation of the Tao.

The Limitation of Shallow Understanding

The complete and enduring way is the Way of Tao. It embraces all of the universal and divine truth and is sufficient unto itself. However, many people, ignorant of this and greedy and fearful of missing out on something, hop from one new way to another, one Master to another, and thereby achieve nothing of substance or depth. It can be likened to a person digging one shallow well after another in search of water. The result will be endless thirst and eventual death from dehydration. Yet, by singularly following the integral Way of Tao, one will be able to achieve the essence of truth and spirituality.

The Limitation of the Belief in a Final Destruction

In this universe, nothing exists without changing. In the phenomenal or material side of the world, things seem to appear and disappear. In the insubstantial or spiritual side of the world, things seem not to even happen. From this we learn the principle of the infinite Tai Chi. We come to know that there is constant change without end, and death is only metamorphosis.

The Unlimited Way

A simple yet careful observation and a deep understanding will reveal that all pursuits, other than embracing the infinite Tao, are limited and shallow. It is really so much easier to follow that which is in harmony with nature and grounded in truth. What could be more natural than taking time to sit quietly and allow the mind to clear itself? Or to accumulate the early morning energies through slow, rhythmic, graceful movement? Or to recognize within yourself a response with the sun, moon, and stars? These are all aspects of the Integral Way of Tao. Through such cultivation and self-discipline you can achieve a calm, clear mind; a peaceful, open and happy heart; and a healthy and vibrant body.

However, a proper attitude toward self-discipline is necessary. It need not be regarded as doing something you do not like, but rather as a method of focusing and refining your own energy and spirit to achieve harmony and balance within and without. If you are experiencing much resistance to something, do not persist. Little help can come from continually trying to force yourself to do something you do not understand. Discipline, like anything else in life, can be as natural as water running downhill. Taoist discipline, like the nature of Tao itself, can be a joyful and spontaneous commitment. If done in the spirit of "wu-wei," which is non-action or allowing the natural flow of things on their own course, then surely nothing could possibly stand in the way of achieving the highest state of unlimited oneness with the supreme Tao.

The Precious Taoist Sword For Breaking the Chains of Laziness and Inertia

The Heavenly bodies of sun, moon, and stars
    are spontaneously moving in their orbits.
The earth, turning on her axis,
    moves unceasingly, facing sun and moon,
    knowing her own path among her sister planets.
In following her own nature,
    she receives light and life.
The seasons follow one another.
Day and night rise and fall without fail.
The moon joins in the journey,
    and all that lives on earth is responsive.
Continuously changing, growing and evolving,
    the universe is just so.

Between Heaven and earth,
    humanity is moving on the axis of its spirit.
Never ceasing, it follows the Heavenly order within.
With form and mind, the spirit can express itself.
In order to become responsive to the natural order,
    one must work diligently.
  Daily life and self-cultivation,
    must work in parallel.

Maintain an even balance.
Slowly but steadily move forward.
To know when to be active and when to rest
*   is to be one with Tao.*
To be idle is to waste the gift of life.
Indolence and laziness curb the spirit.
They bring stagnation to the body's energies.
Energy stagnation causes sickness.
Laziness and energy stagnation combined
*   will manifest disease.*
Do not court disease by laziness!

Be still.
Being still,
*   activity comes forth in a natural way.*
You will be useful and lively
*   and never exhaust yourself.*
You will be gentle and loose,
*   firm, but not rigid,*
*   and will experience true rest.*
The Creative Spirit never ceases.
You appear to be active,
*   yet your work is effortless.*
Moving on the axis of your spirit,
*   in non-action,*
*   you will connect with the eternal oneness*
*   of the universe.*
Following your true nature,
*   you will find your place,*
*   shining brightly as all the stars.*

Your physical life will be firm and long.
Selfless, you will inexhaustibly move
*   forward and upward in the eternal Tao.*

Chapter 21

Breaking the Cortex of Ego

1. Tao is colorless and void. Yet from it come all the wonders of the universe. The Way to follow the Tao is to find its deep core within the great nature of stillness. Through quiescence you can unite yourself with the Great Reality. All religious philosophies are mere creations of the intellect. If you follow the creations of humankind you will find that you have only scratched the surface of the true nature of Reality.

If you can trace your way back to the source found in your deep reflections, it will not be difficult to know the ultimate truth. The Way of self-cultivation requires a proper vehicle to carry you from the fragmentation of being to the unity of integral being. All the systems we employ are only temporary means to reach Reality. If you become puzzled or confused by these temporary systems, how can you expect to achieve Absolute Awareness? Until you realize that all man-made religions share a common ignorance, you will not have the power of an enlightened intelligence with which you can break through all the veils of color and form and comprehend the origin of the True Nature. Then obstacles will suddenly disappear, allowing your light to penetrate, and you will surely bear the correct fruit and become a shien. But first you must have the proper cultivation, practice and verification. This is the correct Way of a shien.

To cultivate the Tao, we must first purify our entire being. Keep the mind pure and free of all stains. In cultivation of Tao, frequently reassess the judgments you make by firmly maintaining the pure motives found behind your first decision. Do not allow any evil disturbance to enter; do not allow your mind to fluctuate even on the roughest road; keep your mind firm as it travels towards its destination. Do not let the mind float, move or trap itself. It is the defilements of your body and mind which cause the disorders of passion and virtue. With disorder, you will not have peace.

2. Do not mistake illusions for reality. Always use your internal light to look at your own reflections and to illuminate your own darkness. Worldly affairs are definitely an empty dream. All the wealth of the world cannot be valued so much as one hair on your head.

When cultivating Tao, you must lay aside the limitations of body and mind and rid yourself of all illusions. Do not get caught in conflicts between yourself and the world. Only in this way can you hope to find whole and complete freedom. When you come in contact with external objects, forget both yourself and the object. When you can do this successfully, you will no longer be bothered by color and form.

By expelling false phenomena and surpassing all form, you will discover true reality even though its subtle nature is invisible and universal. To arrive at this reality, we cultivate our true nature by removing ourselves from the concepts of form, thereby progressing to the invisible and universal realm of eternal life. The principle of Taoist self-cultivation is simple. The seed of a shien needs to be nurtured in the proper way.

3. It is not impossible to unite with the Tao or to become a newly achieved shien and realize Heaven within and without. The only requirement is that you have a consistently calm mind. Keep it peaceful and transparent like the still water of a clear quiet lake and you will enjoy the subtlety of great bliss. Whether you are confronted with a minor problem or a major disaster, you must remain as calm and still as a Sacred Mountain. Strict discipline must also be maintained when dealing with pleasurable experiences, so that when the unpleasant ones appear, they will not disturb your mind. One cannot gain power from the embellishments of rites and rituals, especially the ones which are designed to impress and please. Your sound mind is a gift of life from nature, so you must use it in a positive and constructive way. If you use the mind for worry or anger or in any other negative or destructive way, it is a misuse of nature's gift. Unite your mind with the Way. Do not let your mind become a malingerer. With a clear mind, you will be able to reach the utmost wonders and mysteries. To have sincerity of mind will make your self-cultivation easy in this very moment. In calmness you can perceive infinity.

4. Once you decide to walk on the path of Tao, the temptations of lust and desire will retreat. If at first the six organs become enemies and obstacles in your path, they will ultimately become the wealth of your cultivation. You must be sincere towards the

Tao. Then you will find a change in your body and heart. So adhere closely to the "Six Don'ts";

Do not think it is your will power which makes the world turn, but look for all the forces, both hidden and apparent which make you turn.

Do not cling to any concept which separates you from the truth.

Do not think anything is "necessary."

Do not set your capability higher than your discipline.

Do not challenge the subtle law of the universe.

Do not think that the ideas in your mind are your own.

5. If you detach yourself from all your thoughts and mental activities, you will be left with a pure mind and will discover the true origin of the shien's family in your own being. Discipline yourself, keep your mind still, and the temptations of the outer world will disappear like melting ice. Directly control each subtle square inch of your mind.

Do not confuse your mind. There are many kinds of preferences which are like dyes that stain your bodily energy and mind. It is difficult for beginners to discipline themselves, but after forming good habits, it will come naturally. You will be rewarded for your own discipline and the true happiness which will then appear is unspeakable. The rounds of life and death will be broken. You will no longer follow the old pattern which has created endless stumbling throughout your life. You will have regulated the moving stream of your consciousness.

6. The physical body is the origin of your suffering and unhappiness; however, it can become the altar for your practice of self-cultivation. Do not think that acting with trickery and deceit is beneficial to your physical body. What you may think is good for your body may only cause damage to your mind. When your mind is damaged, your soul will descend.

The key of cultivating Tao lies in the eyes. Be sure to remove all distractions that drain energy away from them. The colors and forms reflected in your eyes can sometimes become an evil army of destructive obstacles which hinder your self-cultivation. Therefore, not only the eyes, but all six gates (of the senses) must be kept pure. When distraction is kept away from your eyes and ears, you will be able to keep your energy full and your spirit whole. Keep your mind from wandering. The subtle body is like true nature and Heaven; it receives all but holds nothing.

Too much speech is not good. To speak less is favorable; to keep silent is best. When you unite your energy in silence with the mystery of the universe, the wholeness of the universal truth nakedly appears within you. You need to keep the "Three Mystics" of body, speech and mind firmly united in one.

7. The untainted mind is used as a tool for achieving unity. This untainted mind is the basis of all true cultures, civilizations and religions. The Mind can only be comprehended with a still mind. This state is called self-awareness. Eliminate all the diverse and scattered thoughts, and do not give rein to the behavior of this type of mind. If you give in to the impulses of you passions and desires, you will not be able to ascend beyond them. When the mind is kept empty, firm, relaxed and clear as crystal, you will be able to verify and experience the wonders of the eternal realms. By being attached to an empty mind, however, you will still remain outside the Tao. Do not hold on to either emptiness or concepts. This is the correct Way to deal with your mind.

With single-mindedness, harmoniously follow the flow of the great Tao. Then you will have no more anxieties due to your selfishness. The inferiority of your mind is the origin of all trouble and sickness. When the impurities of your mind become active, a variety of negative obstacles arise. When your mind is calm, the shadows of many problems and hardships disappear. When you have no inharmonious mental activity, you will have no serious disease or illness.

8. Take care never to be deceived by the six senses. Frequently clean the gates of your senses. Empty your mind of calculation and scheming down to the lethal hidden roots of consciousness;

for this is where you keep your thoughts and feelings of pain, bitterness, and sadness. By correctly swinging the sword of wisdom, you can cut yourself free from the confines of the cortex of your personality.

Do not let your spirit be enslaved by your sense organs, or become bound by vanity. Love, fame, profit or a high position in society have no more substance than the shadow of the moon reflected on the surface of a lake. Do not let external circumstances disturb you, but always keep calm and enjoy peace. You may be able to verify this part of true freedom, but beware: the real void is not void at all. Only through honest self-discipline will the realization of a shien, an integral being, be true.

9. Try to sit with calmness. The head and body need to be in an erect, upright position. Keep the heart at peace, and the mind silent. Close your eyes and be with your own inner being. Cease working only with the external level of your being that satisfies your worldly desires and deprives others of your true knowledge. To do so creates an imbalance in your being. To keep yourself whole and integrated with the Great Whole, there is no need to hunt for fragments in the external world with which to mend your own broken psyche. It is only with a pure mind that you can become one with Tao and fully enjoy the luminosity of self-cultivation, self-gain, and self-contentment. In this way, you will be allowed to be the seed of a Heavenly shien, the universal integral being.

Understand the elusive and delicate quality of body and mind. It is easy to keep a calm mind and peaceful emotions in the face of ordinary situations, but very difficult when one is faced with a major problem unless you handle it as if you are playing with a bubble. Learn this and you will be qualified to sit in the Lotus and look deeply within yourself. If you are a person with the high clarity of self-awareness, your mind will be firm and unshakable and you will become the true son or daughter of the divine family of shiens.

10. Now you already know not to place so much emphasis on worldly affairs and to keep the mind still so that you can make progress in achieving Tao. As worldly interests lessen, the high intentions of Tao increase. Your mind becomes empty, and Tao becomes confirmed within you. If there is purity in your heart

and mind, then external temptations of negativity and evil can no longer affect you. Only by observing and correcting yourself can you rid yourself of the pain and torture that you normally allow to happen.

All the worldly pleasures and pains that you experience are meaningless, deceiving and overly exaggerated. These illusions, formed by your own mind, cause confusion and bewilderment and prevent you from becoming free. If you can see through these obstacles, then all hindrances in your path will disappear. These obstacles are not a hindrance to an enlightened person.

You must progress step by step to progress efficiently. Idle talk is of no benefit to your self-cultivation. If the righteous Tao is allowed the opportunity to penetrate your being and expand with you, then your way of life will be naturally smooth and straight. You will become whole-hearted and have strong protective powers. You will experience contentment within instead of holding the bitterness of suffering. Take all lives as your own life, for all things share one body with you. This secret of life is so clear. With this you have become the seed of a Heavenly shien.

11. Originally it was possible for everyone to obtain the undecaying body of a supernatural being. But people destroyed themselves by their uncontrolled passions and lust, and drowned in their desire for wealth, fame and sensual love. Even if you could live for a hundred years, the time would pass quickly because of your empty pursuits. If your life is run like a sloppy business, you will end your years with another wasted life. Always keep your mind as empty as the great space of the universal valley. Keep your mind flowing smoothly and freely from sticky impediments like the unobstructed smooth flow of water and clouds. Maintain the same innocence and purity inside as outside. That way, you will achieve wholeness.

The immortal spiritual subtle body is found within you. If you get sidetracked and come to an evil road, no matter how hard you try to achieve self-cultivation, you will be moving against the Tao. Do not mistakenly go begging and searching outside for it. It is not necessary to make a long pilgrimage to find your source. The road to becoming a shien is clearly marked. It is your own impatience and desire that create too many "forks" and blind your real eyes. If you remove all the coverings and obstacles here and now, you will know the origin of your life. In this moment you can experience everything contained in Tao, and become a true child of Heaven.

Do not use your self-cultivation as a tool to hunt for respect from your community. Your self-discipline must show its effectiveness on all occasions, especially in times of great difficulty. We must realize the benefit of self-cultivation in each ordinary everyday situation.

There is no special time set aside just for this. With the calm power gained from our daily practice, we can change what seems to be disaster into blessing. Quietude can transform misfortune into good fortune.

12. To become a man or woman of Tao depends entirely on oneself. To achieve the level of a shien depends entirely on one's own energy. All people have the opportunity for self-achievement, but their efforts are covered by selfish clinging and desire. If you detach yourself from the irrelevance of worldly affairs and not permit your true nature to become stained by even one piece of dust, your true nature will clearly and freely shine through. Then there will be no opportunity for the evil and poisons of the world to create a mass of difficulties and problems for you.

When action is the result of the desires of your mind, you create the continuation of the painful cycles of a non-conscious life, death and re-birth. In order to avoid suffering from the result of your actions, you must rid your mind of all attachment or aversion. If your desire to achieve is too strong, it will disturb your true nature, and instead of ascending toward becoming a shien, you will spiral downward toward chaos and fail to keep your subtle nature intact.

If you have even one impure motive, it will give birth to a disturbance in the mind. This will cause you to lose the Taoist standard of clarity and humility, and you will no longer be able to enjoy what you have already achieved. Alas, all the previous efforts will have been in vain. If you can dissolve the poisons of greed and hatred and remove yourself from the passions of life, they will all be transformed into a sweet dew which will cool and purify you.

13. Do not become attached to the world of colorful dust. One hundred years pass in an instant. You live and die in the time

it takes to snap your fingers. Your temporary existence is like the drop of a pin. Yesterday a man rode his horse through the streets; today he lies sleeping in his coffin. This is the glamour of life. All the stories of a person's heroic life fall one day and become a dream resting under the spring tree.

Make certain that you begin early to cultivate yourself and learn to control this life. It is important to make your mind and body firm. Your must first weed out all the irregular grasses of your mental field, and not allow even one speck of dust to remain on the lens of your mental eye. When the mind becomes transparent and subtle, then your psyche becomes purified and you have dominion over your will.

Accumulating too much wealth is both disastrous and a heavy burden. To gain a high position is dangerous and degrades your true self. Do not live your daily life unconsciously as in a vague dream. Keep to the roots of your daily life.

In order to achieve true happiness, your approach should not be like a fire that flares up quickly, only to become extinguished a moment later. Those of true happiness do not clutch at worldly things. They appreciate all that comes their way, and live contentedly with their invisible, subtle and immortal nature. The real nature of true happiness is not found in the excitement of the worldly stimulation to the senses, but is obtained by gaining an understanding of the subtle laws of the universe. You can be saved by true wisdom. Move rapidly so that you can board this steady spiritual ship to safety.

14. To cultivate the understanding of reality is not difficult. Once one has received the teachings of the Integral Way of Tao, the secret of achievement lies in persistently maintaining a pure mind. Once you begin the Integral Way of Tao, continue to follow this method only, and the wisdom of your soul will shine from the constancy of your good efforts. Following many different approaches disperses your energy, creates chaos and causes a long delay in self-achievement. Self-cultivation generates a firm, calming power. Through it, your efforts and hopes to transcend mundane problems will be realized. Stay with one way from beginning to end. Avoid the temptation to retreat and change to a less potent path.

Any kind of day-dreaming or scattered thinking is wasteful, but trying to contact the real origin of life is truly valuable for self-cultivation. In the ordinary level it is dangerous to follow many different religious teachings. Common sense teachings are more desirable; to only follow the plain truth of nature is best. Moreover, the deepest mysteries are found without any teaching. Too many methods of cultivation create bewilderment. Stick to the Way in order to reach the subtle level of simplicity and purity.

15. When you take off the dirty clothing of your pain and bitterness, your true nature will suddenly and freely appear. Even though the sacred science of the shien is boundless, a persistent follower can reach the distant shore safely. Continue on. Do not stop short of your destination, for once you succeed, it is impossible to describe the wonderful happiness and purity you will experience.

Work day and night in your effort; courageously face all the tests and trials which are your own creations; here and now surpass all discriminations between humanity and Heaven. Then, with one final step, you will be able to cross the bitter sea and reach the other shore. From the very beginning to the very end you must hold fast to this goal. When your cultivation is finally complete, your merit and virtue will be full. Always remember that it is in the emptiness of your mind that the seed of the Heavenly shien can be found.

You can experience and verify the greatness of eternal truth personally, and thereby make a safe voyage through the boundless spiritual ocean. Be aware that your own intelligence can create blindness. Be diligent in changing night into day. It is easiest to practice self-cultivation in a dark, quiet room, separate from others. Blessings from all subtle divine realms will come to you and make you a wise and firm seed of a Heavenly shien.

16. To cultivate Tao, a foundation of virtue is required. Without virtue you cannot unite with Tao. The subtle power does not only come from within ourselves. Heaven, earth, and all living things are interconnected through you. This is because your mind embraces all positive virtues. Without being singled out, you make a contribution to all things. In this way you create a sure immortality with the universal true nature. If you strengthen your virtue first, then you will become naturally firm and incorruptible.

Honesty and sincerity are interconnected, and with this support all the positive subtle energies will protect you. Although your subtle body has form, it is not limited to this form. True wisdom is quiet, independent and fragrant. Persevere to connect with the universal light, and through it you will achieve the fullness and brightness found within your nature.

We must not walk away from creating positive influence in accordance with the needs of others. We must have compassion for the needs of the spiritually undeveloped world. When you become one of the healing lights, or merely a teacher, you provide an example and a healing influence for other beings. The subtle radiance of your smile, your speech, your conduct, and your way of life, all combine to produce many effective and beneficial medicines to remedy all the sick minds and bodies. To maintain kindness, generosity and grace is our heritage from the Heavenly Kinship.

17. In becoming a shien, there is no concern with adding a title or decoration to your personality. The true benefit is found through the efforts of your own deep inner being, and has nothing to do with social reputation. What you gain depends solely upon yourself.

For the Taoist Integral Science to have any practical benefit, and for it to be used properly in the realm of real life, it must be passed on to the right person. To be a Heavenly shien, one must have deep spiritual roots. The choice must be made with care. This is not the same as doing favors indiscriminately for all living things. You need to love and value the Integral Science of Tao, but do not carelessly throw it away. Do not mistake those who are without any spiritual affinity in the true Way of eternity for those who truly have it. The Masters of the Taoist Integral Science bid us, again and again, to fully protect the seeds of a Heavenly shien in a cautious way.

18. Too much self-assurance can be the seed of physical problems. When you know the cause, you know how to behave yourself. Do not think for an instant that the Integral Way of Tao is a mere theoretical system. The improvement of your life depends on honest self-reflection and cultivation. You must develop yourself with an awareness of the powerful force of the external culture which constantly enslaves you. You must,

therefore, make an effort to dissolve your mental formations and see the truth. Be united with the final truth; treat your mind and body with your body and mind. Try to trace all apparent differences back to the one original origin. Through true cultivation, true discipline, true proof and true gain, you can become a shien of the high divine clan.

19. Ordinary worldly religions and teachings attract ordinary minds. These teachings are like an uncultivated vine, growing haphazardly in all directions. Their spiritual illusions and idealistic teachings attempt to describe reality, but fall short by failing to illuminate their own spiritual blind spots. For this reason, these teachings only attract weak spirits who must cling to something even if it only supports their own self-deception. If you follow this crude way and put your trust in worldly religions without the clarity to see that you are being led down the wrong path, you will be waiting until the year of the Donkey for your awakening. Maybe then you will have the opportunity to experience the truth. In Integral Cultivation, we emphasize the experience of self-realization and self-transformation in order to discover the key to the puzzle of oral and written obstacles. First integrate yourself. Then you can help influence your environment. All parts of your body and spirit will eventually become your hands and eyes.

If you can develop your mental ability to the point where it is as round, full and smooth as a pearl, then when feelings of anxiety or danger appear, you will able to shake free from their effect. The subtle body of the Heavenly Law will appear in you and through you because you have succeeded in virtue and sharpness. That way, even while living in the world, you will be able to transcend its mundane problems and difficulties. The crystal clarity appears in the root of your life; all things share the same one body and cannot be separated. "Heaven, Earth, and Humankind are as a union of one, for all have the same origin." Realize this. Then you will become the strong seed of the Heavenly shien.

20. Heaven and earth have the virtue of giving birth to everything. We follow the nature of Heaven and earth in order to return to our Heavenly Origin. In this way, we not only enjoy eternity with Heaven and earth, but we also can unite the

positive energy of all life through our compassion. All worldly people desire life and fear death. But even if you fear death, it cannot be avoided. If you wish to achieve immortality, you must remember that it can only be achieved through many deaths. With the death of your impulsive mind, you can prove that the shadow of life and death is only the surface activity of the unconscious mind. In reality, nothing is born and nothing is destroyed. If you hope to experience the efficacy and the luminosity of your pure mind, the mind of desire must completely die. When your mind dies, your spirit will come alive and you will have unusual and majestic light.

All the children of impurity think that worldly enjoyments are a blessing, and because of this they block the channels of their higher energy. They do not see that death is hiding in the very pleasures they seek. Even though death is not always the immediate result, these unhealthy pursuits greatly diminish their vital essences, and their bodies carry the odors of a corpse. Only the true children of Heaven know the wonderful principle of how to receive life through death.

21. Evil powers can be divided into four categories: external, internal, apparent and hidden. The most difficult to deal with are the hidden poisons because your knowledge of their coming is prevented. Therefore, you must recognize them at their subtle beginning. If you work to mold the sharp and precious sword of wisdom, then you will find it necessary to retreat into the mountains to avoid the temptations of the world. The balance of your life is devitalized by too much inharmonious and dissipated mental and physical activity. If your mental disorders arise, then evil powers will immediately enslave you.

There are very few principles concerning the cultivation of the Tao. The most important one is to keep your pure mind undivided and unscattered. Only through self-discipline will your divine nature develop correctly. This new life of subtle transformation will continue in the process of spiritual evolution, and your immortality will become self-manifesting. Be aware that it is possible to become a thief of your own energy (chi). Therefore, be cautious on the road which you must travel to become a shien.

22. If you gently gather the energy together, quiet your wandering mind and carefully filter your desires, you will protect your vitality and radiate with an auspicious light. All of Heaven and its divinities, all of earth and its people, respect this kind of light. The power that you acquire and are able to utilize is the power that is discovered with your tranquil mind. With calmness comes wisdom. The clouds part, the moon becomes bright, and the light of wisdom radiates in all directions. With the Way, you can surpass the Way. Then there is no other Way, because you and the Way become one.

The deepest and most wondrous silence comes by forgetting the active. It is at this level that you may become the great king or queen of the Eternal Way of Liberation and, at last, enjoy its fruit. True happiness can only come about through painstaking discipline and patience. By courageously utilizing your mental power, you can with-stand the bitterness of anxiety and fear. Put your physical needs beyond consideration, for internal powers are far greater than external strength when it comes to accomplishing real work. True spirit has no worry or fear. It is in this way that you can become an integral being accepted by all Heavens.

23. When you cultivate Tao in the correct way and with a firm will, you need not worry whether or not you are producing the right fruit. The true nature of life is the same in all people. A sage does not have more or less than an average person. Nor is there any difference between rich and poor, superior or inferior, in this respect.

The only difference is whether or not there is the aspiration to cultivate Tao. If you follow the precepts of Taoist Integral Science, cultivating yourself precisely and avoiding any motive or ideal which may pull you in a vicious direction, then all good and positive qualities become firm in you and you can become one with Tao. Even in death you can remain undamaged and realize the truthfulness of eternal life. This undecayed, everlasting spiritual body is the highest true soul which connects the course of the universe.

Because of the wondrous effect of non-action, the spiritual firmness of Tao cannot be washed away by the good or bad luck of daily life. If you can remain impartial, then there can be no cause for worry about impurity. This is the correct Integral Way of a shien. You can firmly embrace the Taoist Integral Science, and strictly, effectively and continually protect the sprouting seed of a Heavenly shien.

24. Taoism is different from all ordinary religious teachings. We think that all beings are born with the basic qualities of organic, rational, and divine nature. The right teaching develops these qualities fully and, therefore, enables one to be fulfilled and to become one with the life of nature. Instead of dismembering ourselves, we must value and nurse the normal vital chi to be a bridge reaching the profundity of the universe. This chi in our being is so great and strong that it is not possible to develop it through books alone.

At birth, you are a perfect person with all three purities, like any universal integral being. To achieve the three purities means to achieve the fulfillment of all three natures of life.

To develop and fulfill your organic nature (energy), means to extend to the Heaven of Great Purity. To develop and fulfill your rational nature (energy), means to extend to the Heaven of Crystal Purity. To develop and fulfill your divine or spiritual nature (energy), means to extend to the Heaven of Utmost Purity. The fulfillment of these three natures of life means to have extended to the three Realms of Purity, and have restored balance and completeness.

The total fulfillment of the original energy is the way of Heaven. It has no beginning and no end. It keeps reviving itself without ever being exhausted. If you do not distort or disturb it by going against its nature, you will receive concrete proof of immortality.

Because of your present situation in this life, you need discipline and cultivation. But it is not necessary to go deep into the mountains and become a hermit in order to do this. You must work with all the changes and circumstances which life presents to you. By utilizing the techniques of the Taoist Integral Science, you will find the support that you need, and in addition, you will attract many benefits to yourself. In order to follow the Integral Way of Tao, you must constantly practice it. If you only talk about it, you will derive no real benefit from it. Do not waste your time going around in circles with mere theoretical notions. You must deepen in the reality of cultivation of the Tao.

25. Whenever you are practicing self-cultivation, you must be very realistic in verifying achievements. Through the Integral Way of Tao, you must first dissolve the idea of self and prove to yourself that beingness and emptiness in the universe are interconnected, and of the same essential nature; that life and death are only superficial phenomena; that the way of life and death is one and not two. If you can control the final energy, then true living goes on endlessly.

In the first stage of self-cultivation, you will suffer because your essences are not yet dissolved. But after the essences in your being are dissolved, they will change to a sweet and fragrant energy. This benefit occurs the moment you break through the three check points (blocks) on your spinal column. The energy then rises up from your reproductive center (sexual system) and penetrating the cortex of the brain, is transmuted into spiritual energy which has the power of regenerating your own vitality.

In your cultivation to become a shien, once you have achieved the "three terms" - full essence, calm mind, and pure spirit - you will have proven that you are already a shien living presently in this world. If you can use your spirit to govern the whole body, you will progress to a higher level. We not only ask that you cultivate the interior with spiritual medicine, but that, in addition, you be able to live harmoniously within your community. In order to live in this world, we must complete the three natures of life and become full with virtue. We will not be successful if we use concepts of failure, intelligence, sharpness or dullness as gauges to measure ourselves. Ask only to maintain purity and to be able to unite with Tao. For this you must carefully guard the Way of a high level shien. A broken ship cannot make a long journey on the ocean. If you depart from the truth and cling to false worshipping, you will find that because of this deception and exaggeration you will end in final darkness.

Although it is an impure and dirt-filled world, you will be able to grow a very pure and beautiful Lotus. Let go of all nonsensical talk and try to keep yourself true with the chi of the Mysterious Oneness.

Chapter 22

The Way of Immortality

1.

From the subtlety of spirit
to the gross composite of matter
span the levels of creation.
The physical can be sensed and perceived.
Subtle truth is harder to know.
The spiritual realm to worldly people
is incomprehensible.
Tao alone is eternal and simple.

Ordinary people see the world
in a shallow way.
Yet in the depth of truth,
its levels are many.
All beings may be classified
into three general categories.
The divisions were made by the masters
who developed the mystical knowledge of Tao.

2.

First, there are the shiens
who enjoy immortality
with pure and light yang energy.

Then comes the balanced human beings with yin and yang.
Once they lose their lives
they become dim ghosts
with only decreasing yin energy.

At the death of a human being
both energies are finally separated.
Yang energy has already left the person.
The remaining consciousness adheres to the bone,
staying with weak matter
under the earth in darkness.

Like the lower spirits and dim ghosts,
who have exhausted their pure, complete energy,
So wholesome human forms become dissipated
by their attachments
to the increasing yin quality.

Through temperance and self-cultivation
one may keep up with
the pure energy of the universe
and follow the Way of innate simplicity.

The foolish think they may get to Heaven
by their selfish way of bribing holy beings
by sitting in churches to mortgage their sins.

The only way to Heaven
is through self-oblivion,
Gradually eliminating one's
yin, heavy, gross accumulation.
Then it is possible to accomplish
the perfect completion to become
pure yang energy.

3.
For better understanding, let us review
the three spheres of energy.
The highest energy is subtle and pure.
It is Heaven,
with shiens and all spiritual beings.
There is no death in this plane.

The second is in the middle,
the harmonious, balanced realm
of humankind.
Before they deprave their original nature,
they are already true beings and sages.
Life and death happen in this level
when damage is done to the harmony
of yin and yang.
The third is the realm
of mixed and heavy energy.

The inertia of the beings of this realm
  makes them very material.
They are lost and sinking beings,
  confused souls who are falling
  because of self-degrading evildoing;
  finally ranking the same as
  the incomplete works of creation.

Human beings are both spirit and matter,
  formed by the subtle and gross.
As the yang energy increases
  and the yin energy decreases,
  one earns one's ascension
  to the Heavenly realm
  to enjoy Heavenly blessing.

When the yin grows, the yang goes away.
One walks along the way of devolution
  close to the realm of shadow.

For the attainment of a shien,
  the formula is clear.
The ancient Masters taught us
  to watch the moon
  as our example in self-cultivation.
When the bright side is growing
  the dark side must be yielding.
If you hold this measure for yourself,
  your eternal way will be broad and flat.

The balanced high human beings
  gather yang energy from the vast universe
  until their spiritual moon is full.
They fly away, ascending from the earthly realm
  to the highest realm of immortality.

The wandering souls drift up and down
  through life and non-life materials
  without the true goal.
The remedy comes
  only when their insight grows.

With Tao as the final destination
all beings find eternal life
and reach for the divine origin.

Souls connected with Tao
live both in the human realm
and in the realm of spirit,
gathering yang energy from
immersion in the eternal oneness.

In following the five phases
of energy evolution,
a soul gathers its form.
In this sphere, physical law operates
and transmutation is eventually unavoidable.

Human form is unstable.
As insight grows, fear of death dies.
Spiritual life evolves
and life and death pass without ado.

Self-cultivation gathers
the breath of eternal youth
and nurtures the essences
from the everlasting.
With pure, yang energy,
promote progression and ascension,
expand the path of harmony,
and finally achieve oneness
with the eternal Tao.

4.

Submerged in desire,
Humans are lustful beings.
Violating the laws of life
They do themselves harm
and so cause their own misfortune.

The temptation to obscure the real Way is great.
Few people make the effort
to lift the veil.

Instead of searching for sensory stimulation
    to combat the imbalance
    of internal secretions,
    follow the constant, cosmic law of life.
Learn the Sacred method of Tao
    to realize your true nature.

For fulfillment of your own being,
    you must look into the depths
    of your very own nature
    to finally discover
    the true source of peace.
Even people of great strength
    cannot lift themselves up by their own bootstraps
Thus, we rely on the ultimate spiritual path
    to guide us,
    restoring our true nature
    and elevating spirit.

Follow the Tao and regain your balance,
    reclaim your own soul.
Even in the mundane world
    the Tao can be found within your reach.
It dances even in the most humble of things.

Only the shiens enjoy absolute freedom.
Self-discipline and self-cultivation
    are the wings which will carry us home.
With the sublime energy of Tao,
    we may dissolve all illusions.

One virtuous being
    can destroy a thousand evils.
One's sincere cultivation
    can brighten the whole universe.

5.
Worldly religions blind the good soul,
    deceiving humankind on a dark route.
The Tao is not a religion.
It is only unadorned truth.

As the polarity of yin and yang
propels unceasing evolution,
a life of blind faith
attracts only conflict and doubt.
When the moment of death arrives,
do we believe in faith or death?

To follow the light of Tao,
the way of eternity,
is to realize the true nature
in every forward step.

Religion is an obstacle to being natural,
having little to do with spiritual truth.
The sacred method of Tao
is the accumulation of human wisdom,
the truth of life handed down
by the enlightened ones.

One may transcend all cultural creations,
break the dusty covering
to meet the immortal forerunners
in the highest divine realms.

6.

People ignorant of cosmic law think
by doing favors with preference
and earning an impressive reputation
one cay buy the salvation of one's soul.
But without self-awareness
and adherence to the law of life
those superficial, worldly things
are proven to be in vain.

Ignorant of reality,
people put on airs of holiness
to enhance their self-importance.
This can only lead one spiritually downward.

Only through self-cultivation
and compliance with cosmic law
can the soul surely and safely
return to its Heavenly home.

7.

To understand Taoist philosophy
is not to become sacred.
Understanding is merely a mental tool.
Spiritual truth can only be touched
with the spirit.

Understanding may even lead you
very far astray.
You think you are where you are not
which inevitably brings you
conflict and doubt.
It is the game a vulgar mind plays.

One must let all mental movement fall away,
and unhesitatingly rejoin with
the eternal Tao.
Joyfully plunge yourself
into the depth of mystical oneness.

The Tao is beyond
all concepts and understanding.
Exhume the spiritual essence
from its bondage in physical limitation.
Then all spiritual treasures
will spontaneously manifest.

8.

Mystical powers used for show
will certainly lead you
to spiritual diminishment.
The spiritual method is a ferry boat
to convey you spiritually
from the troubled waters to the shore.

To embody the boundless Tao
one's spirit must be balanced
and without partiality;
achieving spiritual roundness and fullness.

All lights merge and become one,
as does the spiritual reality.
The true Heaven is impersonal.
The eternal simplicity is the root of all.

9.

These are four stages of the spiritual process.
First, seek the guidance
of a truly enlightened Master,
whose light and protection
can illuminate the darkness of your soul.

Second, learn diligently the sacred method
and increase the true knowledge of inner life.
When your spiritual energy grows
you will become enlightened
and all mysteries will be exposed to you.

Third, cultivate yourself step by step.
From the guidance you gain
in your unceasing pursuit of truth,
subjectively continue the spiritual evolution.
Beware of your inertia.

Fourth, unify the inner and the outer,
attain mystical union with Tao.
Immortality is total and whole.
The real integrity is indistinguishable.

These are four stages for those
newly starting on the spiritual path,
and yet they are one
in any single contact with spirit.

10.

*The world is a group of phenomena
     which seem to appear and then disappear
     in the twilight.
In the subtle realm, changes or constancy
     seem not to exist.*

*The harmonious co-existence
     of the subtle and the phenomenal
     is the cosmic principle
     of the great Tai Chi.*

*Life and death are only
     a divine metamorphosis.
The realm of true spiritual beings
     is beyond death and duality.*

*When one resides in the Tao,
     one is absolute and true.
Being both nature and substance,
     essence and form,
     the infinite and the empty -
     and yet neither -
     words can never capture it.*

*The way of spirit appears
     after the view of duality is dissolved.
The contradictory quality is removed.
The truth is revealed.*

THE THREE INTEGRATED WAYS TO IMMORTALITY

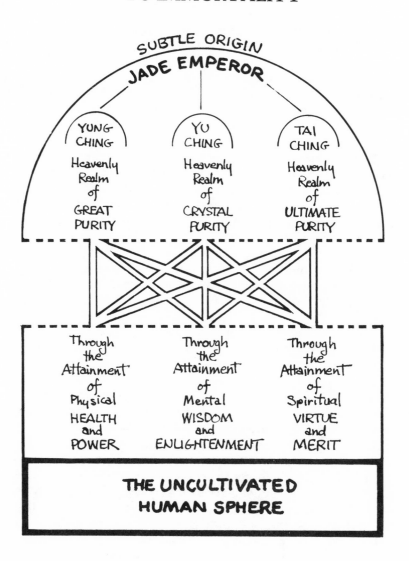

SUBTLE ORIGIN
JADE EMPEROR

YUNG CHING	YU CHING	TAI CHING
Heavenly Realm of GREAT PURITY	Heavenly Realm of CRYSTAL PURITY	Heavenly Realm of ULTIMATE PURITY

| Through the Attainment of Physical HEALTH and POWER | Through the Attainment of Mental WISDOM and ENLIGHTENMENT | Through the Attainment of Spiritual VIRTUE and MERIT |

THE UNCULTIVATED HUMAN SPHERE

Chapter 23

Being a Taoist

The Union of Tao and Man

The Union of Tao and Man is the original ancient Chinese tradition of integral life which has been passed down from the Heavenly beings, the shiens, to the first inhabitants of earth. The adepts in this tradition set precious examples for their students. Members of this tradition are instructed with words, but they also receive continual inspiration from the subtle divine origin on their individual spiritual journeys. This tradition does not depend on rigid doctrine to regulate people in a social sense.

To the adept of this tradition, the term "Heaven" has the spiritual meaning of the transcendence of the relative realm of duality and the attainment of the integral, absolute realm. Refinement of self and the transcendence of the dualistic world are necessary in order to achieve the state of being referred to as "Heavenly shien."

In ancient times, the people who followed, studied and cultivated the Tao lived in the high mountains in order to maintain their unsoiled lives. Mountains symbolize calmness and perpetuity. Through inner peace and calmness, one may experience the wholeness of the universe and connect with the root of all life. Today, the adepts of the tradition of Heavenly shiens do not concern themselves with where they live, but instead endeavor to keep an inner calm wherever they are.

The adepts of this tradition who have already discovered and verified the eternity of life have done so through self-discipline of their own physical, mental and spiritual faculties. Through the high development of these faculties, one may know the everlasting laws of the universe. Through rational, practical and methodical practices of self-cultivation, one can verify the deep truths of the universe within the essence of one's own soul. The Heavenly shiens do not concern themselves with what happens to their physical lives or what benefits their activities. They would rather open themselves to the natural world than try to control it. They do not hold fast to mental concepts and ideas, and thereby dissolve the illusion of an individualized personal self. At any moment they can mentally withdraw from the world of the senses and quietly abide in the deep peace of Tao.

To cultivate the Tao means to practice the Sacred Method of the Integral Way; that is, to follow specific techniques which were discovered by the ancients in order to develop one's physical faculties, to improve one's health, to reform one's mental activity, and to employ one's developed spirit in dealing with all aspects of life. Through the subtle self-control developed by self-cultivation, one can also reach the level of being able to manage one's own life and death. When one is living in the world, one has a peaceful and creative life, both within oneself and with others. When one dies, one knows the right time to go and is prepared to make the transition, because one has already proven that there is no death in the true life, and there is no life separate from the deep, eternal Tao.

There are many schools of religion and philosophy. Taoism is not one of them. Taoists recognize that divinity and humankind function as one entity. They recognize that everything in the universe is the manifestation of Tao. The sun, moon, stars, mountains, rivers, living creatures and plants all have one final source. But because of the dualistic function of the physical world, our awareness of the unity of the spirit with the divine nature has been impeded. In the process of the mental perception of subject and object, human beings individualize and fragment the wholeness of the integral nature of the universe.

Some human beings have evolved to a high enough level where they want to cultivate the Tao and reunite themselves with the integral source. To cultivate the Tao is to spiritually transcend the imprisonment of the ego. Only then is it possible to reach the depths of the real and whole universe, rather than stay attached to the segmented superficial phenomena of the universe. To achieve oneself in Tao means to transcend all and to encompass all things within. The individual ego is a cage. One must also accept the fact that the physical body has its limitations. But if we discipline and cultivate ourselves, we may break through these limitations and experience the fullness and completeness of the universe. Through the practice of the Integral Way, the wonders of everlasting life become the living truth of enlightened men and women.

Whether you recognize or deny this fact, the universal subtle level truly exists. The subtle level supports your own being whether you accept it or not. Even the recognition or denial of this is a special function of your personal subtle level working in you. Intellectuals may argue for either idealism or materialism on the metaphysical level, but we need to recognize that any kind of argument is merely a function of the intellect and is only a difference of point of view. If you follow materialism, the result will be material. If you follow idealism, the result will be idealistic. These are both merely attempts to win influence over others through argumentation. However, in this way one cannot even win influence over oneself because one is trapped within the limitations of one's own framework of the mind. Thus, one who cultivates the Tao never takes the phenomena of the world as the final truth. Nor does one take a part as the whole. One cultivates one's own pure mental and intellectual powers, thereby not only surpassing one's own knowledge but also transcending the psychology of one's daily life, and breaking the boundary of the ego. In order to embody the truth, we must unite our individual lives with Tao. Only then can we enjoy everlasting happiness.

To cultivate Tao is different from participating in a social organization or religious church. Such participation has nothing to do with true life. To cultivate the Tao is a pure experience tailored to fit one's own individual needs. To do or not to do depends on one's own self. It does not relate to other people or things. It is you yourself who needs to shoulder responsibility for your own life. Self-cultivation and the Taoist Way of life are the manifestations of your own true being. To restore this divinity and integrity of one's true being, a beginner who is trapped by worldly life may follow the principles and discovered methods of cultivation and self-discipline which have been handed down by the Taoist Masters of this divine tradition.

Self-discipline means to turn back to the spiritual center in oneself and the universe. This is to live the divinity of wholeness. Refresh yourself by returning to the center of life, the divine origin of the universe. Without self-cultivation, your small bit of vitality becomes transferred and scattered. So the benefits and growth of your true soul are dependent on your own effort and are not concerned with an outside power.

The basic principle for the beginner is that through cultivation, one may experience total liberation and reintegration by connecting oneself with divinity; without cultivation, one cannot. Most beginners hope to gain blessings as a reward for their self-discipline. They ask urgently for results and, if they cannot cause the mysterious level to respond to them immediately, their minds become doubting and they complain about the ineffectiveness of divinity. They externalize the divinity of the universe, and the more they do so, the more they move away from the truth. In reflecting their blindness, they complain about their present situation. Nevertheless, if one hopes to reach enlightenment, one must be free from physical bondage and mental illusion. Then one will prove the subtle connection between the whole universe and the everlasting Tao.

Before you ask Heaven for blessings, you must first reach the level of receiving spontaneous response to your cultivation from the subtle realm. Then all the blessings will come without your strong and mindful ambition. If you ask for a blessing hungrily and strongly, even if you could get it, it would be difficult for it to be a real blessing. Sometimes if you ask impatiently for an immediate response from the subtle realm, it is easy to be fooled by evil spirits or by the performance of another part of one's mind.

If one wishes to fulfill one's life and transcend death, one must first experience the subtle connection of the entire universe. This can be done only through stable, inner calmness. It is not difficult to do. All of the miracles and wonders are within oneself. If you are discouraged by your self-created difficulties, it is you yourself who is stopping the flow of the perpetually changing Tao. There is nothing for you to complain about.

The universal oneness expressed through this ancient tradition differs widely from any man-made dogmas expressed by worldly religious ways. The worldly way worships a sovereign of the universe which is external to oneself and to which one is subordinate. However, through the self-cultivation practiced in this far-reaching spiritual stream, one may restore oneself with the divinity of the universe and become a divine being oneself. The general purpose of this tradition is to enable people to transcend the confines of their egos and unite with the sublime energy of the universe.

The adepts of this tradition may offer themselves in service to the world, but do not seize personal aggrandizement for doing so. Their commitment is to uphold the constancy of a simple life. They live life fully and do not give up any of life's three spheres, neither the physical nor the mental nor the spiritual sphere. The Taoist Way does not degrade the divinity of any aspect of life. Its adepts do not run away from anything, but move forward to complete their lives through self-cultivation.

Some Taoists have a special life purpose. They simplify their lives and concentrate on some special aspect of life. Yet their spirit still contains the fullness of life. Religion, on the other hand, is generally a kind of psychological consolation for social and personal problems. Therefore, it is not the truth of life. Only absolute truth will lead one to immortal life.

There are three main aspects of human nature. One is the organic nature, one is the rational nature, and one is the divine nature. With the first, people maintain an ordinary worldly life. With the second, people know the common laws of existence. With the third, people know enough to purify themselves and pursue spiritual evolution. The individual operating in the human realm of life emphasizes the organic nature and neglects the other two. The philosopher emphasizes the rational nature and neglects the other two. The worldly religious leaders tend to emphasize the divine and neglect the other two.

The Taoist keeps and develops the fullness of human nature in all three of its aspects: organic, rational and divine. So the tradition and sacred method of the "Union of Tao and Man" include all three aspects of human nature. The right Way of life for a person is to live the fullness of life. To realize the fullness of nature is to be a complete person. A complete person is a true person. Therefore, we call this person a man or woman of Tao.

The growth of human nature is accomplished in three stages. The first is organic; the second, rational; the third, divine. In reality, these three aspects are one. These stages may be thought of as being phases of childhood, adulthood and the mature stage. Worldly religions are the product of the first and second stages. These religions in their positive aspects may act as cradles for humanity. We need to eventually grow beyond the preliminary stages, although some people have no desire to do so. We recognize the need these religions fulfill and the emotional protection they offer people, but what to do they achieve? They never get beyond the blind spot in a person's own nature. They mistake this blind spot as divinity, and worship it as an outside sovereign. There are few religious leaders who can even break through their own blind spot and achieve the width and depth of the existing universe.

Some aspects of the Taoist disciplines and training may seem on the surface to resemble these worldly religions; however, we do not stop at the point of our own blind spots. What is needed most is the breakthrough, and once this is achieved, all the secrets of the universe become crystal clear. Then you are not subject to an outside spiritual sovereign and can accept full responsibility, not only for your own life, but also for the universe. This is the real independence of being a shien, and integral being and person. This is why our discipline is different. This is the precious value of the Integral Way and Taoist culture handed down to us through our ancient masters.

The Fundamental Mental Discipline From the Ancient Taoist Tradition of the Union of Tao and Man
Tao is the unnameable name of the Subtle Origin and primal energy of the universe. We recognize the Subtle Origin of the universe as the mysterious mother of existence and non-existence. Ultimately, these three are actually one. This undivided oneness is the ultimate truth. The differentiated manifestation of the universe is naturally so; it was neither created nor designed. There is no single, personified creator. Tao, the primal energy which exercises and develops itself, brings forth all the manifestations of the universe. The original energy becomes the law of its manifestation.

Everything manifested and unmanifested is a spontaneous expression of the nature of the Subtle Origin; no intentional design is needed. As the universe evolves, it develops an energy net for its own subtle connection. The universal development may be viewed as a cyclic or recycling process of endless productivity. All individual beings and things are under the influence of the energy net in the vast arena of the universe. The energy net is the natural administrative system. Its control is usually stronger for the less spiritually developed beings. The development of all things and beings is predetermined in a general way; details of individual development, however, vary.

If we indulge in our strong passions, emotions, desires and ambitions, the influence of the energy net will be strong, because these cause the response of mechanical force. If your energy is light, the influence of the energy net will also be light. If you lead your life normally and in harmony with the universe, you will experience no sign of the existence of an energy net at all.

In this universe, each life is responsible for itself. Nobody can use forceful emotion to assign another human being, or any being, to be their spiritual savior. Spiritual aid sometimes comes in the form of kind and highly evolved natural beings who subtly stretch out helping hands. One may also have good fortune when one's energy moves to a favorable section of the cycle. Great awareness is needed to discern when this is the case.

The Way of Tao is absolute. Whether one is aware of Tao or not, one receives one's life's energy from Tao. Some follow Tao consciously, and others follow it unconsciously. Yet with or without awareness, Tao is the essence of all life. To be ignorant of Tao is to live in blindness. To know Tao is to see clearly. Therefore, we follow only the absolute, nameless, original oneness of the universe, which is the essence of our lives. If we violate the Tao, we annihilate our own lives. We cannot exist without Tao. We reject all man-made names and religious concepts which were created for the segmented mind. They cause confusion and obstruction to our direct experience of truth. The eternal Way is gentle. Brute force is the low-level teaching of some religions or political systems. It is never the truth of integral life.

Our inner incentive is to clarify and purify our own spiritual being. The outwardness of our internal achievement is to extend care and kindness to all beings and things. We refine our emotions and desires to be as light as possible in order to maintain ourselves as high level beings. We do not indulge in passionate love or hate. Temper and passion are by no means our ruler. In this way we avoid any downfall. We also avoid religious emotionalism. As a spiritual child, religious emotionalism may function to initiate one's journey back to the source. But as a spiritual adult, religious emotionalism will prevent one's real growth and union with Tao. To follow Tao is to follow the integration of the universe with harmonious, life-giving energy; to follow religious emotion is to form prejudice and to nurture hostility. As a consequence of this, people invite death.

We practice simplification in our lives, particularly with regard to our energy. Thus, we do not scatter our energy or distract our minds with frivolous, unnecessary activities. We avoid wasting energy through arguments, restless nonsense (busy work), fidgety behavior and meddling into other's affairs. In this way, we preserve the integrity of our spirit and enjoy harmony with the universe. We keep a Taoist hermit spirit in the busy worldly life.

We bravely and earnestly face the bare truth of our lives. We do not mistake Taoist cultivation as an escape from the reality of life, as may be the case in some religions. A simple, plain and natural life is essential to spiritual completeness. The special expression wu wei[1] describes the highest Way of our correct integral evolution.

We take the constant virtue and normalcy of the universe as the model of our lives. The guideline of a Taoist life is to keep a clear mind and have few desires.

We in no way practice either ignorant asceticism or wantonness. We enjoy the beauty, richness and nobility of life and practice the principles of right purpose, right method and right timing according to the universal subtle law of energy response. This sacred spiritual tradition can be maintained only by disciples who lead disciplined, simple and righteous lives. Initially, this discipline is rendered to the awakening disciples by the Master. An aspect of self-discipline is the abstinence from drugs, coffee, excessive alcohol and other similar substances which are an obstacle to spiritual refinement. The developed individual is guided directly by the Tao. If one does not heed this guidance, one loses the Tao.

Sincerity, purity of heart and good deeds can lift an ordinary life to the divine realm. However, we do not disrupt the simplicity of life to create artificial opportunities to do good. This kind of effort is unnecessary, for a simple life in itself is divine. To learn, Tao, fundamentally, is to live a simple, natural and essential life. It means we deny trivialities and avoid unnecessary activities. This is how we have enough energy to accomplish the total integration of our spirit.

The clarity, purity and harmony of your own energy is the reality of union with Tao. Heavy energy (including emotional force and psychological cloudiness) is an obstruction to true spiritual growth. Taoism is not an ordinary religion. Most religions depend on the psychological weakness of human

---

[1]Wu Wei is the Taoist principle of non-making or non-deviation. The way to realize this principle is to simplify the daily marginal activities and live deep in the core of life. Then the transcendental purity and peace lift one above the mechanical forces of the external, physical world.

beings. Some use hypnosis in their attempt to help and to control people's cloudy minds. Hypnosis uses only part of the mind. Taoist cultivation is to integrate one's wholeness of being with the wholeness of the universe. Mistaking emotionalism for spirit, most religions foster self-assertiveness, prejudice, development of ego and hostility. Truthfully, this is the pitfall of spirit. Sons and daughters of Tao must be above this and all things.

Sanity is the essential foundation for learning Tao. It is the basis for the development and subjective evolution of one's own being. Without a sound body and mind, there is no hope of attaining Tao.

Chapter 24

A Traditional Taoist Initiation And Other Ceremonies

The Statement of My Initiation

At the time of my initiation I presented this statement to my father, who was my teacher:

I have been travelling a long time and know not where to find the true Tao. For many years I have been adrift, like a ship without a rudder. Because the wheel of worldly events never stops turning and the troubled waters are endless, I have become confused and have fallen into bitterness and despair. Now I come to your door and ask you to kindly show me the true way. Please have compassion for me. As I enter your court, I ask the Tao and my Heavenly Mother and Father of my Heavenly Family to please accept and save me.

In your court there is a lamp. It is not an ordinary lamp, for it has an eternal flame. In the center of the flame can be seen the hearts of many Heavenly beings. This is an auspicious time for initiation into the sacred shrine. I know it is difficult to transcend oneself, so today as I approach Tao with empty heart and mind, I vow to diligently cultivate myself to answer your Heavenly grace. Your wandering child is finally returning home.

My Letter of Petition for Initiation

Every time I realize that I am in the world as a member of humankind, I feel that it is the grace from the mysterious universe that makes me a human. I very much appreciate this life with the sun, moon, stars and trees. I know this life is an act of grace, but I do not know where or whom to thank. I frequently nourish my heart to seek the Tao, but still know not the right road to it. Many times I have lost the Way, and am constantly struggling in troubled waters. Although my ears have heard many things, my heart remains confused. Time passes quickly and life is so short. I feel that it will be forever lost and I will have no opportunity to serve Heaven and live according to the Tao. I have often wanted to help people and be of benefit, and my will was strong to become one with the Tao, but there was no road to find the Master. Now I feel privileged to learn your ancient Taoist teachings. From the beginning until now, many thousands of years have seen these teachings handed down from Master to Master.

With the help of these simple truths of life and death, people can obtain the sphere of everlasting life. We, in our turn, will also hand down these eternal truths. Everything under Heaven and of earth has its being in Tao and only humankind has the opportunity to know it. If one cultivates and knows the Tao, then one is truly an exalted being. Today, I, your child, come to you for this sacred and rare opportunity.

True man and Master of the Sanctuary of the Eternal Breath of Tao, impart to me the secret truths of the Tao of life and death, and how to become an integral person. I will earnestly try to do everything you instruct.

I, your child, also ask Grandmaster to observe and guard me. I bring this letter before the Jade Emperor and the Most exalted Master of the Tao and the divine beings everywhere, to witness my self-cultivation. I humbly ask Your Holiness to have pity on me, an earthly creature, and support my successful cultivation of Tao.

I vow to change the evil within me to good, and will reform my wrong doings in order to cultivate only good fruit. I will try to avoid falling into bitterness in other lives, and hope to bear everlasting blissful fruit. For this I ask our Master's instruction.

I resolve to become a pure and everlasting channel of Tao. I will always show people the right road and help them follow the Way. I will alert foolish people of danger, how to know right from wrong and how to cultivate a tranquil life. I will forever be a refuge for the needy, building a road for all people to go upward.

Our Tao is handed down from the ancient Masters and is not the product of time or environment. This path is transmitted from one generation to another, because our ancient Master loves all life. Therefore, I have this sacred opportunity to gain Tao. This is what I, your child, very much want and desire.

I lift my head to receive the graceful light turned toward me.

Invocations Used During Initiation

INITIATION INVOCATION
I request the dispersion of impurities,
*   and the elimination of evils and demons,*
*   the source of misfortune and trouble.*
Heaven's generals plan their mysterious moves.
The movement of stars, the lightning of the divine water,

all respond from the Highest Heaven,
and echo from the earth below.
The God of thunder claps and rolls.
The wind and clouds fly to meet each other.
Chyan and K'un take their positions,
and all dimensions develop into fullness.
The ghosts are frightened and the vicious are sad.
All divine spirits come to guard when the pure law appears.
All noxious influences are exterminated.
and happiness comes as quickly as the command
comes from the Mysterious Mother of the Ninth Heaven.

PURIFICATION IN THE SHRINE

The purity of Heaven and earth,
and the essence of the sun and moon
appear with the power to subdue all evils,
to dissipate the impure vapor
and replace it with brightness.
The divine power of water can remove all misery and suffering.
Because the sacredness of the shrine
holds the absolute sovereign,
the offering of water has wonderful powers.
When the water of wisdom is applied,
it makes the Heaven pure, the earth pacified,
and the divine law efficacious.
The inside and outside of the body are cleansed.
So it is commanded by the most Exalted Master.

PURIFICATION AND ENLIGHTENMENT BY WATER

Nine phoenixes as Heavenly energy soar and roam,
benefiting things and beings in all directions.
Angels usher and guard me,
and take me freely to the Heavens
with the privilege of being a man or woman of Tao.
I have the honor of having an audience with the Jade Emperor
and the magnificent Queen of the West Jade Pond.
So nine phoenixes disperse all my impurities.
And it should be done as quickly as the command comes
from the sovereign of the Imperial Heaven.

PURIFICATION BY FIRE

This is not an earthly fire.

It is a sacred flame handed down by our masters.
May this sacred and eternal flame consume all my earthly
desires and strengthen my own spiritual flame.
May it always illuminate my heart and dispel
all my bitterness and darkness.
With this fire, the sacred flame will be forever bright.

PURIFICATION AND SANCTIFICATION OF SPEECH
The original chi becomes many divine beings;
these divine beings make me holy.
With this invocation of the divine realm,
the evils will forever depart
and make my inner light pure
and my outer light simplified and rectified.
My nine orifices will become bright
and my chi will become one with the Tao.
I obtain the right to transmit the Tao,
knowing all the while that it is a secret
that can never be told.
I ask by the name of the most revered Master
to forbid my mouth to speak evil.
I will never try to tell the mystery of the Tao
and will strive to be holy,
so that there will only be good effects from my speech.
By the name of the Mysterious Mother of the universe,
I forbid my mouth to speak evil
or reveal the mystery of the Tao to others.

The Vow of My Ordination of Fulfilling the Heavenly Duties

Since the great ancient times, Tao has been manifesting, and the absolute way has been transmitted through many generations. The Divine Heavenly Realm does not abandon people, it is people who turn away from the Divine Immortal Heaven. We all receive our life from Heaven. It is because we have received Heaven's benevolence that we are able to receive the correct way of self-cultivation. Through Heaven's kindness, we are able to melt our old selves and rebuild a new self, so that our vicious qualities are dissolved and our kind qualities become purer each day. Our sluggishness and mental obstacles disappear and our hearts become bright with inner light. Through our diligent cultivation, there are many subtle spiritual responses which benefit our lives and transform our old ways. Our chi becomes pure and our hearts unite with oneness.

Because our activities are simple and clear, our lives become virtuous. With pure determination we are directed to return to the truth. Our hearts reach straight toward Heaven. The mystical secret of Heaven, earth and humanity manifests before us. The secret profundity of spiritual truth and the sacred meaning of the mystical wonders become clear. When this profound decree is uncovered, we can directly travel the clear and bright road. The gold and jade scriptures are our daily influences. We have deep gratitude for receiving this great fortune. In order to transcend our unrefined worldly habits and sweep away our sensory illusions and obstacles, we recapture our root, and thus the path of the shiens is nearby.

Self-dedication During the Ordination

We are glad to be on the correct path of self-cultivation, which is the fundamental foundation for achieving the Tao. Therefore, we do not hesitate and falter again. We no longer wander alone or stray from the Tao. We are no longer wandering spirits or homeless ghosts because we are already on our enlightened path of brightness. From now on, we cast away our old, heavy impurities and retain clarity. We initially borrow the unreal to cultivate the real. Thus, we travel the path of Tao without swerving from it throughout the rest of our lives. No matter where we are, we engrave it in our bones and plant it in our hearts. In particular we perceive:

The boundless grace from the Divine Immortal Realm cannot be repaid through our gross body. If our Grandmaster does not have the mercy to pilot us across the river, we can never reach the other side. If we get across, we vow to help others within our reach to get across. What a pity it is if we do not help others of readiness, for people are still drowning and suffering in the bitter sea with the guiding light of a pilot. Therefore, we vow deeply to follow the divine subtle light as our heart and to continue the Master's guidance by being a shrine of divine energy. In this way we may be a bridge for helping others across the river. Virtuous people can enter from here to obtain the sacred teaching for achieving enlightenment. We will gather talented and capable people to become the court of the sages and the virtuous, and to turn worldly people toward the shien's non-dualistic Way. We must increasingly cultivate positive virtues so that we may radiate a positive influence to the world. We shall transcend all mental delusions in order to fulfill the obligation of passing on the light and guiding others.

There are many incomplete worldly religions which perpetuate the delusion of humankind. How can one who is deluded awaken another to clarity? Today's world is full of traps and detrimental influences. How can those who are not stripped of delusions avoid harm? By following the absolute Way of Tao which is passed down directly from Heavenly Immortals, we can receive and embody the heart of harmonizing Heaven, actualize the will of harmonizing Heaven, and carry out Heaven's wishes. We look upon the lives of others and our own life as one, and we forgive the mistakes of others as we grow beyond our own mistakes. As we travel on the absolute way, we subtly influence others to become positive and egoless, as one would manage a boat through troubled waters. While we are deluded, we are carried across by our Master. When we become enlightened, we carry ourselves and other across. Those who have realized the truth know that their root of life is handed down from Heaven and thus is harmoniously connected with Heaven, the root of everlasting life. The immortal seeds of our being need good care and continued cultivation so that they will grow through all difficulties and barriers, and enjoy sufficient and complete growth.

The unceasingly positive and constructive virtues of the great Tao truly benefit all life. A disciple of tien shien, the Heavenly Immortals, the absolute beings of the universe, should cultivate virtue, and then manifest this radiant light to illuminate the dark world. For this reason, we vow to all of our Masters who have rejoined this everlasting fountain and handed down this tradition to cultivate immortal seeds. We vow with utmost sincerity to illuminate and dissolve all appearances of suffering and delusion. We are supported by the heart of harmonizing Heaven to open the correct gate of life, and to indicate a path for those who want to ascend to the absolute realm. In this way, the Heavenly heritage will be passed on. The sacred altar of the shiens will continue eternally, with forms and without forms, the sacred path will endure, and the Heavenly loving gate will always be open. We vow to become a sacred vessel of divine energy, honoring Tao as our highest model. We will revere Heaven and its offspring. We will cultivate ourselves with dedication and diligence. We will offer our light to others and extend our virtue to them. We eliminate all greed and negative qualities from our being. Only those who are sincere and spiritually prosperous can be carried across. We will not swerve from righteousness because of worldly pleasures. To do so would be to trade the boundless and eternal for the limited and transient.

This sacred spiritual tradition has been extended by the Heavenly shiens and Heavenly-hearted people, and is dedicated and protected by all Masters. We in turn offer ourselves to the eternal Tao and abide by uniting with the Subtle Origin of the universe. Together we shall build a ladder to Heaven and offer ourselves as a sacred ship to carry across all who are attracted through spiritual affinity. We shall devotedly transform ourselves day by day so that we may gather the virtuous light from the egoless Heaven, which will in turn radiate from us to the world.

My Dedication to Universal Life, Presented in My Ordination

We are fortunate to be piloted by our Master who was piloted across by our Grandmasters. Our Grandmasters had their origin in the divine universal Immortals. Humans also receive their life energy from the universe. The universe is not human imagination, nor is it humankind's conceptual creation. Humankind is held in the embrace of the universe, and also receives its life guiding energy (chi) from the nature of the universe. Provided one has a sincere heart to return to the origin through one's body, the entire universe and the self can merge into oneness.

The universal efficacy (ling) never dies. It is only human beings who become deluded and lose the connection. Therefore they fall into the lasting cycle of sensory desire, wandering and scattering in disorder. A soul may be born with the body and mind of an animal or a human being, depending on the level of development it attained or on how much its development regressed. It is constantly transforming through birth and rebirth without end. Those who have the awareness to return to the universal truth can immediately transcend this cycle.

If one returns to one's true nature, then the universe and humankind can unite into oneness. One's spirit can enjoy itself freely and without restraint in the absolute realm of eternity.

This has been experienced by all of the Masters personally, and is a safe and smooth path paved by them. Therefore, those who follow have the blessing to receive transmission. Through our divine Master, we can step out of the realm of dense desires and rise above all other things. There is no other way to the realm of absolute truth.

It is not that everyone does not grow with the development of the subtle light of spirit (ling ming - the responsive purity and clarity), but it is only that one cannot recognize its presence within oneself. One knows nothing about the precious treasure within oneself and searches daily in vain for worldly fame or exhausts oneself by grudgingly maintaining a livelihood. All day long, muddled and confused, one ignores the true light (chen ling), thereby falling into the dark abyss of sensory desires and unknowingly becoming as rigid as a living corpse deprived of its divine energy (ling chi). Through the mercy of our Grandmasters, the love of our Master, the virtue of the shiens and their brilliant teachings, we can realize all our past ignorance, keep above the abyss of untamed desire, and rejoin the true origin with utmost sincerity. Then our old sins are cast away.

We rejoin the non-dualistic Way,
enjoy the non-deviation from the Subtle Origin,
and dissolve the self in the original Oneness
with the determination of no self-retaining.
Our minds are awakened from the depth of decay.
Without deceit or pretense
we cultivate the harmonizing light to reach all.

My Reflection of Self, Presented at My Ordination

Though human beings embody divine nature, they still remain entangled in the realm of muddy and clear. This means their chi is still impure, half light and half gross. They are tortured by the ever-changing phenomenal world without, and the biological desires within. Therefore their beings can be easily misled, and they do not know how precious and noble it is to have their lives as human beings. This is either because they do not realize the intrinsic divine nature of clear, pure chi is within themselves, or that the divine nature has long been smelted out of shape and has vanished.

This is the result of excessively indulging in following the drives of desires which enslave and imprison one in the body, so that one cannot liberate oneself from it. In order to save the drowning soul, the pure and correct Way of understanding and the precise method of cultivation are employed. This is different from the common religious way. Common religions often are just like poisonous drugs which kill the disease, but leave behind new illness as a side-effect. They just like two drunks trying to help each other, and then both fall down.

We are fortunate to be able to receive the profound teachings passed down from our Grand Masters and Masters. We deeply recognize that in the past we were just like animals and beasts, knowing nothing more than to fill the abyss of desire and living without the light to strengthen our divine spirit. Therefore we lived and died like animals. However, although we now still maintain the same physical form, our way of life is greatly changed. We use our body as our shrine in order to fully recognize our Heavenly egoless nature as true shiens. We cultivate ourselves diligently in order to transform ourselves back to Heaven. Although we still live in the same world as animals and beasts, we do not die as animals and beasts. Though all other living beings are equal to us, our destiny is not the same.

The path from the Tao is straight and reaches directly to our heart. The light of our inner wisdom shines open to the right Way, so there are no more blinding barriers between Heaven and us. The life of our spirit is reborn and our divine light again restored. We realize the Tao and know to cultivate just as we know how to return home after being lost. In order to transcend the cycle of birth and rebirth through the Sacred Method, we must first transform ourselves. We can break through our bodily prison and break apart the net of sensory desires which has chained us. From now on we can surpass the realm of worldly desires and head straight for the Heavenly Capital. All the things that have happened to us in the past are gone forever when the last instance has passed. And for all the things to come again is like being reborn from this moment forward.

In the past we have lived in the external world of sensory pursuit. Because of greed, we had worries, pain, guilt and disharmony. Since we vow to sincerely follow the non-dualistic Tao, from now on, in all things we do, we are revitalized. The revitalization of our good life gives us clear and bright insight, and joyous contentment with our present being. From now on we truly accept the Heavenly egoless joy and peaceful constancy in life.

We are born on behalf of Heavenly origin and, though we dwell in the world of mortals, we devote ourselves to be the living model of true egoless Heaven. Daily we devote and offer ourselves to the pursuit of virtue for the sake of returning ourselves to the Divine Subtle Realm. With piety we have the graceful light of the non-dualistic Tao as our guide. I sincerely make this vow to the Divine Immortal Realm.

This body we are using does not belong to us permanently. It is the result of the interaction of the chi of light spirit and Heavenly physics. Our spiritual nature is handed down to us from the Divine Subtle Realm. Why is it that we lead our lives delusively as in dreams? In the midst of this material world the deluded mind exhausts itself by endlessly chasing ups, downs, gains and losses. At the moment the servant of death knocks at the door, it is too late to regret that our life has been passed in vain. Today we are enlightened through our illusions by our benevolent Master, so we vow to strengthen our original life source anew from the root. We inherit this pure, clean, divine nature from Heaven. It needs to be returned without contamination. We do not stain it with dirt and filth or soil it with flaws and corruption. It is borrowed from divine Heaven and is handed to us for temporary use. Only fools try to possess it forever.

We originally come from nothingness and possess nothing. Our only wish is to become eternally one with the harmonizing Heaven. Henceforth we are awakened in the middle of our dream. After awakening there is nothing which can be recognized as the ego. We vow deeply in our hearts to offer our lives as a dedication to the reintegration of Heaven, earth, and humankind. Every worldly deed, whether for ourselves or for others, is devoted as offering to the Subtle Origin. We offer our worship as a straight response with absolute sincerity. We try our best to integrate our lives. All the shiens in every Heaven are our witness. Our vow is vast and deep as mountains and oceans. Thus our heart is rooted firmly. We never dare evade our responsibility out of greed. Because the net of Heavenly laws cannot be escaped, we always maintain Heaven's ever-permeating righteous chi.

Spiritual Connection and Recognition

Anyone who, after reading some of Master Ni's English works on Taoism, is interested in practicing the Taoist Way of Life might like to connect with other people who enjoy Taoist learning. They can make contact with one of the centers, such as the one in Atlanta, join a study group of Master Ni's work, or learn further about the teachings of Tao through the Degree Program of the College of Tao. Also, those who have already experienced the Taoist Way of Life may receive recognition of being a Taoist through the College of Tao or one of the affiliated Taoist Centers.

The traditional approach of initiation may still apply to students, yet the nature of initiation is non-committal. The meaning of initiation is not to make one belong to another person or to a group, but to guide one to return to one's own impersonal, spiritual center as an integral being. In the Initiation Ceremony, Master Ni passes three major practices of spiritual integration as Three Spiritual Treasures of Taoism. They are valuable as lifetime practices.

Ceremony for the Renewal and Enlightenment of Body, Mind and Spirit

Let us begin the dedication to our Grandmasters and Masters. Please take your positions. (nine gongs) Let us read aloud together:

As Tai Chi divides, Heaven and earth are spontaneously
*   Manifested.*
The clear and light energy becomes the Heavenly realms.
The dark and heavy energy becomes the earthly realms.
In humankind, the energies of Heaven and earth unite.
We cultivate the Tao in order to evolve to be subtle,
*   divine beings.*
The Tao is transmitted to us through our divine Masters,
*   and through studying the sacred books of Tao.*

May the Jade Emperor, the source of all Heavenly shiens,
*   who resides in the golden shrine of the highest*
*   Heavenly realm, please accept our dedications.*

(three salutations or bows)

May all divine, spiritual beings before Fu Hsi
(300,000 years ago),
Semi-gods before the great Yu, (the Emperor of the Sha
Dynasty 2,205 B.C.),
And all inspired sages and emperors afterwards,
please accept our dedications.

(three salutations or bows)

May the powerful spiritual energy of wealth, health,
peace, bliss and longevity,
The Heavenly shiens who respond to our sincerity,
and all divine guardians
within and outside our shrine,
Please accept our dedications.

(three salutations or bows)

May the harmonizing spiritual energy of love union,
please accept our dedications.

(one salutation or bow)

Let us now read together the *Taoist Classic of Obedience to the Eternal Way:*

The creative energy of Heaven is our paternal source.
The receptive energy of earth is our maternal source.
All people are the offspring of the same universal origin.
Within my own nature are the same virtues as those
of the inspired sages.
My spiritual potential here and now is as great as
it was for the sages of all times.
The elders of my spiritual family are the divine beings
in the position to restore order and harmony in my life.
I have respect for those who are in their winter years
and help them to live even longer.
I treat the young ones kindly and help them to have
a good youth.
The sick and the needy are also my brothers and sisters,
so I will protect them under my wings.

I will assist the talented and will not waste my
own talents.
If I enjoy a good life and have many things to give
to others, it is nature displaying its
benevolence through me.
If I have little and undergo many difficulties, it is
nature building me stronger.
Only by realizing my pristine nature can I fulfill
the true significance of life.
To ignore the true significance of life is to
sacrifice my spiritual integrity.
To violate the benevolence of my true personality
is to undermine my own natural well-being.
By knowing the principles of change and always doing
my best, I may be in harmony with the enduring
will of the universe.
I gratefully accept what life presents to me and
do not cling to sorrows or try to run away
from facing the reality of my life.
With courage I follow Tao and obey the subtle
universal law.
Rather than lose myself by seeking the luxuries of
worldly life, I cultivate my positive, spiritual
energy in order to actualize a good life.
In my life, I follow only what is good and thus
never stray from my true nature.
When I die, my energy returns to the infinite
source of life.
There is never a question of my existence or non-existence
because beingness and non-beingness are the two
aspects of my nature.
I confirm the benevolence of the universe with my
selfless service to all beings.
The benevolent universe sustains me with eternal life.

Let us read this song together:

From the five directions comes the true, positive
energy which brings a thousand blessings.
All disasters are eliminated and ten thousand miseries vanish.

The spirits of the three origins protect me and
the eyes of the ten thousand shiens watch over me.
My life is peaceful and trouble-free because I
unite my heart and mind with the eternal Tao.
The balancing, universal will and my will become one.
Because your younger brothers and sisters, sons and
daughters follow the Tao and use this radiation
as their vantage point, the divine spiritual
beings often visit our shrine.
With one hundred salutations, your humble disciple is
bathed in divine energy forever.
We pray your longevity will be boundless and your
spiritual effectiveness will continue eternally.

(three salutations or bows)

Taoist Marriage Ceremony

Tao is one.
It is the perfect harmony of the universe.
Tao divides itself into Heaven and earth,
or yang and yin.
It manifests in men and women
as the subtle yang and yin energies.
Men and women complement each other
and each contains an integral part of the other.

As Taoists, a man and woman build
Their earthly relationship on
the refinement of their subtle energies.
They cultivate together
to reach the state of perfect harmony.
Therefore, their relationship remains untouched
by the constant changes of earthly life.
They unite their virtue in Tao
and their union is everlasting.

_____,do you recognize _____as your wife?

(answered with the striking of one handbell to another)

_____, do you recognize_____ as your husband?

(answered with the striking of one handbell to another)

With this, dear _____ *and* _____ ,

I pronounce you husband and wife,
and bless your marriage to become
a perfect union in Tao.

(affirmed with the striking of their handbells to each other three times.) [This means consonant harmony as a husband and wife.]

The Simple Standpoint of the Reunion of Tao & the Integral Person

We embrace the prime, divine energy only, which is titled Tao. We follow the Tao by renouncing all distorted images and descriptions. We accept spiritual, religious creations as secondary explanations or illustrations, but as no more than that. We will not let them become obstacles to our true achievement of the spiritualization of our being.

We do not doubt the Tao, just as we do not doubt our own true nature, which inherently contains all goodness, beauty and truth. We are wholly equipped by the universe with body, mind and spirit. We are a complete manifestation of the Tao itself. To fulfill our true nature is to fulfill the eternal Tao. We will never go against the Tao or violate the Tao. Nor will we hurt our life by our ignorant behavior or negative thinking, which we will gradually come to understand and eliminate through the growing self-awareness developed through our constant self-cultivation.

This is our primary purpose in which we are guided by our divine teachers of the Union of Tao and Man.

Chapter 25

Talks by Master Ni

Initiation to Be a Taoist
[This talk was given by Master Ni prior to an initiation ceremony during the winter of 1977.]

One can initiate oneself as a Taoist, or if one looks for spiritual direction and recognition, one can be initiated through a teacher.

This teaching of Tao has existed for thousands of years, as far back as our knowledge reaches. We maintain this Shrine of the Eternal Breath of Tao as a school to embrace the teachings and beings it represents. All of us relate for one purpose: to reach for the truth, to seek the spirit itself. When I say truth, perhaps in your mind you think it is something that can be described. To a Taoist, any description is just an expression of what is and is not the essential truth itself. Some of you are close to the final truth. Some of you are just guessing. What is the truth? The truth is not outside you. It is within you. The truth is that from subtle energy you are manifested into being. This is truth itself, and you needn't bother to look for another truth. The truths you find outside yourself are just explanations and verifications of your existence, your beingness. You must remember one thing. This one truth is our common bond. It is universal truth. The universal, subtle energy has been positively transformed into beingness. All living and non-living things are manifestations of this universal nature. The highest beings are those in which the subtle, universal energy has been highly refined until there is no trace of unrefined energy left.

You may then ask, if the universal truth is within my own nature, why have I bothered to come to hear you tell me this? The reason is obvious. Although your essential nature is from the Subtle Origin of the universe, though your many years and many lives in the world, you have forgotten this and now suffer mental, spiritual and physical weakness. You no longer can embody the eternal Tao. Your mind, your thought processes, have created this separation. Every time you use your mind, it goes in a different direction, away from or against the Tao. You are continually separating yourself from the eternal Tao. It is degrading.

The quiet nature of beingness is the universal Tao itself. It is the state which existed before Heaven and earth were created. This shrine keeps the wordless teaching of the Tao which came before Heaven and earth were born. Because you are chained and shackled to the worldly life, you have forgotten the true nature of your own origin. So you have pain or feel uneasy. You sense you have lost something for which you now search. This search is the beginning of all spiritual traditions and philosophies. However, in religion and philosophy, intelligent people invent stories and come to teach you. All sages and spiritual heroes are only taking the water from the ocean to sell to the ocean.

A Taoist is a different kind of teacher. I have already told you that you live in the spiritual ocean. Surrounding you are all the waters. You do not need to buy more water from others. The idea of divinity is not an external supreme being. The Taoist who achieves self-awareness proves that divinity is a manifestation of his or her own eternal energy under different titles. The eternality is within you, but you have lost it. You undermine it with an improper way of life. You are divine beings, but you degrade your own dignity, your own sovereignty and your own sacredness by your unnatural way of life. All improper actions and thought are against your own holiness. This is the main trouble of all humanity.

Friends frequently look to be initiated by men with the desire to keep their own godhood, their own true nature, and to learn daily those things that go against the true nature of their being and the universe. Do you know which part of your thinking and your living goes against the eternal Tao? For this purpose, we have special studies and special methods to cultivate ourselves, to rectify ourselves.

As a Taoist, when you live in this world, you are the supreme energy of the universe and you enjoy eternality. You are the Tao. The Tao is you. Hearing me speak as such may stimulate your pride. This is harmful to you but it happens only because of misunderstanding. These words that I speak to you before you have true enlightenment are only words and are not the reality. If you have true cultivation and enlightenment yourself, then everything comes to be your own truth.

Today at this initiation, I would like my new friends to understand exactly what I say to you: The spiritual sovereign who initiates you is not me. It is you. All you have to do is to uncover your own true nature. The universe is in a continual process of evolution, but this evolution is imposed upon us from without because of the need to adapt to the ever-changing environment. You want to transfer the factual evolution of the universe to be self-aware, spiritual evolution. The high being is within you. You can prove it in your daily life. What kind of being are you? The child of what spirituality are you? Are you the spirit from a branch or do you come directly from the root of the universe?

Before you become initiated, I hope you will be honest with yourself. The Taoist Way is mainly one of self-cultivation. You must be willing to take responsibility for yourself, your soul and your spirit. I do not say that I am God or your savior. I say that with your full cooperation and effort, or effortlessness, there is hope for your self-salvation. The Taoist Way is one of taking responsibility for your own salvation and spiritual evolution.

If you are willing to take responsibility for your own salvation and self-refinement, why do you need to come here? You need direction after having been lost for so long. Besides, you need someone else who is on the way and who can recognize you as a companion. You need to initiate a pure, spiritual alliance with others like yourself. When you understand all of this, you are welcome to be my spiritual friend.

I recognize that all of you have a serious purpose in life, but no achievement in this moment. This initiation may give you a better chance. Today's world is troubled and is no longer natural. The main purpose of this initiation is to learn how to equip your bare mind and bare spirit with the tools necessary for dealing with life, spiritually and physically.

I love you all, but I can teach you only when you are ready. I welcome your interest in this initiation to become a disciple of the eternal Tao. I also welcome my old friends who wish to be reinitiated in order to reaffirm their adherence to the Tao.

Chinese New Year
[This was taken from the 1979 Chinese new year's letter to all of Master Ni's students and friends.]

This year, 1979, is the year 4679 according to the Yellow Emperor's Calendar. The Chinese calendar is mostly concerned with seasonal changes. It combines two systems of recording time: one is a lunar system and one is a solar system. The Yellow Emperor, whose reign began in 2,698 B.C., was the first emperor in Chinese history who established an official method of recording time. The emperors were the unified cultural center of the society at that time.

There was a great sage named Da Chow who was appointed as a minister of the Yellow Emperor. He was assigned the task of formalizing the ancient knowledge of astronomy based on the revolution of the Heavenly bodies for the purpose of establishing a unified calendar. He adopted the system of the "Heavenly Stems and Earthly Branches." The Heavenly Stems are ten divisions of the revolution of the high sphere of universal energy, and the Earthly Branches are twelve divisions of the revolution of the energy sphere relevant to earthly cycles.

When the two cycles are combined, yang with yang and yin with yin, sixty divisions result. This system of universal energy cycles became the basis for the time system of years, months, days and hours. The new year starts with the new moon cycle of springtime. "Spring Day" is the new cycle of the revolution of the earth around the sun.

The Yellow Emperor chose the first year, month, day and hour of this new system of recording time for his official inauguration as the Emperor of China. He followed a long succession of cultural development in China and former Emperors such as Fu Hsi and Shen Nung.

At the time, the beginning of a Chinese year started on the first day of the eleventh month around the time of the winter solstice, for it is then that the earthly energy starts to expand after its contraction since the summer solstice. This is one valuable illustration of the *I Ching* principle that when yang comes to its peak, yin begins. In autumn, the vital energy of the earth starts to withdraw deep into the earth. We become aware of this by observing that all the leaves fall and branches become dry because the life force of all plants withdraws to the roots. In the spring, the energy moves forward again to the surface of the earth.

Later in Chinese history, the Emperor Yu decided to use the Spring Day as the beginning of the cycle of a new year, for this is the time when all things come back to life and grow again. He was an expert in astronomy and the great hero who dealt with the vast deluge of that time. Emperor Yu, as an effort of the whole society, led a group of people to fight the deluge by opening water channels. He led his men day and night to chisel channels to let the water go to the ocean. One of the main works, a channel called the Dragon Gate, is still in existence at the upper side of the Yellow River, being an example of the architectural feats performed by this great man.

Yu's father had died in the process of trying to fight the deluge, so his son continued the work. He spent years fighting the deluge. He was so busy that when he had a chance to pass by his own village, even though his wife and sons beckoned him to come home, he turned away. He could not forget all families and all children to be with his family. When he finally succeeded in stemming the deluge, he was appointed by the benevolent Shun to succeed him as the emperor of China. Emperor Yu became an unselfish model of life.

I mention the benevolent Yu because he is my working model, as well as having been the model for many past Masters. He vowed that if he could survive that disaster, then all people should survive, and that if this were not possible, then he should be the first one to suffer calamity. I took his vow as my sacred vow when I was asking enlightenment. Today we do not have a visible deluge, but we have an invisible deluge of cultural and religious, as well as personal, mental and emotional confusion. We need to fight the deluge and help humankind out of its troubles. Therefore, today's Taoists cannot merely cultivate and enjoy themselves without facing the responsibility of the world around them. We must be aware that we are on the verge of a great deluge. My students must achieve awareness of the unnatural lifestyle of present day societies, and first save themselves in order to fight the enormous deluge of confusion. The benevolent Yu is a good model for contemporary Taoists, for we need to fight all kinds of deluges. Even in the twentieth century, human beings in a group sense they still need someone to change their diapers from the artificial flood of their own making.

Glossary

Ba Gua (or pa gua): Eight *gua* or trigrams, or an arrangement of the eight trigrams. Also may refer to Cosmic Tour *Ba Gua Zahn* (also expressed in Chinese as *Pa Kua Chang)*, an exercise done in a circular movement.

Book of Changes: See also *I Ching*. The legendary classic *Book of Changes* or the *I Ching* is recognized as the first written book of wisdom. Leaders and sages throughout history have consulted it as a trusted advisor which reveals the appropriate action in any circumstance.

Chi (also spelled *Qi* or *Ki*): *Chi* is the vitality or life energy of the universe and resides within each living being. In humans, it provides the power for our movements of body and mind, immune system, and all organ functions.

Chuang Tzu: A Taoist sage who lived around 275 B.C. and wrote an influential book called *Chuang Tzu*.

Dao-In (or Do-In): A series of movements traditionally used for conducting physical energy. The ancients discovered that *Dao-In* exercise solves problems of stagnant energy, increases health, lengthens one's years, and provides support for cultivation and higher achievements of spiritual immortality.

Huang Ti: See Yellow Emperor.

I Ching: An ancient book that teaches about the changes and unchanging truth of nature, human society, and individual life. It is also a method of divination which uses the 64 hexagrams originated by Fu Shi. Information about the hexagrams was recorded in a book by the same name which is translated into English as *Book of Changes*.

Jing (Ching or Tsing): The gross or "raw" level of energy; can be refined to *chi*.

Kou Hong, Master: Also known in Chinese as Pao Poh Tzu or Bao Boh Tzu. Living 283-262 C.E., during the Jing Dynasty. A balanced personality who provides a model of high spirituality. Pao Poh Tzu or Bao Boh Tzu is also the name of the book attributed to him.

Lao Tzu: Also expressed in Chinese as Lao Zi, Lao Tze, or Lao Tse. Achieved master who continued the teaching of natural truth. Author of the *Tao Teh Ching* and *Hua Hu Ching*. (Active around 571 B.C.E.)

Meditation: A way of focused or concentrated awareness which unites the mind with the body and gathers one's energy. A time of quieting the mind which can take place sitting, standing, lying, or moving.

Nei Ching (or Neijing): Ancient book of health, medical, and spiritual knowledge attributed to the Yellow Emperor translated in English as *The Yellow Emperor's Classic of Medicine*. Consists of two parts, *Suwen* (Questions of Organic and Fundamental Nature) and *Lingshu* (a technical book on acupuncture).

Pao Po Tzu: See Kou Hong, Master.

Sen (shen): Spirit; also the high or pure level of energy, which can be refined from *chi*.

Shien: An immortal, a spiritually achieved individual.

Su Wen: See *Nei Ching*.

T'ai chi: The ultimate union of the two forces inherent in nature, *yin* and *yang*.

T'ai Chi Movement: Also known in Chinese as *T'ai Chi Chuan* or *Tai Ji Quan*. Ancient Chinese exercise for harmonizing body, mind and spirit, whose connected movements somewhat resemble a graceful dance. Consists of many different *chi kung* movements put together sequentially and arranged with the principles given by the *Tao Teh Ching* and *I Ching*.

T'ai Chi Principle: The principle of alternation of opposites, also called the *Yin/Yang* Principle, the Universal Law, or the Law of *T'ai Chi*.

Tao: The invisible, Integral Way. Profound truth of life.

Tao Teh Ching: Also expressed in Chinese as *Dao Deh Jing*. An influential book written by Lao Tzu as an attempt to elucidate Tao, the subtle truth of life. Considered a classic, it is among the most widely translated and distributed books in the world.

Tan Tien (or *Dan Tien*): Translated as "field of elixir," this is more an area than a specific point on the body. It is generically used to refer to several centers of the body where energy is stored: the Upper *Tan Tien* or Heavenly Eye Point, the Middle *Tan Tien* or center of the chest, and the Lower *Tan Tien* or area around four finger-widths below the navel. *Tan tien* also frequently refers specifically to the Lower *Tan Tien*.

Virtue: High individual qualities of the human character such as moral excellence, righteousness, balance, patience, wisdom, and responsibility.

Wu Wei: The principle of "doing nothing extra" or "inaction in action," "doing just enough," "non-doing," or "harmonious action."

Yellow Emperor: Known in Chinese as Huang Ti (2698-2598 B.C.E. reign), emperor of China credited as being the founder of Chinese medicine and achieving immortality.

Yin and Yang: Terms which describe opposites, the two ends of either pole, or duality. *Yang* relates to the male, outward, active, positive, fiery, energetic side of life or nature of a person. *Yin* relates to the female, inward, passive, negative, watery, cool, substantial side of life or nature of a person.

About Hua-Ching Ni

The author, Hua-Ching Ni, feels that it is his responsibility to ensure that people receive his message clearly and correctly, thus, he puts his lectures and classes into book form. He does this for the clear purpose of universal spiritual unity.

It will be his great happiness to see the genuine progress of all people, all societies and nations as they become one big harmonious worldly community. This is the goal that inspires him to speak and write as one way of fulfilling his personal duty. The teachings he offers people come from his own growth and attainment.

Hua-Ching Ni began his spiritual pursuit when he was quite young. Although spiritual nature is innate, learning to express it suitably and usefully requires worldly experience and a lot of training. A hard life and hard work have made him deeper and stronger, and perhaps wiser. This is the case with all people who do not yield to the negative influences of life and the world. He does not intend to establish himself as a special individual, as do people in general spiritual society, but wishes to give service. He thinks that he is just one person living on the same plane of life with the rest of humanity.

He likes to be considered a friend rather than have a formal title. In this way he enjoys the natural spiritual response between himself and others who come together in extending the ageless natural spiritual truth to all.

He is a great traveller, and never tires of going to new places. His books have been printed in different languages, having been written at the side of his professional work as a natural healer – a fully trained Traditional Chinese Medical doctor. He understands that his world mission is to awaken people of both east and west, and he supports his friends and helpers as Mentors. All work together to fulfill the world spiritual mission of this time in human history.

Teachings of the Universal Way by Hua-Ching Ni

NEW RELEASES

Spring Thunder: Awaken the Hibernating Power of Life - Humans need to be periodically awakened from a spiritual hibernation in which the awareness of life's reality is deeply forgotten. To awaken your deep inner life, this book offers the practice of Natural Meditation, the enlightening teachings of Yen Shi, and Master Ni's New Year Message. BSPRI 0-937064-77-7 PAPERBACK, 168 P $12.95

The Eight Treasures: Energy Enhancement Exercise - by Maoshing Ni, Ph. D. The Eight Treasures is an ancient system of energy enhancing movements based on the natural motion of the universe. It can be practiced by anyone at any fitness level, is non-impact, simple to do, and appropriate for all ages. It is recommended that this book be used with its companion videotape. BEIGH 0-937064-55-6 Paperback 208p $17.95

The Universal Path of Natural Life - The way to make your life enduring is to harmonize with the nature of the universe. By doing so, you expand beyond your limits to reach universal life. This book is the third in the series called *The Course for Total Health*. BUNIV 0-937064-76-9 PAPERBACK, 104P $9.50

Power of Positive Living How do you know if your spirit is healthy? You do not need to be around sickness to learn what health is. When you put aside the cultural and social confusion around you, you can rediscover your true self and restore your natural health. This is the second book of *The Course for Total Health*. BPOWE 0-937064-90-4 PAPERBACK 80P $8.50

The Gate to Infinity - People who have learned spiritually through years without real progress will be thoroughly guided by the important discourse in this book. Master Ni also explains Natural Meditation. Editors recommend that all serious spiritual students who wish to increase their spiritual potency read this one. BGATE 0-937064-68-8 PAPERBACK 208P $13.95

The Yellow Emperor's Classic of Medicine - by Maoshing Ni, Ph.D. The *Neijing* is one of the most important classics of Taoism, as well as the highest authority on traditional Chinese medicine. Written in the form of a discourse between Yellow Emperor and his ministers, this book contains a wealth of knowledge on holistic medicine and how human life can attune itself to receive natural support. BYELLO 1-57062-080-6 PAPERBACK 316P $16.00

Self-Reliance and Constructive Change - Natural spiritual reality is independent of concept. Thus dependence upon religious convention, cultural notions and political ideals must be given up to reach full spiritual potential. The Declaration of Spiritual Independence affirms spiritual self-authority and true wisdom as the highest attainments of life. This is the first book in *The Course for Total Health*. BSELF 0-937064-85-8 PAPERBACK 64P $7.00

Concourse of All Spiritual Paths - All religions, in spite of their surface difference, in their essence return to the great oneness. Hua-Ching Ni looks at what traditional religions offer us today and suggests how to go beyond differences to discover the depth of universal truth. BCONC 0-937064-61-0 PAPERBACK 184P $15.95.

PRACTICAL LIVING

The Key to Good Fortune: Refining Your Spirit - Straighten Your Way *(Tai Shan Kan Yin Pien)* and The Silent Way of Blessing *(Yin Chia Wen)* are the main guidance for a mature, healthy life. Spiritual improvement can be an integral part of realizing a Heavenly life on Earth. BKEYT 0-937064-39-4 PAPERBACK 144P $12.95

Harmony - The Art of Life - The emphasis in this book is on creating harmony within ourselves so that we can find it in relationships with other people and with our environment. BHARM 0-937064-37-8 PAPERBACK 208P $14.95

Ageless Counsel for Modern Life - Following the natural organization of the *I Ching*, Hua-Ching Ni has woven inspired commentaries to each of the 64 hexagrams. Taken alone, they display an inherent wisdom which is both personal and profound. BAGEL 0-937064-50-5 PAPERBACK 256P $15.95.

Strength From Movement: Mastering Chi - by Hua-Ching Ni, Daoshing Ni and Maoshing Ni. - *Chi*, the vital power of life, can be developed and cultivated within yourself to help support your healthy, happy life. This book gives the deep reality of different useful forms of *chi* exercise and which types are best for certain types of people. Includes samples of several popular exercises. BSTRE 0-937064-73-4 PAPERBACK WITH 42 PHOTOGRAPHS 256P $16.95.

8,000 Years of Wisdom, Volume I and II - This two-volume set contains a wealth of practical, down-to-earth advice given to students over a five-year period. Volume I includes 3 chapters on dietary guidance. Volume II devotes 7 chapters to sex and pregnancy topics. VOLUME I: BWIS1 0-937064-07-6 PAPERBACK 236P $12.50 • VOLUME II: BWIS2 0-937064-08-4 PAPERBACK 241P $12.50

The Time is Now for a Better Life and a Better World - What is the purpose of personal spiritual achievement if not to serve humanity by improving the quality of life for everyone? Hua-Ching Ni offers his vision of humanity's dilemma and what can be done about it. BTIME 0-937064-63-7 PAPERBACK 136P $10.95

Spiritual Messages from a Buffalo Rider, A Man of Tao - This book is a collection of talks from Hua-Ching Ni's world tour and offers valuable insights into the interaction between a compassionate spiritual teacher and his students from many countries around the world. BSPIR 0-937064-34-3 PAPERBACK 242P $12.95

Golden Message - by Daoshing and Maoshing Ni - This book is a distillation of the teachings of the Universal Way of Life as taught by the authors' father, Hua-Ching Ni. Included is a complete program of study for students and teachers of the Way. BGOLD 0-937064-36-x PAPERBACK 160P $11.95

Moonlight in the Dark Night - This book contains wisdom on how to control emotions, including how to manage love relationships so that they do not impede one's spiritual achievement. BMOON 0-937064-44-0 PAPERBACK 168P $12.95

SPIRITUAL DEVELOPMENT

Life and Teaching of Two Immortals, Volume 1: Kou Hong - A master who achieved spiritual ascendancy in 363 A.D., Kou Hong was an achieved master in the art of alchemy. His teachings apply the Universal Way to business, politics, emotions, human relationships, health and destiny. BLIF1 0-937064-47-5 PAPERBACK 176P $12.95.

Life and Teaching of Two Immortals, Volume 2: Chen Tuan - Chen Tuan was an achieved master who was famous for the foreknowledge he attained through deep study of the *I Ching* and for his unique method of "sleeping cultivation." This book also includes important details about the microcosmic meditation and mystical instructions from the "Mother of Li Mountain." BLIF2 0-937064-48-3 PAPERBACK 192P $12.95

The Way, the Truth and the Light - *now available in paperback!* - Presented in light, narrative form, this inspiring story unites Eastern and Western beliefs as it chronicles a Western prophet who journeys to the East in pursuit of further spiritual guidance. BLIGH1 0-937064-56-4 PAPERBACK 232P $14.95 • BLIGH2 0-937064-67-X HARDCOVER 232P $22.95

The Mystical Universal Mother - Hua-Ching Ni responds to the questions of his female students through the example of his mother and other historical and mythical women. He focuses on the feminine aspect of both sexes and on the natural relationship between men and women. BMYST 0-937064-45-9 PAPERBACK 240P $14.95

Eternal Light - Dedicated to Yo San Ni, a renowned healer and teacher, and father of Hua-Ching Ni. An intimate look at the lifestyle of a spiritually centered family. BETER 0-937064-38-6 PAPERBACK 208P $14.95

Quest of Soul - How to strengthen your soul, achieve spiritual liberation, and unite with the universal soul. A detailed discussion of the process of death is also included. BQUES 0-937064-26-2 PAPERBACK 152P $11.95

Nurture Your Spirits - Spirits are the foundation of our being. Hua-Ching Ni reveals the truth about "spirits" based on his personal cultivation and experience, so that you can nurture your own spirits. BNURT 0-937064-32-7 PAPERBACK 176P $12.95

Internal Alchemy: The Natural Way to Immortality - Ancient spiritually achieved ones used alchemical terminology metaphorically to disguise personal internal energy transformation. This book offers the prescriptions that help sublimate your energy. BALCH 0-937064-51-3 PAPERBACK 288P $15.95

Mysticism: Empowering the Spirit Within - "Fourteen Details for Immortal Medicine" is a chapter on meditation for women and men. Four other chapters are devoted to the study of 68 mystical diagrams, including the ones on Lao Tzu's tower. BMYST2 0-937064-46-7 PAPERBACK 200P $13.95

Internal Growth through Tao - In this volume, Hua-Ching Ni teaches about the more subtle, much deeper aspects of life. He also points out the confusion caused by some spiritual teachings and encourages students to cultivate internal growth. BINTE 0-937064-27-0 PAPERBACK 208P $13.95

Essence of Universal Spirituality - A review of world religions, revealing the harmony of their essence and helping readers enjoy the achievements of all religions without becoming confused by them. BESSE 0-937064-35-1 PAPERBACK 304P $19.95

Guide to Inner Light - Modern culture diverts our attention from our natural life being. Drawing inspiration from the experience of the ancient achieved ones, Hua-Ching Ni redirects modern people to their true source and to the meaning of life. BGUID 0-937064-30-0 PAPERBACK 192P $12.95

Stepping Stones for Spiritual Success - This volume contains practical and inspirational quotations from the traditional teachings of Tao. The societal values and personal virtues extolled here are relevant to any time or culture. BSTEP 0-937064-25-4 PAPERBACK 160P $12.95.

The Story of Two Kingdoms - The first part of this book is the metaphoric tale of the conflict between the Kingdoms of Light and Darkness. The second part details the steps to self-cleansing and self-confirmation. BSTOR 0-937064-24-6 HARDCOVER 122P $14.50

The Gentle Path of Spiritual Progress - A companion volume to Messages of a Buffalo Rider. Hua-Ching Ni answers questions on contemporary psychology, sex, how to use the I Ching, and tells some fascinating spiritual legends! BGENT 0-937064-33-5 PAPERBACK 290P $12.95.

Footsteps of the Mystical Child - Profound examination of such issues as wisdom and spiritual evolution open new realms of understanding and personal growth. BFOOT 0-937064-11-4 PAPERBACK 166P $9.50

TIMELESS CLASSICS

The Complete Works of Lao Tzu - The *Tao Teh Ching* is one of the most widely translated and cherished works of literature. Its timeless wisdom provides a bridge to the subtle spiritual truth and aids harmonious and peaceful living. Plus the only authentic written translation of the *Hua Hu Ching*, a later work of Lao Tzu which was lost to the general public for a thousand years. BCOMP 0-937064-00-9 PAPERBACK 212P $13.95

The Book of Changes and the Unchanging Truth - Revised Edition - This version of the timeless classic *I Ching* is heralded as the standard for modern times. A unique presentation including profound illustrative commentary and details of the book's underlying natural science and philosophy from a world-renowned expert. BBOOK 0-937064-81-5 HARDCOVER 669P $35.00

Workbook for Spiritual Development - This is a practical, hands-on approach for those devoted to spiritual achievement. Diagrams show sitting postures, standing postures and even a sleeping cultivation. An entire section is devoted to ancient invocations. BWORK 0-937064-06-8 PAPERBACK 240P $14.95

The Esoteric Tao Teh Ching - This totally new edition offers instruction for studying the Tao Teh Ching and reveals the spiritual practices "hidden" in Lao Tzu's classic. These include in-depth techniques for advanced spiritual benefit. BESOT 0-937064-49-1 PAPERBACK 192P $13.95

The Way of Integral Life - The Universal Integral Way leads to a life of balance, health and harmony. This book includes practical suggestions for daily life, philosophical thought, esoteric insight and guidelines for those aspiring to help their lives and the world. BWAYS 0-937064-20-3 PAPERBACK 320P $14.00 • BWAYH 0-937064-21-1 HARDCOVER 320P $20.00.

Enlightenment: Mother of Spiritual Independence - The inspiring story and teachings of Hui Neng, the 6th Patriarch and father of Zen, highlight this volume. Intellectually unsophisticated, Hui Neng achieved himself to become a true spiritual revolutionary. BENLS 0-937064-19-X PAPERBACK 264P $12.50 • BENLH 0-937064-22-X HARDCOVER 264P $22.00.

Attaining Unlimited Life - Most scholars agree that Chuang Tzu produced some of the greatest literature in Chinese history. He also laid the foundation for the Universal Way. In this volume, Hua-Ching Ni draws upon his extensive training to rework the entire book of Chuang Tzu. BATTS 0-937064-18-1 PAPERBACK 467P $18.00; BATTH 0-937064-23-8 HARDCOVER $25.00

The Taoist Inner View of the Universe - This book offers a glimpse of the inner world and immortal realm known to achieved individuals and makes it understandable for students aspiring to a more complete life. BTAOI 0-937064-02-5 218P $14.95

Tao, the Subtle Universal Law - Thoughts and behavior evoke responses from the invisible net of universal energy. This book explains how self-discipline leads to harmony with the universal law. BTAOS 0-937064-01-7 PAPERBACK 208P $12.95

MUSIC AND MISCELLANEOUS

Colored Dust - Sung by Gaille. Poetry by Hua-Ching Ni. - The poetry of Hua-Ching Ni set to music creates a magical sense of transcendence through sound. 37 MINUTES ADUST CASSETTE $10.98, ADUST2 COMPACT DISC $15.95

Poster of Master Lu - Shown on cover of Workbook for Spiritual Development to be used in one's shrine. PMLTP 16" x 22" $10.95

POCKET BOOKLETS

Guide to Your Total Well-Being - Simple useful practices for self-development, aid for your spiritual growth and guidance for all aspects of life. Exercise, food, sex, emotional balancing, meditation. BWELL 0-937064-78-5 PAPERBACK 48P $4.00

Progress Along the Way: Life, Service and Realization - The guiding power of human life is the association between the developed mind and the achieved soul which contains love, rationality, conscience and everlasting value. BPROG 0-937-064-79-3 PAPERBACK 64P $4.00

The Light of All Stars Illuminates the Way - Through generations of searching, various achieved ones found the best application of the Way in their lives. This booklet contains their discovery. BSTAR 0-937064-80-7 48P $4.00

Less Stress, More Happiness - Helpful information for identifying and relieving stress in your life including useful techniques such as invocations, breathing and relaxation, meditation, exercise, nutrition and lifestyle balancing. BLESS 0-937064-55-06 48P $3.00

Integral Nutrition - Nutrition is an integral part of a healthy, natural life. Includes information on how to assess your basic body type, food preparation, energetic properties of food, nutrition and digestion. BNUTR 0-937064-84-X 32P $3.00

The Heavenly Way - Straighten Your Way (*Tai Shan Kan Yin Pien*) and The Silent Way of Blessing (*Yin Chia Wen*) are the main sources of inspiration for this booklet that sets the cornerstone for a mature, healthy life. BHEAV 0-937064-03-3 PAPERBACK 42P $2.50

HEALTH AND HEALING

Power of Natural Healing - This book is for anyone wanting to heal themselves or others. Methods include revitalization with acupuncture and herbs, *Tai Chi, Chi Kung (Chi Gong)*, sound, color, movement, visualization and meditation. BHEAL 0-937064-31-9 PAPERBACK 230P $14.95

Attune Your Body with *Dao-In* - The ancient Taoist predecessor to *Tai Chi Chuan*, these movements can be performed sitting and lying down to guide and refine your energy. Includes meditations and massage for a complete integral fitness program. To be used in conjunction with the video. BDAOI 0-937065-40-8 PAPERBACK WITH PHOTOGRAPHS 144P $14.95

101 Vegetarian Delights - by Lily Chuang and Cathy McNease - A lovely cookbook with recipes as tasty as they are healthy. Features multi-cultural recipes, appendices on Chinese herbs and edible flowers and a glossary of special foods. Over 40 illustrations. B101V 0-937064-13-0 PAPERBACK 176P $12.95

The Tao of Nutrition - by Maoshing Ni, Ph.D., with Cathy McNease, B.S., M.H. - Learn how to take control of your health with good eating. Over 100 common foods are discussed with their energetic properties and therapeutic functions listed. Food remedies for numerous common ailments are also presented. BNUTR 0-937064-66-1 PAPERBACK 214P $14.50

Chinese Vegetarian Delights - by Lily Chuang - An extraordinary collection of recipes based on principles of traditional Chinese nutrition. Meat, sugar, dairy products and fried foods are excluded. BCHIV 0-937064-13-0 PAPERBACK 104P $7.50

Chinese Herbology Made Easy - by Maoshing Ni, Ph.D. - This text provides an overview of Oriental medical theory, in-depth descriptions of each herb category, over 300 black and white photographs, extensive tables of individual herbs for easy reference and an index of pharmaceutical names. BCHIH 0-937064-12-2 PAPERBACK 202P $14.50

Crane Style Chi Gong Book - By Daoshing Ni, Ph.D. - Standing meditative exercises practiced for healing. Combines breathing techniques, movement, and mental imagery to guide the smooth flow of energy. To be used with or without the videotape. BCRAN 0-937064-10-6 SPIRAL-BOUND 55P $10.95

VIDEOTAPES

Natural Living and the Universal Way (VHS) - *New!* - Interview of Hua-Ching Ni in the show "Asian-American Focus" hosted by Lily Chu. Dialogue on common issues of everyday life and practical wisdom. VINTE VHS VIDEO 30 MINUTES $15.95

Movement Arts for Emotional Health (VHS) -*New!* - Interview of Hua-Ching Ni in the show "Asian-American Focus" hosted by Lily Chu. Dialogue on emotional health and energy exercise that are fundamental to health and well-being. VMOVE VHS VIDEO 30 MINUTES $15.95

Attune Your Body with *Dao-In* (VHS) - by Master Hua-Ching Ni. - The ancient Taoist predecessor to *Tai Chi Chuan.* Performed sitting and lying down, these moves unblock, guide and refine energy. Includes meditations and massage for a complete integral fitness program. VDAOI VHS VIDEO 60 MINUTES $39.95

***Tai Chi Ch'uan*: An Appreciation** (VHS) - by Hua-Ching Ni. - "Gentle Path," "Sky Journey" and "Infinite Expansion" are three esoteric styles handed down by highly achieved masters and are shown in an uninterrupted format. Not an instructional video. VAPPR VHS VIDEO 30 MINUTES $24.95

Self-Healing *Chi Gong* (VHS Video) - Strengthen your own self-healing powers. These effective mind-body exercises strengthen and balance each of your five major organ systems. Two hours of practical demonstrations and information lectures. VSHCG VHS VIDEO 120 MINUTES $39.95

Crane Style *Chi Gong* (VHS) - by Dr. Daoshing Ni, Ph.D. - These ancient exercises are practiced for healing purposes. They integrate movement, mental imagery and breathing techniques. To be used with the book. VCRAN VHS VIDEO 120 MINUTES $39.95

Taoist Eight Treasures (VHS) - By Maoshing Ni, Ph.D. - Unique to the Ni family, these 32 exercises open and refine the energy flow and strengthen one's vitality. Combines stretching, toning and energy conducting with deep breathing Book also available. VEIGH VHS VIDEO 105 MINUTES $39.95

T'ai Chi Ch'uan **I & II (VHS)** - By Maoshing Ni, Ph.D. - This style, called the style of Harmony, is a distillation of the Yang, Chen and Wu styles. It integrates physical movement with internal energy and helps promote longevity and self-cultivation. VTAI1 VHS VIDEO PART 1 60 MINUTES $39.95 • VTAI2 VHS VIDEO PART 2 60 MINUTES $39.95

AUDIO CASSETTES

Invocations for Health, Longevity and Healing a Broken Heart - By Maoshing Ni, Ph.D. - "Thinking is louder than thunder." This cassette guides you through a series of invocations to channel and conduct your own healing energy and vital force. AINVO AUDIO 30 MINUTES $9.95

Stress Release with Chi Gong - By Maoshing Ni, Ph.D. - This audio cassette guides you through simple breathing techniques that enable you to release stress and tension that are a common cause of illness today. ACHIS AUDIO 30 MINUTES $9.95

Pain Management with Chi Gong - By Maoshing Ni, Ph.D. - Using visualization and deep-breathing techniques, this cassette offers methods for overcoming pain by invigorating your energy flow and unblocking obstructions that cause pain. ACHIP AUDIO 30 MINUTES $9.95

Tao Teh Ching Cassette Tapes - The classic work of Lao Tzu in this two-cassette set is a companion to the book translated by Hua-Ching Ni. Professionally recorded and read by Robert Rudelson. ATAOT 120 MINUTES $12.95

BOOKS IN SPANISH
Tao Teh Ching - En Español. BSPAN 0-937064-92-0 PAPERBACK 112 P $8.95

Order Form

SEVEN STAR COMMUNICATIONS

name_____

street address_____

city_____ state_____ zip_____

country_____ best time to call_____

phone (day)_____ (evening)_____

Credit Card Information (VISA or MasterCard Only)

Credit Card No._____

Exp. Date_____

Signature_____

Quantity	Price	Title	5 Letter Code	Total

	Sub total	
	Sales tax (CA residents only, 8.25%)	
	Shipping (see left)	
	Total Amount Enclosed	

Mail this form with payment
(US funds only) to:

**SevenStar Communications
1314 Second Street
Santa Monica, CA 90401 USA**

Credit Card Orders:
call **1-800-578-9526**
or fax **310-917-2267**

E-Mail Orders:
taostar@ix.netcom.com

Other Inquiries
1-310-576-1901

Shipping Charges

Number of items	Domestic		International			
	UPS Ground	4th Class Book Rate US Mail	Surface Rate US Mail	Air Printed Matter US Mail	Air Parcel Rate US Mail	UPS Int'l Air
First item [1]	4.50	2.00	2.50	7.50	12.00	46.00
Each Additional item	0.50	0.50	1.00	5.00 [3]	6.00	6.00

NOTES
1 BOOK OF CHANGES (I CHING) because of weight, counts as 3 items, all other books count as one item each.
2 US Mail Air Printed Matter Table to be used for European destination only. All others use Parcel rate.
3 Limit of 4 items only for this service.

DELIVERY TIMES
UPS Ground: 7-10 days, Insured
4th Class Book Rate USmail: 5-8 week, Uninsured
Surface US mail (Overseas): 6-9 weeks, Uninsured
Air Printed Matter USmail (Overseas): 2-4 weeks, Uninsured
Air Parcel Rate USmail: 2-4 weeks, Insured
UPS International Air: 4 days, Insured

Spiritual Study and Teaching
Through the College of Tao

The College of Tao (COT) and the Union of Tao and Man were formally established in California in the 1970's, yet this tradition is a very broad spiritual culture containing centuries of human spiritual growth. Its central goal is to offer healthy spiritual education to all people to help individuals develop themselves for a spiritually developed world. This time-tested "school without walls" values the spiritual development of each individual self and passes down its guidance and experience.

COT does not use an institution with a building. Human society is its classroom. Your own life and service are the class you attend; thus students learn from their lives and from studying the guidance of the Universal Way.

Any interested individual is welcome to join and learn for oneself. The Self-Study Program that is based on Master Ni's books and videotapes gives people who wish to study on their own, or are too far from a teacher, an opportunity to study the Universal Way. The outline for the Self-Study Program is given in the book *The Golden Message*. If you choose, a Correspondence Course is also available.

A Mentor is any individual who is spiritually self-responsible and who is a model of a healthy and complete life. A Mentor may serve as a teacher for general society and people with a preliminary interest in spiritual development. To be certified to teach, a Mentor must first register with the Universal Society of the Integral Way (USIW) and follow the Mentor Service Handbook, which was written by Mentors. It is recommended that all prospective Mentors use the Correspondence Course or self-study program to educate themselves, but they may also learn directly from other Mentors. COT offers special seminars taught only to Mentors.

If you are interested in the Integral Way of Life Correspondence Course, please write: College of Tao, PO Box 1222, El Prado, NM 87529 USA.

If you would like more information about the USIW and classes in your area, please send the following form to: USIW, PO Box 28993, Atlanta, GA 30358-0993 USA

☐   I wish to be put on the mailing list of the USIW to be notified of educational activities.

☐   I wish to receive a list of Registered Mentors teaching in my area or country.

☐   I am interested in joining/forming a study group in my area.

☐   I am interested in becoming a member or Mentor of the USIW.

Name:_____

Address:_____

City:_____State:_____Zip:_____

Country:_____

Phone, Fax and/or E-mail_____

Herbs Used by Ancient Masters

The pursuit of everlasting youth or immortality throughout human history is an innate human desire. Long ago, Chinese esoteric Taoists went to the high mountains to contemplate nature, strengthen their bodies, empower their minds and develop their spirits. From their studies and cultivation, they gave China alchemy and chemistry, herbology and acupuncture, the I Ching, astrology, martial arts and T'ai Chi Ch'uan, Chi Gong and many other useful kinds of knowledge.

Most important, they handed down in secrecy methods for attaining longevity and spiritual immortality. There were different levels of approach; one was to use a collection of food herb formulas available only to highly achieved Taoist masters. They used these food herbs to increase energy and heighten vitality. This treasured collection of herbal formulas remained within the Ni family for centuries.

Now, through Traditions of Tao, the Ni family makes these foods available for you to use to assist the foundation of your own positive development. It is only with a strong foundation that expected results are produced from diligent cultivation.

As a further benefit, in concert with the Taoist principle of self-sufficiency, Traditions of Tao offers the food herbs along with SevenStar Communication's publications in a distribution opportunity for anyone serious about financial independence.

Send to: Traditions of Tao
1314 Second Street #200
Santa Monica, CA 90401

Please send me a Traditions of Tao brochure.

Name _____

Address_____

City_____State_____Zip_____

Phone (day)_____(evening)_____

Yo San University of Traditional Chinese Medicine

"Not just a medical career, but a life-time commitment to raising one's spiritual standard."

Thank you for your support and interest in our publications and services. It is by your patronage that we continue to offer you the practical knowledge and wisdom from this venerable Taoist tradition.

Because of your sustained interest in natural health, in January 1989 we formed Yo San University of Traditional Chinese Medicine, a non-profit educational institution under the direction of founder Master Ni, Hua-Ching. Yo San University is the continuation of 38 generations of Ni family practitioners who handed down their knowledge and wisdom. Its purpose is to train and graduate practitioners of the highest caliber in Traditional Chinese Medicine, which includes acupuncture, herbology and spiritual development.

We view Traditional Chinese Medicine as the application of spiritual development. Its foundation is the spiritual capability to know life, diagnose a person's problem and cure it. We teach students how to care for themselves and others, emphasizing the integration of traditional knowledge and modern science. Yo San University offers a complete accredited Master's degree program approved by the California State Department of Education that provides an excellent education in Traditional Chinese Medicine and meets all requirements for state licensure. Federal financial aid and scholarships are available, and we accept students from all countries.

We invite you to inquire into our university for a creative and rewarding career as a holistic physician. Classes are also open to persons interested in self-enrichment. For more information, please fill out the form below and send it to:

> Yo San University of Traditional Chinese Medicine
> 1314 Second Street
> Santa Monica, CA 90401 U.S.A.

❑ Please send me information on the Masters degree program in Traditional Chinese Medicine.

❑ Please send me information on the massage certificate program.

❑ Please send me information on health workshops and seminars.

❑ Please send me information on continuing education for acupuncturists and health professionals.

Name _____

Address _____

City _____ *State* _____ *Zip* _____

Phone (day) _____ *(evening)* _____